Political Traditions and UK Politics

Political Traditions and UK Politics

Matthew Hall
Honorary Fellow, POLSIS, University of Birmingham, UK

© Matthew Hall 2011

All rights reserved. No reproduction, copy or transmission of this publication may be made without written permission.

No portion of this publication may be reproduced, copied or transmitted save with written permission or in accordance with the provisions of the Copyright, Designs and Patents Act 1988, or under the terms of any licence permitting limited copying issued by the Copyright Licensing Agency, Saffron House, 6–10 Kirby Street, London EC1N 8TS.

Any person who does any unauthorized act in relation to this publication may be liable to criminal prosecution and civil claims for damages.

The author has asserted his right to be identified as the author of this work in accordance with the Copyright, Designs and Patents Act 1988.

First published 2011 by
PALGRAVE MACMILLAN

Palgrave Macmillan in the UK is an imprint of Macmillan Publishers Limited, registered in England, company number 785998, of Houndmills, Basingstoke, Hampshire RG21 6XS.

Palgrave Macmillan in the US is a division of St Martin's Press LLC, 175 Fifth Avenue, New York, NY 10010.

Palgrave Macmillan is the global academic imprint of the above companies and has companies and representatives throughout the world.

Palgrave® and Macmillan® are registered trademarks in the United States, the United Kingdom, Europe and other countries.

ISBN 978–0–230–29202–4

This book is printed on paper suitable for recycling and made from fully managed and sustained forest sources. Logging, pulping and manufacturing processes are expected to conform to the environmental regulations of the country of origin.

A catalogue record for this book is available from the British Library.

Library of Congress Cataloging-in-Publication Data

Hall, Matthew, 1975–
   Political traditions and UK politics / Matthew Hall.
     p. cm.
   Includes index.
   ISBN 978–0–230–29202–4 (hardback)
    1. Great Britain – Politics and government – History. 2. Political participation – Great Britain – History. I. Title.

JN231.H355 2011
324.0941—dc23
                                                                                                 2011018683

10 9 8 7 6 5 4 3 2 1
20 19 18 17 16 15 14 13 12 11

Printed and bound by CPI Group (UK) Ltd, Croydon CR0 4YY

This book is dedicated to the memory of Philip Hall

Contents

Acknowledgements	viii
Introduction	1
1 'Variations on a Theme': Political Tradition in Explanations of British Politics	7
2 Tradition or Traditions?	51
3 Exploring Tradition	92
4 The British Political Tradition Revisited	122
5 The British Political Tradition and Political Life in the UK	152
6 The Participatory Tradition	173
7 The Nationalist Tradition	194
Conclusion	216
Notes	221
Bibliography	252
Index	267

Acknowledgements

The idea for this book arose as part of research I undertook part-time from 2004 to 2009 at the University of Birmingham. Its foundations, however, can be traced back much further. My interest in politics and history began in the 1980s at the height of Thatcherism. For me, witnessing the Miner's Strike, the abolition of the GLC and later, the Poll Tax, whilst listening to the likes of Billy Bragg and Paul Weller raised numerous questions concerning the nature of UK politics and society. I am pleased to have the opportunity to acknowledge the contribution made by numerous people over the years to my attempts to find some semblance of answers to those questions.

First, I'd like to thank Amber Stone-Galilee and Liz Blackmore of Palgrave Macmillan, and the anonymous reviewer who read the draft chapters of the book, for their support, advice and enthusiasm in bringing this project to fruition.

On a personal level I would like to offer my warmest thanks to my friends and family who have been with me throughout this. In particular, honourable mentions go to my Mum and Dad for their constant support and encouragement over the years as well as for their help in fostering my interests in all things 'political'; my sister Jo for buying me Emile Burns's *Introduction to Marxism* for Christmas in 1988 so I 'would know what I was talking about'; to Mandy and the rest of the Bishops, who supported me through so many years in ways I can never fully say thank you for; and to Taryn whose immeasurable kindness, intellectual prowess and proofreading skills were instrumental in the final moments of completing my thesis and the production of this book. Thanks for everything one and all!

Numerous people have contributed, many inadvertently, to the interpretation offered below. Teaching politics and history has allowed me to engage with, and hopefully inspire, those on their own intellectual journey. Words I read many years ago seem most appropriate here: 'Those who teach also learn and those who learn also teach.' To my students I offer my thanks for debating, discussing and often disagreeing with my interpretations.

During my A levels I encountered two fundamental sources of influence and inspiration. The first, Dr John Burgess, inspired and challenged me sufficiently to want to continue my studies at degree level.

The second was the publication of Charter 88's demands for constitutional reform. Coming across this as I first sought to understand and critically engage with the UK's political system had a profound influence on me, shaping and driving my concerns regarding democratic practice in the UK.

I was hugely fortunate as an undergraduate at Sheffield University in the early 1990s to encounter a number of truly outstanding political analysts. Amongst these the work of Martin Smith, David Marquand and Andrew Gamble has influenced my own. In the History Department, I was privileged to be taught by Professor Ian Kershaw. It was in his seminars on the Nazi regime that I first encountered the centrality of questions concerning intention and structure.

At Birmingham University as an MA student I pursued my interest in the inter-war period. Here, I'd like to extend my gratitude to John Grenville who oversaw my research. Whilst dealing with an entirely different historical topic, this further extended my understanding of issues surrounding agency and structure. Furthermore taking Chris Wickham's course on Historical Methods introduced me to the work of E. P. Thompson and many other great works of historical interpretation.

A number of colleagues assisted and supported me throughout my research and the writing of this book. Stuart McAnulla generously engaged with me throughout. I am grateful to him for allowing me to cite from his unpublished paper 'Understanding Tradition in British Politics and Beyond' (2007). Nicky Smith was hugely supportive of the project and offered invaluable advice to me as I sought publication. Colin Thain was also crucial in assisting me as the project came to fruition. I'd also like to thank Mark Goodwin and Martin Monahan for their suggestions. This said any errors or mistakes in the interpretation below remain my own.

Two final acknowledgements remain. To Peter Kerr I owe an enormous debt of gratitude. It was Pete who initially steered me towards the concept of political traditions and the work of Bevir and Rhodes. Throughout my research and the writing of this book he has been a constant source of advice and support, generously giving his time and consideration to my various questions and requests. In particular, his critical engagements with my ideas has proven invaluable as I have refined the arguments and interpretations offered below.

Lastly, it is to Dave Marsh that I owe the greatest debt. When I began my research I could not have asked for a more engaged and inspirational advisor than Dave. His intellectual rigour, drive and desire to continually develop and refine his understanding proved to be both challenging and inspiring. Dave's original work on the BPT clearly inspired the interpretation offered below, as it has the work of a number of his former students. The idea of a British Political Tradition allowed me to bring together the various ideas, concerns and understandings I had previously developed into an interpretation of British political life over time. However it was his encouragement for me to stretch myself and try to write the best work I could that made the most telling contribution. For this, for his reviewing of my work and for his constant support, encouragement and engagement I offer my most profound and heartfelt thanks. This book is a modest token of my lasting respect for, and thanks to, him.

Introduction

Various changes that were instituted by the Labour government during its tenure between 1997 and 2010 have marked a significant moment in the history and development of the British political system. These changes, which Tony Blair described as 'the biggest programme of change to our democracy ever proposed' (Blair 1994), have seen reform of numerous aspects of the institutions and processes of British politics. Since 1997 we have witnessed the reform of the House of Lords (1999), the introduction of both the Human Rights Act (1998) and the Freedom of Information Act (2000), the creation of a Supreme Court for the UK (2005) and devolution for Scotland and Wales (1998). Amongst these there has seemingly been a lack of uniformity of approach or intent. For example Scottish devolution was introduced with speed and without any significant attempt to de-radicalise the original proposal. However Freedom of Information was significantly de-radicalised and electoral reform for Westminster did not occur (Marsh and Hall 2007; Marsh 2008a).

Taken together, such is the impact of these changes and those that have been left unresolved that further reforms of the British political system now appear likely. Indeed the somewhat unprecedented Conservative-Liberal Democrat coalition formed in 2010 announced in its first Queen's speech various constitutional reforms including fixed-term parliaments, the power of recall, a largely elected second chamber and a referendum on the introduction of the Alternative Vote for Westminster elections. Explaining the eventual fate of these reforms, if and when they occur, will raise further questions regarding change and continuity in British politics.

Any consideration of recent developments in British politics encounters two notable trends in accounts of British political life. Firstly the majority of explanations of the British political system have been characterised by reference to the Westminster Model (WM). The WM has been, until recently, the dominant organising perspective in British politics (Gamble 1990; Kerr and Kettell 2006) for those attempting a broader explanation of the British political system. In the past the WM was often seen as a paradigm that should be exported around the world. However in recent years the WM has become increasingly contested (see for example Rhodes 1997; Marsh, Richards and Smith 2001; Bevir and Rhodes 2003; 2006b). The development of new approaches such as the 'Differentiated Polity Model' (DPM) (Rhodes 1997) and the 'Asymmetrical Power Model' (APM) (Marsh, Richards and Smith 2001) has provided a fresh challenge for analysts of the British political system. All explanations of British political life over time must now respond to the criticisms of the WM offered by these new approaches and see to demonstrate how it remains in any way relevant to British politics. Rather than accept this model as a reality as much political analysis has done (Norton 1984; Hanson and Walles 1990), or see it as 'the other' to now be rejected as the 'governance thesis' does (Rhodes 1997; Bevir and Rhodes 2003), we should seek to identify the ideational underpinnings of the institutions, process and discourses of that narrative through the notion of 'political traditions'. In doing so we can more fully explain both the key features of British political life and change and continuity over time.

Alongside the dominance of the WM, a tendency towards British exceptionalism has characterised many accounts of Britain's political development.[1] Conventional analyses of the British political system often neglect detailed consideration of the complex range of dynamics that produce outcomes. This is particularly, though not exclusively, the case with discussion of change and continuity over time. Conventional accounts have tended towards the Whig interpretation of history, emphasising the linear, gradual development of British political life over time. In this a tendency towards exceptionalist accounts of the British mode of democracy that allege the superiority of Britain's historical development can be detected. Taken together, the focus on Whiggish developmentalism and the WM has promulgated a distorted picture of power and democracy within Britain. In particular we can find a tendency towards emphasising the essential pluralism of British politics, rather than highlighting the persistent patterns of structured inequalities and elitism which dominate British society and its political relations.

British exceptionalism in developmental terms remains evident in many overviews of the British political system (see for example Wright

2000). However views steeped in the Whig interpretation of history fail to capture the complexity of the process of change and continuity over time. They tend to ignore the peculiarity of the British mode of political development (Anderson 1964). They also tend to afford the political (and socio-economic) elites a benign and benevolent role that fails to adequately identify or explain the interplay of the socio-economic and the political. The role of the political and social elites has been distorted or forgotten via the Whig narrative, as have their motives. Rather than being groups that were fearful of the idea of democracy itself and unwilling or reluctant to yield their power and influence, they are all too often transformed into the benevolent, interest-free overseers of the gradual extension of democracy (Bagehot 1867; Norton 1984). Conventional approaches not only mask the underlying continuities in who rules Britain but also ignore the possible manufacturing and promotion of consent through the promulgation of the WM narrative. By focusing on the notion of predominant and competing political traditions we can more fully understand the development of British political life over time.

Nor do references to 'the essential political homogeneity of the British people' (Hanson and Walles 1990: 3) accurately portray the reality of British political life historically. Political ideas, attitudes and cultures can and do become dominant and widely accepted. However to suggest that consensus alone is the hallmark feature of British politics significantly underplays a history of ideational conflict and contestation over time. Indeed the hard-fought struggle for some semblance of democratic governance based upon universal suffrage has been supplanted by a narrative of 'evolutionary' development towards a stable and efficient political system based upon democratic elections and responsible and reasonable governance.

This latter point returns us to the relationship between the structures and practices of British government and the broader economic and social strata in UK society. This has been an area of analysis all too often neglected by introductory textbooks and mainstream analyses of the British political system. Indeed the tendency to overlook or even ignore the importance of socio-economic elites within British politics has been amplified by the alleged 'decline of class' and the rise of postmodern approaches in academic circles. Contra this trend the approach to political traditions below seeks to reassert the importance of socio-economic factors historically in the framing of the institutions, processes and practices of the British political system. Indeed the continued relevance of notions concerning structured inequality and asymmetrical power relations should be recognised, as should their impact upon both the institutions and process of British government, and crucially, on outcomes. The predominant ideas, institutions and processes of British politics both reflect and reinforce broader inequalities in British society and contain inherent biases towards certain groups and particular types of political strategy.

This book therefore has two fundamental concerns. Firstly in order to tackle the issues emanating from the failings of traditional accounts of British politics it seeks to critically consider the usage to date of the concept of political traditions in relation to British politics. Secondly it develops a critical concept of the predominant and competing political traditions operating in Britain. Here the aim is to suggest how the institutions and processes associated with the WM can be better conceptualised as emanating from ideas that were a product of the structured inequality of UK society historically and from ideas that reinforced those inequalities. Over time these institutions and ideas became the dominant prism through which politics and political developments were viewed. The book also seeks to offer a concept of how change and continuity in British politics may be explained by stressing the centrality of conflict and contestation in driving historical change and continuity. Furthermore it develops the idea of asymmetrical resonance of political traditions over time, explained in part through reference to contingent events. As such the book is set out as follows:

Beginning with a brief overview of the WM, Chapter 1 unpacks and evaluates existing conceptualisations of the British Political Tradition (BPT). Considering first the classical approach to the BPT found in the work of Oakeshott (1962), Birch (1964), Beer (1965) and Greenleaf (1983a; 1983b; 1987), we will then review a more critical but underutilised approach to the concept found in the work of Marsh and Tant (1989), Tant (1993) and Evans (1995; 2003). From an appreciation of these approaches we can identify the strengths and weaknesses of the concept and suggest why it has been either ignored, underutilised or taken for granted until recently.

In Chapter 2 our attention will turn to the recent work on political traditions, namely that of Bevir and Rhodes (2002; 2003; 2004; 2006a; 2006b; 2006c; 2008a; 2008b) and Marquand (2008). In particular the former's 'new interpretivism' invokes a controversial discussion of tradition to explain outcomes in British politics which is gaining widespread consideration and credence.[2] In particular the usage of the notions of competing traditions by both Bevir and Rhodes, and Marquand is an interesting and welcome development.

Chapter 3 critically explores the concept of tradition by considering how it has been and is best viewed, thus remedying one of the major omissions of work on political traditions to date. Particular emphasis will be placed upon considering how traditions are maintained, reinforced or adapted over time. The contention is that traditions perform functions in relation to the wider social, economic, cultural and political relationships in society and they help to perpetuate patterns of dominance and inequality over time. Predominant and competing traditions operate within society and the interaction between them offers much to those attempting to explain socio-political outcomes. Throughout this chapter tradition will be considered in relation to key meta-theoretical relationships such as structure and agency, the material and ideational, institutions and ideas, and change and continuity. This chapter closes with a consideration of the idea of a political tradition and the possible heuristic value of this concept.

Chapters 4 and 5 revisit the idea of a British Political Tradition (BPT) and offer a detailed explanation of the development of the predominant political tradition in the UK. Chapter 4 considers the development of that tradition historically and its key discourses and architects. This tradition is based upon two discourses which emphasise an elitist concept of democracy, and two further discourses concerning change and national distinctiveness. In Chapter 5 we will then turn to the relationship between the predominant tradition and the institutions of British governance. Finally the relationship between the BPT and structured inequality in the UK will be considered. Throughout these chapters the emphasis will be on the link between the dominant ideas in British politics and the ideas, values and interests of socio-economic and political elites in the UK.

Chapter 6 focuses on a competing political tradition which emphasises a more participatory concept of democracy, thus contesting central tenets of the predominant tradition. This competing tradition can also be traced back through British history and it is possible to identify its key architects and discourses. We will also focus on the challenges emanating from this competing tradition over time and briefly consider the relationship between this tradition and actors in British politics. The contestation between the predominant tradition and this competing tradition can help to explain the development of political outcomes over time, including many recent constitutional reforms.

Chapter 7 focuses on challenges emanating from the nationalist tradition in British politics. This has emphasised different concepts of how territorial politics should be conducted in the UK. Once again we can demonstrate how this tradition can be traced back through British history and identify its key architects and discourses by focusing on its expression in the constituent parts of the UK. Contestation between the nationalist tradition and the predominant tradition helps to explain the development of territorial relations in the UK over time.

Of central significance to the issues discussed in this book is the concept of a British Political Tradition and it is to this that we will now turn.

1
'Variations on a Theme': Political Tradition in Explanations of British Politics

Introduction

The British Political Tradition (BPT) is a concept that has been utilised by a number of authors to explain the nature of British politics and the ideas that underpin political practice in the UK.[1] Two points should be noted initially. Firstly the Westminster Model (WM) has been the dominant prism through which the British political system has been described and analysed. For this reason we should start by briefly outlining this model. A range of explanations for the WM's dominance have been advanced (Gamble 1990; McAnulla 2006a; Kerr and Kettell 2006). However until recently, in general terms, there has been a lack of detailed focus on the role of ideas in shaping political institutions[2] (Hay 2002a: 2004).

Having outlined the WM, various conceptualisations of the BPT will be discussed. There is no agreed definition of what constitutes a political tradition and consequently, it is possible to identify differences between authors who advocate the existence of a distinctive BPT. What is clear is that those using the concept all do so to describe and comment upon the ideas and values that have influenced British politics over time. Indeed it is the focus on the ideational, rather than the institutional, that is often seen to differentiate the BPT from the WM.

The Westminster Model

The dominant organising perspective used in explanations of British politics has been the Westminster Model (WM) (see for example Norton

1984; Punnett 1987). Indeed it is clearly articulated in the canonic descriptions of the British political system (see for example Bagehot 1867; Dicey 1885; Jennings 1936). Verney (1991: 637) states:

> The characteristics of the Westminster model... include: strong cabinet government based on majority rule; the importance attached to constitutional conventions; a two-party system based on single member constituencies; the assumption that minorities can find expression in one of the major parties; the concept of Her Majesty's loyal opposition; and the doctrine of parliamentary supremacy, which takes precedence over popular sovereignty except during elections'.[3]

However more recently Marsh, Richards and Smith argue that it has been 'used more as a shorthand, normative, organising perspective to portray a particular image of the British political system, rather than a theoretically, well developed and explicit model of how British politics works' (2003: 306).

In particular the ideational foundations of the institutions and processes narrated by the WM were/are almost entirely ignored or underexplored, despite the fact that these ideas and values have been at the 'core of the theory and practice of British government for (over) three hundred years' (Miliband 1982: 20).

The WM traditionally refers to the institutions and processes of British government and has remained largely constant since Dicey (1885) outlined its main features. According to Dicey the WM is underpinned by the two pillars of the constitution, Parliamentary Sovereignty and the Rule of Law, with the former encapsulating the contention that the Westminster Parliament:

> under the English constitution, has the right to make or unmake any law whatever, and, further, that no person or body is recognised by law as having a right to override or set aside legislation to override or set aside the legislation of Parliament. (1885: 37–8)

As Gamble (1990: 407) notes in the UK: 'Parliamentary sovereignty meant that the public agencies which made up the state were subordinate to the will of Parliament and were obliged to enforce its decisions.' This potential for Parliament and the party that dominates it to wield its influence over the UK has meant that the WM and its underlying assumptions have been hugely influential on views of and approaches to British politics amongst politicians and commentators alike, a point we will return to shortly.

Although there is not an agreed, definitive version of the WM (Rhodes 2000; Richards and Smith 2002), a number of features are identified by most authors. Lijphart (1999) identifies the following features of the Westminster Model:[4]

- A concentration of executive power in one party
- cabinet dominance
- a two-party system, where parties produce manifestos and seek a mandate to govern (parties are able to control their supporters in the legislative)
- majoritarian (disproportional) electoral system
- unitary, centralised government
- interest group pluralism
- concentration of legislative power in Parliament
- constitutional flexibility
- a central bank controlled by the executive.

To this we could add, as Richards and Smith (2002) do:

- the doctrine of ministerial responsibility
- a permanent, neutral and anonymous civil service.

Gamble (1990) highlights the extent to which the Westminster Model encapsulates a Whiggish approach to change and continuity over time to which many political scientists 'were largely sympathetic' (1990: 411). In this view change needed to be evolutionary' and able to celebrate 'the practical wisdom embodied in England's constitutional arrangements' (1990: 409). The WM emphasised a unilinear, gradual evolutionary development for the institutions and processes of the British political system. Echoing this observation, Kerr and Kettell (2006: 7) argue that the WM:

> was based on an intrinsically Whiggish conception of the political order dating from the Glorious Revolution of 1688, maintaining that this had bequeathed the nation a series of balanced, harmonious, and yet flexible constitutional arrangements, which had enabled it to adjust to social, political, and economic change in a gradualist and evolutionary manner and which had thereby enabled it to avoid the

kind of upheavals and revolutionary politics that had been seen in other states.

Thus the WM suggested a degree of British exceptionalism politically whereby Britain's political development was seen as essentially superior to that found elsewhere, particularly on the European continent and in the USA.

Furthermore Richards and Smith (2002) argue that the WM encapsulates a view of the nature of power in the British political system. In the WM power is viewed as concentrated at Westminster and exercised in a top down manner in which the government governs in the interests of the nation.

In recent years the WM has come in for sustained criticism and it can certainly be argued that many of the features of the model have or are changing. However whether the underlying ideas and discourses that have informed that narrative are changing is debatable.

Recent debates

The WM has been the subject of sustained criticism and alternative narratives have been developed (Rhodes 1997; Smith 1999; Marsh, Richards and Smith 2001; 2003; Bevir and Rhodes 2003; Marsh 2008a).[5] Indeed the WM has been 'roundly dismissed as 'over simplified', as holding 'crude assumptions about the nature of power' and of creating 'false dualities' (Judge 2005: 24). Furthermore Marsh, Richards and Smith (2001: 247) correctly suggest that:

> the Westminster Model present(s) a false picture of how the British political system works. The key features – parliamentary sovereignty, ministerial responsibility and collective responsibility – do not function as the model suggests. However unsurprisingly, it is the view of democracy shared by actors in the core executive... it legitimises their authority and power. As such it affects how the system works. It shaped the process of constitutional and organisational reform and continues to maintain elite rule.

Thus the inaccuracy of the description found in the WM has been increasingly noted. Smith demonstrates how the descriptions given in the WM have been questioned in terms of their accuracy for many years. He notes that 'In the 1960s and 1970s a number of institutional and behavioural accounts questioned the simplicities of the Westminster

Model but they did so largely in terms of traditional approaches, questioning the accuracy of its description but not the principles underlying its approach' (1999: 118).

Examples of this can be found in works such as Mackintosh (1977) or King (1985). Furthermore the peculiarity of the British State itself has been recognised by some. For example Anderson (1964) suggests that the British State is more accurately seen as an 'Ancien Regime' due to the lack of bourgeois revolution in the UK. Many pre-industrial, pre-modern institutions and processes remained in place such as the House of Lords and the monarchy's involvement in the political process.

However the recent questioning of the WM and its assumptions has been driven by a combination of empirical and theoretical challenges (Smith 1999). For example the New Right and their civil service reforms led to changes in both the structure and practice of government bureaucracy. Indeed the increased use of think tanks and political advisors is seen as indicative of a changing role for the civil servant at Whitehall. Smith points to the internationalisation of government through the development of supranational organisations such as the EU, the WTO and the World Bank, as well as the growth of multinational corporations and financial institutions. Finally he suggests that marketisation within parts of the British state has led to both fragmentation and the growth of external constraints on those within the core executive marketisation has thus challenged some of the alleged workings of the WM.

Beyond the general observations above, two specific yet interrelated criticisms have been aimed at the WM.

Governance

In recent years, numerous authors have suggested that we have witnessed a shift from government to governance (see for example Rhodes 1997; Pierre 2000; Bevir and Rhodes 2003; 2006b). Governance is a notoriously difficult term to define and one that is also contested. Richards and Smith (2002: 14) define governance as:

> a descriptive label that is used to highlight the changing nature of the policy process in recent decades. In particular it sensitizes us to the ever-increasing variety of terrains and actors involved in the making of public policy. Thus 'governance' demands that we consider all the actors and locations beyond the 'core executive' involved in the policy-making process.

Governance is therefore broader than the notion of government in that it includes non-state actors from the public, private and voluntary sectors. In particular the boundaries between state and non-state actors have become blurred or opaque. Governance is characterised by interactions between network members who exchange resources and negotiate shared goals. Network members interact with each other in a game-like fashion where these interactions are regulated by agreed, negotiated rules. Finally these networks are self-organising and thus not accountable to the state. Most significantly in the context of our present discussion, the governance thesis does not privilege the state as sovereign. Instead, contra the WM and its central doctrine, Parliamentary Sovereignty, it can only steer these networks and even then only imperfectly.

In relation to the WM therefore 'governance' suggests a break with past explanations of British politics and the development of 'a new process of governing' (Rhodes 1997: 15). Furthermore a range of developments linked to the rise of governance have undermined the core assumptions of the WM. These include:

- challenges to Parliamentary sovereignty emanating from the EU and the advent of globalisation
- the rise of managerialism in the public sector, privatization, and the advent of agencies and quangos – this had led to a blurring of the lines of accountability
- challenges to the unitary state via devolution
- when combined, the above points suggest the hollowing out of the State at the centre
- the decline of Cabinet government in the face of policy-active prime ministers such as Thatcher and Blair
- the failure of ministerial responsibility to operate as the model suggests.

As a consequence of these changes Rhodes (1997) suggests that the WM is no longer an adequate organising perspective for British politics and he develops the Differentiated Polity Model (DPM). McAnulla (2006a: 35) identifies six features of the DPM:

- A hollowed-out state where the state has lost its powers in various ways. Through EU integration and globalisation it has lost power to supranational organisations. The state has also lost power to both agencies and the private sector.

- A segmented executive where government departments have substantial input into policy and decision-making is segmented rather than integrated by the Prime Minister. Furthermore there are divisions on policy within the government.
- Power-dependency where actors are reliant upon each other for success. This serves to limit the potential for any one actor or group to dominate.
- Intergovernmental relations where the focus is on a wide range of relationships between central and regional or local government, and the public sector. Decision-making involves exchange between actors at a central and local level.
- A focus on governance rather than on government. In this view, actors beyond the core executive play a key part in the formulation and implementation of policy.
- Policy networks where various interests seek to influence the policies in a specific area of activity. There are no clear boundaries between networks and government departments do not have a privileged position within networks.

Multi-level governance

The notion of Multi-Level Governance (MLG) is an increasing feature of discussions about territorial politics and governance in the UK (Gamble 2000; Hay 2002b; Flinders 2006). Indeed Pierre and Stoker (2009: 29) suggest that 'governing Britain – and indeed any other advanced Western democratic state – has thus become a matter of multi-level governance'.

MLG means an increasingly complex governmental and policy process where authority is distributed both vertically and horizontally across a variety of institutions at a sub-national, national and supranational level. The distribution of power across and between institutions is a hallmark feature of this new concept. It should also be noted that of equal importance in this 'disaggregated state' are both state and non-state actors such as the private sector, voluntary organisations and community groups. Crucially, MLG is characterised by dramatically different features to the Westminster Model (WM).

Flinders (2006) highlights the three areas of distinction between the two concepts. Firstly the WM was based upon the general principles of centralisation, control, hierarchy and clear lines of accountability, whereas MLG emphasises disaggregation, heterarchy, steering and multiple lines of accountability. Secondly the WM emphasised the absolute and inviolable sovereignty of the Westminster Parliament whereas MLG emphasises relative sovereignty. Finally the internal dimensions of the UK state identified by both models are also different according to Flinders. Whilst the WM stressed parliamentary sovereignty, a unitary state and a strong centralised executive who governed directly, MLG sees a quasi-federal state where new working practices and skills such as inter-institutional bargaining in a segmented executive, delegated governance and fragmentation are hallmark features. As such the two models stand in stark contrast to one another and MLG provides a major challenge to the WM.

Moreover those who use MLG tend to use it 'not just as a descriptive or analytical term to describe change but also as a normatively superior mode of allocating authority' (Bache and Flinders 2004: 195–6) to the WM. MLG is seen as both an accurate description of recent political developments and 'a good, superior and beneficial mode of governance' (Flinders 2006: 132). Here we might ask on what other basis is this superiority of MLG grounded? Advocates of MLG offer no critique of the WM beyond the fact that it fails to explain the complexity of relations today. In a sense they are guilty of not explaining their position fully. Furthermore the accuracy of the WM as a description of British political life was highly debateable anyway. This point can be illuminated through a brief focus on one of the key facets of the WM, the Unitary State.

The Unitary State

The UK has historically been, and remains, a composite state with a complex pattern of territorial politics (Holliday 1999: 119). Traditionally the UK has been seen as a unitary state. Although this term is rarely defined (Mitchell 2002: 239) it is a core feature of the WM (see for example Dicey 1885). A unitary state can be defined as a state or country that is governed constitutionally as one single unit, with one constitutionally created legislature. The political power of government in such states may well be transferred to lower levels, to regionally or locally elected assemblies, governors and mayors. However the central political authority retains the principal right to recall such delegated power.

Dicey (1885) focused on the unitary state contra other potential territorial relations such as federalism which he saw as flawed and offering few, if any, benefits (Evans 2003). In particular he highlighted the need for national unity as being far easier to achieve under a unitary constitution. Dicey did not deny the existence of pre-union institutions and practices when describing UK territorial relations; instead he believed the key aim was to achieve 'unity of government,'[6] that is to say, British government. The unitary state, with its obvious link to the central Diceyian principle of Parliamentary Sovereignty, was essential to achieve this. However whilst widely cited works on British politics focused on the unitary constitution with sovereignty at the centre, regional variances were often overlooked or taken for granted (Paterson 2000; Macinnes 2008). Thus traditional descriptions came to equate territorial relations in the UK with a narrow, unsophisticated 'unitary state paradigm' in which national unity directed by the centre was emphasised, whilst difference at the periphery was downgraded or ignored. Such was the dominance of this view that it featured in numerous descriptions of the British political system (see for example Jennings 1941; Bogdanor 1979; Norton 1984).[7]

However Mitchell (2002) suggests that despite achieving an almost 'mythological status', the unitary state is a more problematic and underconceptualised term than its previously unquestioned status would suggest. More recently, the term 'union state' (Rokkan and Unwin 1982) has come to feature more prominently in the discussion of territorial politics in the UK[8] and offers a more accurate description of territorial relations in the UK. It recognises the high degree of centralisation in the UK political system. However it maintains that integration was less than total, with some pre-union institutions continuing to exist and other new institutions being created. As such it allows for the notion that competing approaches might exist, develop and eventually contest the predominant approach. It also implies that the existence of such institutions served a function for elites either for recruitment or because they did not threaten the broader aim of creating a unified British government. More broadly the 'union state' allowed for the, at the very least, partial integration of Scottish and Welsh elites into a newly created British socio-economic and political elite post 1707 (Colley 2003). Indeed Mitchell (2007) suggests that 'viewed from Scotland and the rest of the periphery, the UK was never a unitary state but a state of the unions' (McGarvey and Cairney 2008: 24).

Furthermore Bulpitt argues that the period between 1926 and the early 1960s was one in which 'national and local politics were largely divorced from each other' (1983: 235). This again suggests a more nuanced position than the simple view promulgated as part of the WM. In Bulpitt's view, territorial relations in this period are best characterised as a 'dual polity'. By this concept he means that as long as central government controlled the policies of 'high politics' – essentially finance, defence, and foreign policy – it was prepared to leave the administration of what it regarded as 'low politics' to the localities and other groups. The idea of the UK as a 'dual polity' suggests two points relevant to developing a more nuanced and accurate view of territorial relations in the UK than that offered by the WM. Firstly the potential for executive dominance remains central to the idea of a dual polity; however it may not be consistently actualised. Centre–periphery relations in the UK were dominated by the centre via its control of key policy areas. Indeed it is worth noting that the centre had control of the policy areas that define the nation-state and, thus could, and did, assert both its dominance and a sense of 'Britishness' through this. Secondly the administration of low politics by the periphery occurred within parameters set by the centre, Westminster, in most areas. As Mitchell (2002) suggests, for the most part, the centre governed as it saw fit.

From the brief discussion above it can be seen that the WM can be criticised both as incapable of fully capturing the realities of recent changes in British politics and also for offering an inaccurate description of British political life historically. However despite these criticisms, the WM must still be considered for one reason.

Continued relevance?

Despite its inability to accurately describe how UK institutions work and interact 'the most important feature of this model is that it reflects how most politicians and officials perceive the system' (Richards and Smith 2002: 248). Thus it continues 'to inform and condition the way in which (these) actors operate' (Richards and Smith 2002: 248). It is this that is worthy of note. In their detailed study of central government Marsh, Richards and Smith argue that 'whilst there have been changes in intra and inter Whitehall relationships, they have not undermined many of the traditional assumptions that the practitioners have about the workings of the system' (2001: 233).

On this, Oliver notes that, even allowing for the primacy of EU law, 'Parliamentary Sovereignty is still regarded as sacrosanct, by both the UK Courts and by the political elites' (2003: 8). Furthermore canonic texts such as Bagehot (1867), Dicey (1885) and Jennings (1936; 1941) are still widely cited as authoritative texts, despite the questionable accuracy of their descriptions of the British political life in the past.[9] However rather than accept these descriptions we should seek to understand how the conventions and practices described therein have been inculcated and promulgated over time, to the point where they have become 'common understandings' of the British political system.

Rather than viewing the WM as an accurate description of the reality of British political life it is best viewed as a narrative of the British political system. In this view the WM was/is actually a widely believed and promulgated self-image of the institutions and processes of British politics underpinned by discourses concerning representation, responsibility, gradual change and national distinctiveness. This 'legitimising mythology' (Richards and Smith 2002: 48) is centrally significant when explaining the process by which recent developments such as devolution have developed. Even Rhodes, one of the sternest critics of the WM admits that it 'embodies political traditions which continue to shape political behaviour' (1997: 199). Thus the importance of the WM lies in relation to how actors understand the British political system, rather than the accuracy of the description it offers.

If we return to the unitary state for a moment, a similar point can be made. As with other aspects of the WM, actors across both the UK and the political spectrum came to believe that this was both an accurate description of UK territorial relations and one that delivered (Mitchell 2002). Indeed the unitary state's potency lay less in its accuracy and more in the widespread, and largely unquestioned, acceptance this discourse achieved. Even as late as the early 1990s the unitary state remained uncontested in many explanations of territorial relations in the UK.[10] It undoubtedly had a profound impact upon the attitudes of political actors from both the Conservative and Labour parties, although for differing reasons. Thus the unitary state became the dominant explanation of UK territorial relations and one that was largely viewed as positive and beneficial. Having been established by the Act of Union 1707, centre–periphery relations soon became clearly understood and taken for granted in the UK (Holliday 1999). The role of the lower levels of governance within the UK was primarily to ensure integration wherever possible. In essence, the notion of the unitary state quickly became accepted amongst the principle actors at Westminster and in the regions. The pre-1998 example of devolution in UK politics, Stormont, seems to confirm this analysis. The aim of Stormont was to encourage conformity to the same standards as Westminster (Mitchell 2002: 243).

Having outlined the WM and some issues surrounding its efficacy as an explanatory framework for British politics, we will now turn attention to a perspective that focuses explicitly on the ideational underpinnings of British political life rather than its institutions, the BPT.

The British Political Tradition

As stated earlier, the British Political Tradition (BPT) is a concept that has been deployed by a diverse range of authors from various methodological and normative perspectives (Beer 1965; Birch 1964; Greenleaf 1983a; 1983b; 1987; Marsh and Tant 1989; Tant 1993; Evans 1995; 2003). Although there are differences between their conceptualisations, what unites these authors is a desire to focus on the notion of political tradition and the ideas that underpin the institutions and processes of British government. In doing so, they attempt to offer a more theoretically informed view of the development of the British political system over time.[11] Despite this, such a perspective on British Politics has all too often been ignored. The majority of authors have favoured either explicitly or implicitly the Westminster Model as an explanatory framework without considering how those institutions and processes came into being or, crucially, what ideas and views of democracy underpin them.

Classical approaches to the British Political Tradition

Here we can identify the views of Michael Oakeshott and three key texts: Anthony Birch's *Representative and Responsible Government* (1964), Samuel Beer's *Modern British Politics* (1965) and W. H. Greenleaf's, *The British Political Tradition* (1983a; 18983b; 1987).

Oakeshott

The BPT has often been seen as non-ideological. Such a view is advanced in the work of the conservative thinker Michael Oakeshott (1962). The origins of this view can be traced back much further to that key conservative thinker Edmund Burke (1790). Oakeshott was concerned with tradition in its broadest sense and believed that it offered the surest guide to political action. He believed that 'every political community...can be said to have developed a tradition of political life' (Kenny 1999: 277). Ideologies acted only as 'simplifications of richer and more nuanced sets of practices, values and ideas designed to facilitate political argument and understanding (Kenny 1999: 278). For Oakeshott, the BPT was not a consistent doctrine or ideology. Rather it was a set of intertwined practices, values and ideas. It was characterised by the 'pragmatic handling of social problems, an aversion to the intrusions of rationalist dogma and a commitment to the rule of law which enables a flourishing of what he termed, a vital civil association' (Kenny

1999: 278). Oakeshott suggests that these values were deeply rooted in day-to-day aspects of political life and debate in Britain and can be seen particularly in the core institutions, practices and beliefs of British politics. They are then handed down from generation to generation, thus constituting a political tradition.

This characterisation of the BPT as an indigenous, distinctive set of non-ideological values, ideas and prejudices, with its attendant rejection of rationalism, has a long history within British political discourse. Indeed we can find it powerfully expressed in Burke (1790). Moreover it underpins widely read works such as Norton (1984). Three key points are notable here. Firstly it is possible to detect what Kenny (1999: 278) refers to as a 'high minded version of a frequently uttered piece of common sense wisdom – that ideology is in fact alien to British culture and experience and has had largely harmful consequences when imported'. Secondly it is based upon appeals to a sense of political distinctiveness rooted in indigenous national characteristics. Finally it is the non-ideological nature of the BPT that sets it apart from other political traditions, particularly those found in Europe. Indeed this argument underpins the claims to British exceptionalism and a superior developmental path that has been prevalent in many key works on British politics.

Birch

Anthony Birch (1964) offers an influential interpretation of the BPT that has found expression in some of the most widely read textbooks on British Politics.[12] Birch argues that the BPT has been shaped by certain notions regarding democracy and, in particular, debates about the nature of 'representation' and 'responsibility'. These two notions have, according to Birch, fundamentally shaped the practice of British politics and constitute the BPT.

Representation

An approach to representation has developed in Britain as a result of debates conducted in the 19th century between the Whigs and the Tories and their descendants: the Liberals and Conservatives. Birch identifies three meanings for the term. Firstly he argues that it has often denoted 'an agent or delegate, a person whose function is to protect and if possible advance the interests of an individual or group on whose behalf he is acting – irrespective of who they are, how they are chosen, or how much discretion they are allowed, their function is to look after the interests of the organisation, group or person they represent' (Birch 1964: 14).

Secondly representation can refer to persons and assemblies who have been freely elected. These elected representatives have some obligation to advance interests and views of electors. However there is no constitutional imperative for this and the conventions of British politics do not compel elected representatives to act as an agent or delegate of his/her constituents. It is notable that only a small minority of MPs or political commentators have ever argued that MPs should act as delegates (Birch 1964: 227). On this we can see that the net result of this has been a minimal role for the electorate and a great deal of discretion for both representatives and the government once selected.

Thirdly Birch suggests that representation is used to discuss the extent to which Parliament can be considered a microcosm of the society it claims to represent. Parliament may represent the nation in a demographic sense, although it should be noted that representation in this sense is in no way perfect or fixed. The 2005 reduction in the number of Scottish seats at Westminster from 72 to 59, and the concerns regarding equalisation of constituencies by the Conservative party clearly demonstrate this point. However the debates of the late 18th and early 19th centuries did not see it is as essential or desirable that Parliament was a microcosm of the society it represented. Indeed this was something that was to be avoided. This definition of the term representation has not been seen as necessary or desirable in the British system of government because it is contended that political actors will act responsibly.[13]

In discussing representation in the UK the importance of the thought of Burke (1790) and the idea of trusteeship have proven to be of central significance. The importance of this approach to representation will be discussed in Chapter 4. Suffice it to say here that it has been the predominant ideational prism through which MPs have both seen and narrated their role as representatives of the people.

Therefore for Birch the product of the almost continuous debates concerning representation occurring from the end of the 18th century and throughout the 19th century was a situation where 'no single theory of political representation' (Birch 1964: 227) developed. Crucially, Birch argues that representation is counter-balanced against the need for politicians to be able to govern.

Responsibility

The other key facet of the BPT identified by Birch is 'responsible government'. Birch contends that the debate concerning responsible government did not become fully realised until the 20th century.[14] From that point onwards there was a stringent debate about what constituted 'responsible government'.[15] Birch suggests that 'responsible government' has three meanings.

Firstly it has meant responsiveness to public demands and shifts in public opinions. Birch argues that the recognition of this obligation is what distinguishes democracy from dictatorial and autocratic regimes (Birch 1964: 18). Secondly responsible government means that government has a moral duty to act as the guardians of national interest and to pursue policies that are 'wise', even if policies do not meet with immediate approval from the electorate. Thus responsible government is equated with strong government; initiatory and decisive government is seen as effective government. The willingness of British governments to risk unpopularity by taking decisions in the national interest is often invoked to illustrate governments acting responsibly. Finally responsible government is equated with accountability. Responsibility is used to describe 'the accountability of Ministers, or of the government as a whole, to the elected assembly' (Birch 1964: 20). Conventions such as Individual Ministerial Responsibility and Collective Ministerial Responsibility exist to ensure this, as do mechanisms within Parliament such as Prime Minister's Question Time.

In effect, the BPT equates responsible government with leadership and prudence. Indeed Birch argues that 'The British political tradition would clearly determine the order as first consistency, prudence and leadership, second accountability to parliament and the electorate and third, responsiveness to public opinions and public demands' (1964: 245). This is demonstrated by the 'belief that a government should not be deterred from pursuing policies which it thinks are right by the fact that they are unpopular' (Birch 1964: 244).

Thus for Birch, it is the ideas of representative and responsible government that form the BPT. Crucially, this tradition and its consequences are characterised by Birch in a positive light. As he famously states:

> Everyone knows that the British Constitution provides for a system of representative and responsible government. These characteristics are almost universally regarded as both desirable and important...The concepts of representation and responsibility are indeed invoked in almost every modern discussion of how countries ought to be governed. (Birch 1964: 13)

Three points should be made about Birch's analysis before moving on. Firstly Birch undoubtedly focuses attention on the debates surrounding the development of the British political system and how these were fundamental in shaping much of what followed. This in itself is important, although the debates concerning the British political system and their outcome can be more persuasively characterised somewhat differently.

Secondly he does not focus on the extent to which his central notions of 'representation and responsibility' have been inscribed into the institutions and processes of British government (Marsh and Hall 2007). Birch leaves uncharted the important question of the relationship between institutions and ideas. This constitutes both a major omission and a significant weakness of his analysis. By not adequately explaining how the notions of representation and responsibility influenced and informed the development of the institutions and processes of British government, the reader is left with, at best, a partial account.

Finally he offers a perspective that stresses the importance of continuity in British politics. For example he states that 'fresh theories have not replaced the old, but have tended to take place alongside old ones as strands in the British Political Tradition' (Birch 1964: 227). Here the emphasis on continuity and the under-theorisation of how the BPT might develop over time is problematic, a point we will return to in greater depth later in this chapter.

Beer

Samuel Beer's *Modern British Politics* (1965) offers another widely read analysis that also suggests the existence of a distinctive BPT. Indeed Moran states that this book 'was the most influential advanced text in the teaching of British politics for a generation' (2006: 139). Authors including Marsh and Tant (1989) and Batters (2005) point to similarities between Beer (1965) and Birch (1964). Beer (1965) undoubtedly shares Birch's belief that ideas play a fundamental role in explaining political outcomes. Like Birch, he sees debates concerning representation, and to a lesser extent responsibility, as central to the development of the British political system and its institutions and processes.

However we should be wary of homogenising the work of these two authors (Batters 2005). Beer's contention that there is a distinctive BPT differs from Birch's in two important respects. Firstly Beer (1965) describes the BPT as a political culture. Indeed he suggests that the BPT is 'a body of beliefs widely held in British society' (1965: xii). Secondly he describes the BPT as an arena in which some tensions and conflict about moral and political questions have been and continue to be, played out (1965: xii).

Despite these important differences, Beer does afford significance to debates concerning representation, albeit as part of a broader debate about authority and the legitimate distribution of power (Batters 2005). For Beer, the ideal parliamentary representative is conceived of in liberal terms (Marsh and Tant 1989). The BPT favours politicians who were independent in the sense that their consciences and opinions defined their political actions and affiliations. As such, for Beer, the BPT defines the ideal MP as 'an independent rational man' (1965: 39) and this reflects Burke's view about the proper role of the representative that so decisively shaped the debates of the late 18th and 19th centuries.

Beer is also explicitly concerned with the implications of debates concerning representation for the subsequent development of the institutions and practices of British government (Batters 2005). When discussing the proper role of government emphasised in the BPT, Beer identifies the executive as the 'central initiating, directing, energizing body' (Beer 1965: 14). Quoting L. S. Amery, he states that 'British government ... is an independent body which on taking office assumes the responsibility of leading and directing Parliament and the nation in accordance with its own judgement and convictions' (1965: 96). He goes on to suggest that this forms both the theory and practice of British government to date, in that this notion 'was preserved [as] an element around which the vast powers of modern cabinet could collect' (1965: 14). He also notes the extent to which there has been consensus between the parties of government over a range of points including 'the main contemporary practices of party government and functional representation' (Beer 1965: 387).

Thus Beer, like Birch, identifies the centrality of notions of representation and the proper role of government as being central to the BPT. Significantly, he believes that this tradition – and the view of democracy that it incorporates – asserts that, while governments must be representative, they must also be able to govern. Whilst focusing, like Birch (1964), on the centrality of debates concerning representation and responsibility in the 18th and 19th centuries is important, these notions can be more persuasively characterised somewhat differently.

The undoubted strength of Beer's approach to the BPT is that he conceptualises that tradition somewhat differently to Birch by discussing it as a political culture. This suggests that it has permeated beyond the political elite into the populace at large who recognise its alleged benefits and this opens up consideration of how it has been inculcated and reinforced over time.

Contra Birch (1964), Beer also offers some focus onto how the central ideas of representation and responsibility influenced the institutions and processes of British government. However his view of this process is underdeveloped and under-theorised. The implication of Beer's work is that ideas shape institutions in a unilinear fashion. Here, there are two key points. Firstly it can be argued that his concept of change and continuity is also underdeveloped and under-theorised, a point we will return to later. Secondly Beer's view can be critiqued for being crudely idealist, that is to say, it gives much importance to ideas in influencing political outcomes. However the relationship between institutions and ideas requires far greater theorisation if persuasive explanations of the development of institutions over time are to be advanced. It is on this basis that Beer's account should be criticised, rather than on his focus on ideas generally.

Greenleaf

W. H. Greenleaf's three volumes, *The British Political Tradition* (1983a; 1983b; 1987), is the other defining work of the classical literature of the BPT. It should be noted here that Greenleaf's novel approach is rooted in a definition of political tradition linked to political ideology and, thus needs to be partially differentiated from the work of Birch (1964) and Beer (1965). For Greenleaf, the BPT is characterised by a trans-ideological tension between Libertarianism and Collectivism. Notably, Greenleaf's conceptualises this tension in terms of dialectical conflict between opposing forces.

Kenny (1999: 279) suggests that Greenleaf takes his initial conceptualisation of tradition from Oakeshott (1962). Greenleaf views a tradition of political activity as implying 'a unity in diversity: a complex amalgam of different forces and opposing choices and therefore internal tensions, which is at the same time in a continual state of flux and development but which nevertheless constitutes a recognisable whole' (1983a: 13).

However Greenleaf's focus upon the dialectical tension between libertarianism and collectivism saw him move beyond the non-ideological claims of Oakeshott in explaining key features of the BPT. This tension between opposing tendencies within British politics, signified by the rising of *the tides of collectivism* in the late 19th century (Dicey cited in Kenny 1999: 279), can be used to explain political developments in

Britain. As Greenleaf states: 'the dialectic between the growing processes of collectivism and the opposing libertarian tendency is the one supreme fact of our political life as this has developed over the past century and a half' (1983b: 3). Greenleaf defines Libertarianism as an assemblage of values, whose core is the belief that there is a natural harmony in society that exists without recourse to state intervention. Its four central characteristics are:

- a stress on the importance of the individual, and freedom from social and political supervision
- a commitment to limiting the legitimate arena for government intervention
- a fear of concentrations of power
- a commitment to the security offered by rule of law.

Adapted from Kenny (1999)

Conversely, collectivism, for Greenleaf, is an 'idea of an artificial identification of human interests resulting from legislative and other political regulation' (1983a: 15), usually articulated through a concern with public good and a desire to achieve common security. For Greenleaf the BPT is 'constituted by a dialectic between two opposing tendencies, which, taken together, constitute limits within which the possibilities of politics freely range' (1983a: 28).

Greenleaf's narrative suggests that the BPT had seen a shift from libertarianism towards collectivism as the extent of government intervention and public agency had increased. This was particularly the case in the 20th century as the government took on new powers as a consequence of industrialisation, urbanisation and the need to fight two world wars (Greenleaf 1983a: 78). As government grew in size and scope as a consequence of economic and social developments, political debates in Britain have been decisively shaped by the tension between the demands for individual liberty and greater government intervention (Greenleaf 1983b: xi). In this process the three main ideological traditions, Liberalism, Conservatism and Socialism, had both reacted to and been stimulated by this tension. For Greenleaf, each of these ideologies had adherents to either libertarianism or collectivism within them.

Unlike Birch (1964), Greenleaf is concerned with how the BPT has informed the institutions and processes of British government. He devotes the third volume of his study, entitled *A Much Governed Nation* (1987), to it. Leaving aside the obvious normative connotations of this title, we should note here Greenleaf's argument. In essence, he argues that the dialectical tension between libertarianism and collectivism has had an impact upon the institutions of British government. In particular the rise of collectivism led to the development of numerous new institutions and ways for the state to intervene in the lives of citizens. On the latter point, Greenleaf makes little attempt to hide his views on this extension of state intervention when he asserts: 'the history of the modern British polity thus reveals a continuing parade of institutional modification and invention and a tendency to apply this machinery ever more widely' (1987: 3). Indeed his references to 'a positive frenzy of reform and reorganization' (1983: 3), the moulding to the collectivist purpose, and/or the casting aside of traditional institutions, highlights the extent to which Greenleaf viewed the rise of collectivism as leading to over-government and the adaptation, and often abandonment, of traditional institutions and practices.

Kenny (1999) argues that Greenleaf's approach has been widely read and has inspired some influential analyses of modern British politics. He certainly makes an intriguing contribution to discussions about the BPT by focusing attention on the broader philosophical ideas within which British political actors have operated. More importantly, he offers the suggestion that the institutions and processes of British government have been inscribed with the ideas of the BPT. Although his conceptualisation of this process has been critiqued for offering an idealist perspective in which the institutions and processes of British government have been inspired by ideas or traditions of thought (McAnulla 2006a), it is here that its major contributions lies. His approach that involves moving outward 'from the intimations of traditions to the practices and institutions it inspires' (Bevir and Rhodes 2003: 21) is undoubtedly overly simplistic.[16] However a view that accepts that there is a relationship between ideas and institutions, but conceptualises it as both interactive and iterative (Marsh 2003), can offer a great deal of heuristic value.

The majority of criticisms of Greenleaf's view of the BPT are directed at its substance. Bevir and Rhodes (2003) dispute Greenleaf's analysis in a number of ways. Firstly they critique his view for offering an essentialist conceptualisation of the BPT that reifies traditions and ignores the possibility for change within traditions. They suggest that the components of Greenleaf's version of the BPT act 'as fixed categories, ideal types, into which he forces individual thinkers and texts' (Bevir and Rhodes 2003: 123). Relatedly they critique him for offering an ahistorical view of British political development in which the BPT is static and unchanging over time. Thus they believe that Greenleaf offers an account that focuses only on continuity and not change. Finally they contend that Greenleaf offers a crude idealist perspective in which the institutions and processes of British government have been simply inspired by ideas or traditions of thought (Bevir and Rhodes 2003: 23). More broadly, we might note here, as McAnulla (2006a: 22) does, that 'a range of authors, sometimes dubbed sceptics, argue that ideas tend to be used as instruments or tools that politicians use to manipulate opinion and to gain power'. Kenny identifies a different flaw with Greenleaf's view. He argues: 'The interpretation of political discourse in the nineteenth and twentieth centuries through the push-pull of libertarian and collectivist expressions gives rise to inadequate intellectual history as these categories are too starkly drawn to account for the unfolding patterns of thought which straddle and undermine this divide' (1999: 280).

Essentially, Greenleaf's analytical framework oversimplifies the interaction between divergent political ideas by reducing it to the simple prioritisation of one view over another, which is unlikely to be the case. In contrast, it could be argued that it is through the process of interactive and iterative conflict between competing sets of ideas that the process of change and development, as well as entrenchment and affirmation, in the BPT and British politics can be explained.

Two final observations on the conceptualisations of the BPT offered by the authors above are important. Firstly despite the differences raised between the various usages of the BPT, they are unified on one point. From Oakeshott to Greenleaf they all discuss the BPT and how it has functioned over time in a positive and sympathetic tone (Tant 1993: 90). Indeed central to all their concepts is a belief that the BPT has served Britain and the British well. For example Birch endorses Quintin Hogg's view that 'the British on the whole prefer to see a strong government of which they disapprove, rather than a weak government whose political structure is more complex and whose power to govern is limited' (1964: 244). Here, he is implying that the BPT is both desirable and desired by the British populace. Thus it is a positive force within British politics. Such a view is not too far distanced from the exceptionalist accounts of Norton (1984), Punnett (1987) and Hanson and Walles (1990), all of whom focus on Britain's distinctive, and allegedly superior, developmental path. Indeed the classical literature on the BPT may have assisted in the perpetuation of this view.

Secondly there is insufficient theorisation of meta-theoretical issues in the work of all those adopting a positive view of the BPT. None of the authors adequately discuss or theorise the relationships between structure and agency, the material and the ideational, institutions and ideas, and continuity and change. This failure to address meta-theoretical issues is, as Marsh and Stoker (1995; 2002) and Hay (2002) claim, a weakness of much literature in political analysis and one we will return to in more detail shortly.

Having outlined the major positive approaches to the BPT, we will now turn our attention to more critical approaches to the concept.

Critical approaches to the British Political Tradition

Here, we can identify a range of works: David Marsh and Tony Tant's *There is No Alternative: Mrs Thatcher and the British Political Tradition* (1989), Tant's *British Government: The Triumph of Elitism* (1993) and Mark Evans's, *Charter 88: A Successful Challenge to the British Political Tradition?* (1995) and *Constitution Making and the Labour Party* (2003).[17]

Marsh and Tant

Marsh and Tant (1989) provide a view of the BPT that emphasises what they see as its fundamentally elitist nature. They contend that British democracy is essentially a top down version of democracy based upon elitist concepts stressing the need for strong government and executive dominance, rather than responsive government. Indeed they suggest that 'executive dominance...has consistently marked the British Political Tradition' (1989: 9).

Like Birch (1964) and Beer (1965), Marsh and Tant stress the notions of 'representative and responsible' government. As regards representation, they (1989: 8) suggest that debate and deliberation were viewed in the 18th and early 19th centuries as the province of the elected few. They argue that this Burkeian concept of representation has, until very recently, been fundamental in informing the views of the majority of politicians, regardless of their ideological persuasion. As such, they believe that we should view representation at Westminster as based upon ideas concerning elitism, rather than popular accountability.

Similarly, they suggest that responsible government in the UK revolves around strong government, rather than responsive government (Marsh and Tant 1989: 4). In their view, this is underpinned by a view of democracy that is 'an elitist or top down view' (1989: 4). In particular they highlight the importance of the idea that 'the Government acts as the trustees and guardians of the nation's well-being' (1989: 8). The direct consequence of this elitism is that 'strong, decisive and centralised government is always emphasised' (Marsh and Tant 1989: 8).

There are two aspects of the BPT identified by Marsh and Tant (1989) which are important here. Firstly they offer a perspective that, on the surface, seems to focus on history and continuity over time. They note that 'virtually all writers on the British political tradition note the extent to which continuity rather than radical change marks succeeding dominant ideologies' (1989: 6). Secondly they suggest that notions concerning harmony and order have proven to be essential to sustaining the BPT (1989: 7). On the basis of these observations about the fundamental elitism of the BPT, they proceed to analyse the Thatcher governments, concluding by paraphrasing the mantra of the first Thatcher administration.

In a number of ways the analysis offered by Marsh and Tant (1989) should be viewed as pioneering. Firstly they offer us a critical, if brief, account of the development of the British political system in which they highlight the essentially elitist nature of British politics in theory and practice. Importantly they also highlight the relationship between how notions of representation are conceptualised and how the role of government responsibility is then seen. Secondly they suggest that an elitist view of democracy has been translated into institutional arrangements. Thirdly they emphasise the importance of a historically informed perspective for explaining contemporary developments. Finally they suggest that we should consider how the British political system has been narrated over time by identifying broader ideas concerning harmony and order as essential features of the BPT.

However their work is by no means definitive. Like classical accounts of the BPT they do not sufficiently address meta-theoretical issues. Moreover we can also identify more specific criticisms. Firstly their analysis is not fully realised. For example they suggest that 'in Britain the participatory strand of democratic thought has had very little influence' (Marsh and Tant 1989: 4). They do not however fully explore how or why this might be the case. They also offer us the possibility that the dominance of the BPT may be linked to the interests of the dominant groups in British society, but do not explore this relationship. At the same time, it can be argued that their perspective focuses too much on continuity. Certainly, Marsh and Tant (1989) privilege continuity and do not theorise or account for change over time. Of course, this does not mean that their perspective cannot explain change or the potential for change but rather that they have not theorised or explained how it would do so.

Tant

Tant (1993) builds upon the perspective advanced by Marsh and Tant from an explicitly radical democratic perspective. Tant rightly asserts that this elitist democracy has been presented by many authors as legitimate, distinctive, naturally British and ultimately superior to the versions of democracy and the processes which have developed in other Western democracies. In Tant's view 'the most striking feature of the British political tradition and governmental practice is its elitist nature' (1993: 4).

For Tant the UK has, historically, had a system of government rooted in a belief in the virtue of a 'top down' or elitist system of government. He again suggests that the central notions of representation and responsibility can be more properly seen as elitist in their nature. He also suggests that this elitism can be found in the fact that, to date, only a limited number of individuals affect decision-making in the British political system, but, nevertheless, this elite sees itself as acting in the national interest (Tant 1993: 5–6). Once in power the executive will, in most instances, be in a position to force through its policies and the electorate will only be able to have an indirect say every four to five years (Tant 1993: 113).[18] Furthermore Tant argues that MPs are under no constitutional obligation to take any notice of the views of their constituents (1993: 110) and parties do not even have to implement their manifesto commitments (1993: 114).[19] Underpinning this view is the notion that efficient and effective government can only be achieved if we trust the elite to perform decision-making virtually free from public interference. Thus Tant suggests, 'government and only government was the arbiter of the national interest sustained through the tradition of strong, centralised, independent and initiatory government' (1993: 6).

Crucially for Tant, debates concerning the British system of government have tended to focus upon who should govern and on what basis should their authority rest, rather than on how government should be conducted. Highlighting this point, he contends that 'what has never been effectively questioned is whether government, in whatever guise, has the right to make decisions independently and on behalf of the people' (1993: 90).

From this perspective, Tant then develops two further observations on the impact of the BPT. Firstly he focuses on the extent of secrecy endemic in the BPT. Given that the government is the sole arbiter of the national interest, the immediate consequence has been that Britain developed one of the most secretive governments in the Western world. Government maintained control over the release of information to the point where, historically, even the courts did not have the power to compel disclosure. The standard argument has been that this secrecy is essential to protect the anonymity of civil servants. It is also suggested that it is needed for efficient and responsible government. The BPT suggests that:

> the people's representatives (require) to have a large amount of discretion and autonomy in decision-making on behalf of the people and in their ultimate interests... In this view government is a specialised vocation; government must therefore be unfettered, free and independent, in order to make sometimes difficult decisions in the national interest. (Tant 1993: 44)

Focusing upon the elitism that underpins British political institutions and practices, he also explores how more radical, participatory challenges to the BPT, both historically and in recent times, have been defeated. In particular Tant discusses the early Labour party and the more recent Campaign for Freedom of Information (CFOI) as challenges based around more participatory views of democracy. For Tant, the implications of this elitist form of government are unequivocal. He suggests that the last two centuries have seen the thwarting of a range of movements that have attempted to initiate a more participatory version of democracy and government in the UK. In particular he highlights the 'constitutionalisation' of the Labour party as a key example (1993: 125–191). With origins radically different to the Liberals and the Conservatives, Labour, once it became a serious contender for power, quickly came to accept the logic of the BPT. In doing this, the participatory view of democracy that had inspired its initial phase was quickly replaced with adherence to an elitist, or leadership, view of democracy. Since assuming power, the Labour party has moved 'from initially representing a threat to the British constitution it has come to be one of its major guarantors' (Tant 1993: 191).

Tant also argues that the BPT allowed more recent movements, such as the CFOI, to be easily resisted by the Conservative governments of the 1980s who argued that Ministers were already accountable for their actions to Parliament and, consequently the demands of CFOI were unnecessary and inappropriate (1993: 201).

Tant offers a welcome extension of Marsh and Tant (1989) in a number of ways. Firstly Tant's criticisms of the existing literature on the BPT are telling. He rightly asserts that a major weakness of the classical literature and its associated works is an overemphasis on the positive and continuous nature of British political culture in the UK, which he suggests emerge from powerful trends and continuities within British politics (1993 57–9). He rightly contends that this overt focus upon historical continuity and consensus has led to perspectives on British politics that undervalue historical change and, ultimately, prove unsatisfactory when attempting to explain political developments.

Secondly Tant develops the critical view of the BPT by demonstrating, more fully than Marsh and Tant (1989), how the elitist concept of democracy underpins the institutions and practices of the British political system. In particular his discussion of excessive secrecy and how this has developed and is justified is a welcome addition to the debate.

Finally Tant focuses attention on challenges to the BPT, such as the early Labour party and CFOI. He correctly identifies that these challenges were rooted in a more participatory concept of democracy. This is an important addition to the discussion of the BPT in two ways. Firstly it raises the idea that competing views of democracy can be found operating within the UK. Secondly it focuses attention onto the specific groups that might be 'winners and losers' within the BPT.

However Tant's analysis is not without its problems. As with previous analyses, we find a lack of theorisation of meta-theoretical issues. In particular given the tone of his critique, the lack of discussion of an economic dimension of the BPT is telling. More pointedly, we should note that, despite his critique of the classical authors for overly focusing on continuity, he comes dangerously close to doing so himself. His view that the BPT has successfully thwarted all challenges and attempts at radical change suggests that it is largely unchanged over time. Thus Tant emphasises historical continuity and gives little attention to change, or even the potential for change, within the BPT. Here, we should note two points. Firstly not all change need be radical. Secondly British democracy has not remained entirely unadapted over time. Tant does not offer us a way of explaining less substantial changes or adaptations to the British political system through his concept of the BPT. Nor does he adequately conceptualise the relationship between continuity and change. Rather he leaves us with a view that seems to privilege continuity over change. Whilst he is right to contend that central ideas have remained largely consistent over time, adaptations and re-narrations have occurred. This clearly begs the question: Why? To answer such a question we need to move beyond a simplistic dualism between continuity and change and adopt a more nuanced approach (Marsh 2007).

Despite these criticisms Tant (1993) offers much to those concerned with the ideas that have underpinned and shaped British political institutions and practice over time, in particular the essential elitism of British government.

Evans

The third example of the critical approach to the BPT can be found in the work of Mark Evans (1995; 2003). Both these works are informed by the critical approach to the BPT developed by Marsh and Tant. Evans (1995) seeks to explain how constitutional debates have developed in the UK and where Charter 88 can, and should, be located within them. This is not the place for a detailed discussion of Charter 88, but Evans makes some interesting points about the BPT. Influenced by Marsh and Tant, he argues that 'the institutions and processes of the British political system are underpinned by an elitist concept of democracy' (1995: 4). He regards this tradition as an obstacle to the implementation of Charter 88's hegemonic project and one that poses major difficulties for those challenging the dominant elitist view. Evans sees the BPT as something that has to be overcome, rather than as something that cannot be overcome. So, he sees change as possible and his work as part of the process by which a successful challenge to the BPT can be mounted. Indeed in his conclusion he states that 'Charter 88's campaigning energies must re-focus on defeating the elitist conceptualisation of democracy, power and authority which underpins the institutions and decision-making processes of the British political system: (1995: 269).

He contends that Charter 88 has to 'maintain the radicalism of its demands...Only in this struggle can it forge the breakthrough from how we are governed, to how we may govern ourselves' (1995: 270). As such, Evans (1995) suggests that agency will be crucial to driving that change.

Evans (1995) explicitly links the BPT and the WM. He states: 'the Westminster model formed the basis of the British political tradition and provided the political orthodoxy of British government' (1995: 16). He highlights the role that Dicey's model of British politics had in generating the key ordering principles of the British political system, such that continuity, gradualness, flexibility and stability became the 'buzz words' of the BPT. This observation is crucial to the conceptualisation of the BPT offered in Chapter 4.

Evans (1995) also seeks to relate the BPT to the debates about constitutional reform throughout the 1970s and 1980s. The rise of Charter 88, is seen as an example of a more participatory view of democracy challenging the elitist British political system. Two points are relevant here for the forthcoming discussion. Firstly challenges to the BPT to be found within debates about the UK constitution began in the 1960s and increased in their resonance in the 1970s and 1980s (Evans 1995: 19–30). Secondly he suggests that contingent events were integral to this increased questioning of the adequacy and impact of the UK's constitutional arrangements.

Evans's *Constitution Making and the Labour Party* (2003) focuses on Labour party views of constitutional reform and Labour's conversion to, and actualisation, of a constitutional reform agenda. Evans highlights the extent to which 'much of the normative discussion constitutionalism and political tradition in the UK has been couched in terms of elitist versus participatory views of democracy' (2003: 16), thus ascribing a central significance to this dichotomy in explaining outcomes. He also makes three further relevant points.

Firstly Evans (2003) discusses the institutions and processes of British government that have been decisively shaped by the elitist view of democracy focusing on the following features:

- a majoritarian or First-Past-the-Post electoral system
- executive dominance over the legislature
- limited access to government information
- low levels of participation in the system of government
- persistent inequalities of power resources
- a centralised unitary state
- a media system that is vulnerable to manipulation by the government.

(adapted from Evans 2003)

He also links the BPT to established constitutional doctrine in the UK and the three key features of the British constitution outlined by Dicey (1885): unlimited Parliamentary Sovereignty, an uncodified constitution and a Unitary State.

Subsequently Evans goes on to suggest that the survival of the BPT with its elitist view of democracy is 'primarily due to the historic failure of radical British political parties in the last century, such as the Liberals and the Labour Party, to successfully challenge the existing order' (2003: 16). Again we should note here the importance attached to agency or the failure of agents to develop successful strategies to effect change.

Finally Evans (2003) recognises the potential for change in the BPT by emphasising the intended and unintended consequences of constitutional change. His suggestion that 'institutionalization has a momentum of its own' (2003: 6), which he calls 'the dynamic of spill over' offers the possibility of developing a more sophisticated and diachronic concept of change and continuity. It also opens up the possibility for further challenges and changes to the BPT.

The work of Evans (1995; 2003) strengthens the critical approach to the BPT in a number of ways. Firstly he stresses the link between the BPT and the WM and identifies those institutions and processes of British government that are underpinned by the BPT. He also offers us a range of buzz words associated with the BPT which are integral to debates concerning institutional and policy development. Moreover and of fundamental significance, he moves the BPT towards a more sophisticated concept of continuity and change by reference to the role of agency, the importance of contingency and the role of intended and unintended consequences. This is particularly important when attempting to explain contemporary developments such as the fate of Labour's constitutional reform programme.

However as with Marsh and Tant (1989) and Tant (1993), there are omissions in Evans's work (1995; 2003). In particular the economic dimension of the BPT is again left unexplored. In addition, a more thorough conceptualisation of continuity and change would undoubtedly extend the explanatory power of his approach.

In conclusion, the work of Marsh, Tant and Evans is a welcome advance to discussion of the BPT and British politics generally. By identifying the elitist concept of democracy that has underpinned many of the institutions and processes of British politics, as well as the views of political actors, these authors have provided a more critical and persuasive analysis of the BPT than that offered in the classical literature. Moving beyond the somewhat self-congratulatory discussions found in the classical literature and subsequent works influenced by it (Norton 1984; Punnett 1987), these authors have highlighted both the fundamentally elitist nature of the BPT and the existence of a competing participatory tradition in British politics that has, through a variety of guises, periodically challenged the dominant tradition. The fact that these challenges have been successfully overcome is a defining feature of this more critical approach which stresses the historical continuity of British political institutions and practices. Thus in this view, the BPT remains largely, if not entirely, unchanged.

Reviewing the British Political Tradition perspective

As noted earlier, the WM has been the dominant prism through which the British political system has been viewed (Kerr and Kettell 2006;

McAnulla 2006a). Few scholars focus upon the ideas that have underpinned the British political system or paid much attention to the BPT. However with the sustained criticism of the WM (Rhodes 1997; Marsh, Richards and Smith 2001) and the interpretivist challenge of Bevir and Rhodes (2003; 2004; 2006a; 2006b), the BPT is becoming more widely discussed.[20] Now, we should discuss the utility of the concept. In particular we should consider the criticisms developed by Bevir and Rhodes (2003; 2004; 2006a; 2006b).

Inadequate theorising of tradition

The first substantive criticism of the literature on the BPT is that there is no adequate theorisation of tradition. Tradition is treated as a 'commonsense' or taken-for-granted concept that requires no Theorisation. With the exception of Oakeshott (1962), none of the authors discussed above offer a detailed examination of what tradition is, and how and to what purpose it is developed and inculcated. Such an undertaking would necessitate addressing meta-theoretical issues such as the relationship between structure and agency and between the material and the ideational. It would also raise questions regarding the relationship between institutions and ideas.

For his part Oakeshott (1962) offers us a classic example of the conservative view of tradition rooted in a rejection of rationality and a preference for non-ideological approaches to politics. McAnulla suggests that Oakeshott (and others) 'were of course particularly concerned to highlight the distinction between traditions and ideologies' (2007: 8). Oakeshott's portrayal of the BPT as an indigenous, distinctive set of non-ideological values, ideas and prejudices is not persuasive however. Such a view leaves many questions unanswered. Whilst this is not the place to develop a sustained critique of the conservative view of tradition, three points are important here. Firstly Hobsbawm (1983a) develops a more useful conceptualisation of tradition than Oakeshott. Secondly Oakeshott's view of tradition does not adequately address the relationship between traditions and the material world. In particular his view of the BPT ignores the extent to which that tradition can be, and has been, linked to the view of dominant economic, social and political elites. Thirdly Oakeshott's conceptualisation of tradition is overly synchronic and does not adequately explain change and continuity over time.

The critical perspective on the BPT offered by Marsh and Tant (1989), Tant (1993) and Evans (1995; 2003) would benefit from greater theorisation of tradition, given the substance and implications of their argument regarding elitism and the British political system. Theorising tradition would allow these authors to consider the purpose for which that tradition might have been developed, how it was developed and, crucially, by whom.

An idealist viewpoint?

Those who advocate the existence and importance of a distinctive BPT are often criticised for offering an idealist perspective. Some authors would suggest that the perspective offers an overemphasis on ideas and their role. As we saw earlier, Greenleaf (1983a; 1983b; 1987) was criticised for conceptualising British politics in terms of a constant tension between libertarianism and collectivism. McAnulla (2006a: 22) identifies the existence of 'sceptics' who contend that ideas are tools or instruments used by politicians to manipulate opinion and to maintain power. Bulpitt (1983) suggests that politicians are primarily concerned with winning elections and, consequently, with projecting an image of competence and unity. In such a view ideas become essentially devices upon which politicians draw if and when necessary. They are important primarily in the context of pragmatism and opportunism on the part of politicians.

Hay (2002a; 2004) notes the tendency of much Anglophone political science towards a 'much cherished positivism' (Hay 2004: 143) which, epistemologically, leads them to undervalue ideas. Two suggestions can be made here. Firstly the BPT offers an analysis of the development of the British political system that focuses on the importance of ideas which allows a more accurate analysis of the development of the institutions and practices of British politics over time. Indeed the focus on ideas supports a historically rooted approach to understanding contemporary politics. This allows us to more fully explain both change and continuity over time.

Secondly given the 'ideational turn' in Anglophone political science in recent years (Hay: 2004) and the interest in the interpretive approach of Bevir and Rhodes (2003; 2004; 2006a; 2006b; 2008b), the BPT concept may find wider resonance in analyses of British politics.

Therefore the BPT is a perspective that explicitly addresses the failure to take the ideational seriously. Whilst it does undoubtedly require some further theorisation and development, the BPT perspective can offer great heuristic value to those interested in analysing and explaining British politics.

An ultra-structural-institutionalist perspective?

Blyth notes that there is a long-running debate in political science over 'the appropriate role for ideas and institutions' (2002: 292–3). Perhaps unsurprisingly then, contra the concerns regarding idealism, some have rejected the concept of the BPT as an ultra-structural and highly 'institutionalist' perspective. In particular this criticism is aimed at those offering a critical concept of the BPT, such as Marsh and Tant (1989), who have sought more explicitly to link ideas and institutions through their work. As we saw earlier, this approach sees the BPT as inscribed in the institutions and processes of UK government and as having a causal impact on agents and outcomes. In this sense, the BPT is often seen, rather crudely, as having much in common with Historical Institutionalism[21] in that it offers an analysis that focuses on the 'bigger picture', taking ideas and trying to map and measure their influence on institutions and practices over time. Whilst this is not the place for an extended discussion of the strengths and weaknesses of Historical Institutionalism,[22] the following points should be considered. Firstly as Marsh, Batters and Savigny (2004) suggest, there is a tendency to homogenise those advocating historical institutionalism when a range of meta-theoretical and methodological differences exist between its proponents.

Secondly we should note that the alleged commonality between the BPT and Historical Institutionalism is rooted in three major factors:

- There is a focus on both the importance of institutions and practices in shaping the actions and attitudes of actors, and thus outcomes.
- They focus explicitly on the historical, suggesting that, for explanations to be persuasive, they must include a temporal element.
- Both are explicitly concerned with issues around continuity and change, raising the possibility of path dependency.

Critics of the BPT approach argue that its institutionalist tendencies lead to a perspective in which ideas are constraining or even determining the actions of actors. So, the approach is accused of overemphasising structure and negating agency. This criticism suggests that the BPT is portrayed as an unavoidable influence on the actions of actors. Kerr and Kettell note that the interpretivist approach of Bevir and Rhodes aim 'a large part of their critique...at the idea of a strong British political tradition, which influences and determines outcomes' (2006: 13). In fact, Bevir and Rhodes make two main points. Firstly they argue that 'tradition is not an unavoidable influence on all we do, for to assume it was would leave too slight a role for agency' (2003: 33). Secondly they suggest that conventional accounts suffer from a tendency to 'hypostatise' traditions (2003: 33). In contrast, they argue that when the idea of traditions is used 'we must not claim an existence for them independent of the beliefs and actions of individuals' (2003: 33). As such, they contend that the BPT negates the role of agency, overemphasising the role of structures as determinants of the actions of agents.[23]

In response, rather than seeing agents' actions as determined by traditions and structures, the critical approach to the BPT seeks to properly situate agents in their ideational and institutional context. This allows us to move beyond a simplistic dualism between institutions and ideas towards a view that stresses their interactive and iterative relationship (Marsh 2003). Rather than privileging either institutions or ideas, Marsh (2003) advocates adopting a dialectical view of the relationship between institutions and ideas.[24] In suggesting the existence of this dialectical relationship, Marsh completely rejects Blyth's (2002) view that institutions underpin stability and ideas drive change. Here, Blythe is reproducing a simple dualism between institutions and ideas, but the relationship is more complex: 'while ideas are crucial in shaping institutions, institutions are the context within which ideas are interpreted, experienced and changed' (Marsh 2003: 3). This is a more convincing approach to this key relationship and forms part of the view of the BPT offered by Marsh and Hall (2007).

Continuity and change

Explanations of British politics are increasingly criticised for failing to sufficiently explain change and continuity over time (Kerr and Kettell 2006: Marsh 2007). Indeed we might cite the dominance of the WM and the Whig interpretation of British history as central to this tendency (Kerr and Kettell 2006: 7). While Chapter 2 will deal in greater depth with debates concerning the importance of change and continuity to political analysis, some points should be made here. The BPT is often seen as an overly synchronic perspective which privileges continuity over change, presenting a picture of the British political system as essentially unchanging over time. For example Kerr and Kettell (2006: 19) critique both Greenleaf (1983a; 1983b; 1987) and Birch (1964) for producing a view in which 'the overwhelming emphasis within this historical narrative is the persistence of stability, continuity and, central to most accounts, consensus among the political elite' (Kerr and Kettell 2006: 19). Birch discussing the ideas that have shaped British politics, argues that 'they are not modern doctrines, and unless they are understood it is impossible to grasp the nature of the British representative system' (1964: 22). The recent work of Bevir and Rhodes (2003; 2004; 2006a; 2006b) also attacks this synchronic tendency, whilst proposing their interpretivist account in which change is seen as being highly contingent and multi-directional.

Indeed it could be argued that the primary weakness of the BPT concept to date is that it lacks a developed temporal dimension. In particular the critical approach raises the possibility of challenges to that tradition through reference to the existence of a participatory concept of democracy and various movements informed by it, but suggests that all challenges have been thwarted, so continuity appears the inevitable outcome.

However the critical approach to the BPT could overcome such criticisms if it was slightly adapted or extended. Firstly it could acknowledge that although some/most challenges have been thwarted, this outcome is not inevitable. The British political system has changed over time and a range of examples could be cited. Thus we should examine in depth each and every challenge to the dominant tradition and the outcomes of this challenge. Secondly we should also recognise that whilst a challenge may appear to have failed in the short term, it may have opened up the possibility for further challenges in the future. For example the challenge mounted by the CFOI may well have been thwarted in the era of the Thatcher government but within 20 years a Freedom of Information Act, albeit a severely limited one,[25] had been introduced.

Therefore, on the central issue of continuity and change, classical approaches to the BPT over-emphasised continuity at the expense of change, whilst critical approaches left the notion of change under developed. Thus explaining the capacity for, and actuality of, change is a task that authors adopting the BPT have not fully addressed. Given this apparent overemphasis on continuity, we can ask two related questions: Is it possible for the BPT to change or be changed? If the answer is no, what role are we to attribute to agency? Without a sense of the temporal and the dynamic relationship between ideas, institutions and political practice, agency is negated and change within British politics is downplayed. Therefore the BPT perspective needs to develop a more nuanced and sophisticated concept of change and continuity over time if it is to fully explain the development of the British political system. This issue is discussed more fully in Chapter 2.

Ideational conflict and binary oppositions

In the literature on the BPT there has also been a tendency to see binary oppositions between ideas. For example Greenleaf portrays the BPT as characterised by a tension between libertarianism and collectivism, while the critical approach emphasises elitist and participatory concepts of democracy (Tant 1993; Evans 1995; 2003). Most accounts of the British political system, however, see it as characterised by ideational consensus (Kerr and Kettell 2006). Even Birch (1964) and Beer (1965), whilst highlighting the role of early debates concerning representation and responsibility, suggest that there has been consensus since the late 19th and early 20th centuries over these notions. However conflict has always been a feature of the British political system, although it has varied in intensity over time and competing ideas have not resonated symmetrically. As such, to suggest that there is consensus over the ideas that shape British politics is misguided. This notion of ideational conflict and the resonance of ideas forms an important part of the arguments developed in the later chapters of this book. Moreover we should recognise the centrality of ideational conflict over time to any developed understanding of the process continuity and change (Kerr 2002; 2003).

However we should also be wary of overemphasising or overstating these binary oppositions. Kerr (2001; 2002) notes that explanations of British politics suffer from a tendency to invoke binary oppositions such as 'consensus and conviction, Keynesianism and monetarism and social democracy and neo-liberalism' in their explanations (Kerr 2002: 336). This oversimplifies both the complexity of the relationship between ideas and the process of change and continuity over time. Thus when focusing on ideational conflict we should be wary of drawing the lines between competing ideas too starkly.

We need to recognise both the resonance of certain ideas and the way in which they are influenced by other ideas. Two points are crucial here. Firstly ideas remain dominant, in no small part, through their acceptance by the populace. This involves a process of articulation, negotiation and reformation (Gramsci 1971). Or, to put it another way, ideas have to adapt to remain dominant. Thus we should consider what factors promote this dynamic and diachronic aspect. Here we can see the impact of both competing ideas and contingent events as causal factors promoting both change and continuity. Such a recognition raises interesting questions regarding how we conceptualise the motor of change, a point we will return to when discussing the work of Bevir and Rhodes (2003: 2004; 2006a; 2006b).

Competing traditions have an impact on the predominant tradition and consequently it is essential to identify and explain both the success and the failures of these impacts, otherwise there is too much focus on continuity. Only if we acknowledge the interactive and iterative relationship between dominant and competing ideas (Marsh and Hall 2007) can we explain both continuity and change in British politics over time.

Tradition or traditions?

Is there a single tradition operating within British politics? Bevir and Rhodes (2003; 2004; 2006a; 2000b) accuse authors who have utilised the idea of a BPT of essentialism. They reject any suggestion that traditions are fixed (Bevir and Rhodes 2003: 33) and argue that there are four traditions operating within British politics. As such, they contend that we should discuss traditions rather than tradition when discussing British politics. While the work of Birch (1964), Beer (1965) and Greenleaf (1983a; 1983b; 1987) identifies a single BPT, critical accounts (Marsh and Tant 1989; Tant 1993; Evans 1995; 2003) suggest that there is an alternative democratic tradition rooted in a participatory concept of democracy. However the latter fail sufficiently to consider how the two traditions interact and the extent to which that interaction is asymmetrical, a point we will return to in greater depth later. Nor do they recognise the multiplicity of political traditions. Rather, multiple political traditions, based on competing views of democracy and/or a competing view of territorial politics and national identity, operate within the UK.

Conflation with the Westminster Model

The BPT concept and the WM are frequently conflated. The WM has been the dominant view of the British political system historically. However those adopting it have rarely analysed or explained in detail the ideas that underpinned or informed it. Rather the relationship between ideas and institutions was not considered or was taken as read. Consequently the relationship between the BPT and the WM was left largely unexplored in the mainstream literature (see for example Wright 2000).

Similarly, those advocating the BPT have never fully explained the relationship between ideas and institutions. As we saw earlier, Birch (1964) devotes little attention to institutions, whilst Beer and Greenleaf do not sufficiently explain how the BPT found expression in the institutions and practices of British government. The critical approach to the BPT is undoubtedly more concerned with this. However of the published work from this perspective, only Evans (2003) focuses explicitly upon the BPT and its relationship to the institutions of British government. Certainly, greater consideration of the relationship between institutions and ideas is required by those advocating a critical concept of the BPT.

The analytical utility of the BPT concept is limited by this conflation. Indeed the extent to which the WM was the institutional reality or expression of the BPT requires more extensive investigation and explanation. Again, it is crucial to approach the relationship between institutions and ideas as dialectical, that is to say, interactive and iterative (Marsh 2003). If we accept this, one key point follows: that the ideas of the BPT helped inform and shape institutions and structures within British politics narrated by the WM. Thus the WM should be viewed as a narrative of the British political system. In this view key notions such as parliamentary sovereignty and the unitary state are more properly viewed as discourses within the WM narrative.

However the accuracy of the description offered by the WM has rightly been called into question (Rhodes 1997, Marsh, Richards and Smith 2001). In particular the elitist underpinning of those institutions and practices was either left uncovered or ignored. Nor were the asymmetrical power relations and structured inequalities of UK society recognised. From this perspective, as mentioned earlier, the WM narrative offered an image, and a self-image at that, rather than an accurate description of the reality of British political life.

As such the relationship between institutions and ideas in British politics requires greater consideration than it has thus far been afforded to date. Neither overall approach to the BPT sufficiently explains this relationship. This relationship is best viewed as interactive, iterative and reciprocal (Marsh and Hall 2006). Political traditions help to shape institutions and practices, whilst these institutions and practices provide the context within which both dominant and competing traditions operate and develop over time.

Homogenising the authors

The literature on the BPT tends to be homogenised by its critics. For example Marsh and Tant (1989) and Tant (1993) don't explore the differences between Birch and Beer. For example Beer discusses the notion of tradition as a political culture or body of beliefs widely held in British society, whilst Birch does not (Batters 2005). Similarly, Marsh and Tant (1989), Tant (1993) and Evans (1995; 2003) underpin their analyses with reference to broader debates about democracy, whilst Birch and Beer do not (Batters 2005). As such, the literature on the BPT is more diverse in methodological and explanatory terms than is usually noted.

An under-theorised perspective

Much of the existing literature on the BPT is under-theorised, perhaps reflecting what McAnulla (2006a: 3) terms: 'the poverty of theory on British politics'. In particular there is insufficient consideration of three issues: the structure-agency debate, the material-ideational debate and the role of cultural factors.

In the BPT literature, there is a basic divergence between those privileging structure (Marsh and Tant 1989; Tant 1993) or agency (Birch 1964; Beer 1965). To explain continuity in political practices and hierarchies, we must acknowledge that structures and dominant ideas constrain, while not determining, outcomes or, to put it another way, we recognise that there is path dependency. However we should not negate agency, but rather conceptualise the relationship between structure and agency as dialectical. Thus rather than conflate structure and agency, or see them as oppositional, we should consider how they relate to each other.

We might properly then ask where do ideas fit into such an approach? McAnulla (2002) demonstrates how Archer's idea of a morphogenetic cycle examines the relationships between both structure and agency and culture and agency. He (2002: 286–8) describes the morphogenetic cycle as demonstrating a three part cycle of change over time.[26] Such an approach focuses on the interactive and iterative relationship between structure and agency, viewing this relationship as dialectical. McAnulla (2002) also focuses upon how culture or ideas act in relation to continuity and change. The process begins with cultural conditioning, or the cultural-ideational context in which agency occurs and continues with socio-cultural interaction where actors strongly influenced by the cultural or ideational context attempt to effect change. Finally we enter the phase of cultural elaboration or reproduction in which the context is either transformed (morphogenisis) or reinforced (morphostasis). This approach offers great insight into the process of change and continuity, particularly when married to a dialectical view of the relationship. It is this approach that informs our later discussion of the BPT.

There is also scant attention paid to material-ideational relationships in the previous usages of the BPT. The focus on ideational factors in the literature has left their relationship to material factors largely unexplored. Hay (2002: 205–9) argues that contemporary idealists, including interpretivists such as Bevir and Rhodes (2003: 2006) 'invariably confine their analyses to the discursive' (2002: 207). Thus he argues that 'contemporary idealists tend to dissolve the very distinction between the ideational and the material' (2002: 207), privileging the ideational. Conversely, materialism contends that 'the material is dominant in the final analysis' (Hay 2002: 207). As such, Hay argues that much sociopolitical analysis treats the ideational or the material as a dualism. In contrast, he argues that the relationship between the material and the ideational is dialectical. Such an approach is undoubtedly more complex as it focuses on the interactive and iterative relationship between material and ideational factors.[27]

This brings us to the approach advocated by Jessop (1990), Hay (1996) and Kerr (2001; 2002) discussed in Chapter 3. More specifically, we require greater discussion of how the structures of the British political system were informed by the BPT and how they have, in turn, had an impact upon it. Broadly, we should consider how the BPT relates to the wider socio-economic context of British politics. Here we might ask what interests, if any, do the BPT serve? Birch (1964), Beer (1965) and Greenleaf (1983) do not address the question and this is not uncommon in terms of approaches to the British political system (Kerr and Kettell 2006).

Once again the critical approach of Marsh and Tant (1989), Tant (1993) and Evans (1995; 2003) offers the possibility of developing a socio-economic dimension to the BPT, but, in fact, it does not develop it. Indeed an exploration of the socio-economic interests at the root of the BPT is required if we are to fully understand the elitism that pervades the British political system. Those using the concept critically need to address the question of whether there is an economic dimension to the BPT and whether the continued resonance of the core ideas that underpin British politics have helped to serve or foster the interests and dominance of certain groups or institutions in British society (Marsh 2002). Or, to put it another way, how does the BPT relate to the structural inequalities and asymmetries of power that have been evident in British politics over time? As such, we need to recognise that the focus on ideational conflict, without recognising the socio-economic interests, power relationships and structured inequalities that exist in society, fails to address the material-ideational relationship in a convincing manner.

Finally the notion of culture should briefly be considered. As we noted earlier, Beer (1965) conceptualises the BPT as a political culture and, indeed tradition is often seen as part of the broader notion of culture in social analysis. Moran (2006: 144) suggests that Beer uses the term culture in a 'relatively relaxed and flexible' manner and indeed sees this as a strength. However the apparent absence of theoretical rigour might equally be seen as problematic. As Marsh and Hall (2007: 221) note, Beer's notion of political culture is helpful in that it suggests the BPT is a set of beliefs widely held in British society. However this notion of culture requires more detailed conceptualisation than Beer's suggestion that it includes 'values, beliefs and emotional symbols...(which can)...determine behaviour' (Beer 1965: xi). Indeed a more thoroughly conceptualised view of culture and its relation to tradition opens up two key possibilities. Firstly it allows us to draw from Bourdieu (1980) the notion that culture is the field upon which human interaction occurs and also a source of domination which assists in the establishment and maintenance of social and institutional hierarchies over time. Secondly it raises the possibility of discussing the notion of a British political-cultural identity, as advocated by Preston (2004), with the BPT as a key component of that identity.

Archer (1995) suggests that we can distinguish between the structural/material and the cultural aspects of social life and their inheritances over time. She suggests that structural and cultural inheritances have relative autonomy from one another, but both condition the actions and interactions of agents (McAnulla 2002). By adopting Archer's distinction, it would be possible to discuss changes and elaboration in either structures or culture without the need for that change to be replicated in the other. This allows us to develop a far more nuanced explanation of continuity and change than the current literature can accommodate. However as McAnulla (2002: 290) suggests, Archer's approach requires greater theorisation of the relationship between the cultural and the structural over time.

To date, we can therefore suggest that the BPT perspective has been somewhat under- theorised. To offer more persuasive explanations of British politics and political outcomes those advocating the BPT must address these meta-theoretical issues more sophisticatedly if the concept is to receive more widespread acceptance.

The normative element to explanations of the British Political Tradition

The literature on the BPT is also highly normative, which is perhaps not surprising or necessarily problematic. However we need to recognise the normative position of authors when assessing their work and their contribution to our understanding of phenomena. Three points are important here.

The self-congratulatory tone of much of the work on the British politics which emphasises British exceptionalism[28] is readily identifiable. Certainly, a degree of British exceptionalism informs the classical work on the BPT. Oakeshott (1962) sees the non-ideological nature of the BPT as both what differentiates the UK approach from those found on the Continent and what makes the British approach superior. Birch's evident antipathy towards more direct forms of democracy (1964: 227) reflects his belief that the BPT has helped create an effective system that sets UK government apart from other countries. Beer (1965) sees the BPT as widely accepted, and perhaps even revered, amongst the populace. The implication is that Britain has been exceptional in avoiding the rancour and upheaval that has faced other systems. This belief in the superiority of the British developmental path is no better demonstrated than when Norton argues that 'in the past 300 years alone, the nation (Britain) has experienced industrialisation, the advent of democracy, and the introduction and growth of the welfare state – yet the changes have never been such as to be described as revolutionary. They have built upon and have adapted that which had already existed' (1984: 37). The dominance of this Whiggish developmentalism is undoubtedly linked to a reverence for both the BPT and the institutions and processes narrated by the WM.

Secondly we can detect a clear anti-collectivism in the classical position adopted by Beer (1965) and Greenleaf (1983a; 1983b; 1987). Beer's discussion of the alleged growing failure of the British system in the face of collectivism is revealing. As Kerr and Kettell (2006: 9) note, Beer (1982) suggests that the origins of the post-war political and economic crisis in the UK lie in rising collectivism and, particularly, collective bargaining. Indeed Beer (1965: 390) asserts that the growth of collectivism might lead to a bypassing of Parliament and the traditional patterns of government in the UK.

Greenleaf, makes little attempt to hide his normative purpose in his critique of the rising tide of collectivism. Indeed his concerns seem to mirror many of the preoccupations of the Thatcher governments and New Right Conservatives generally. For example he poses the question: 'Why in Britain, has a libertarian, individualist society sustaining a limited concept of government been in so many ways and to such a degree replaced by a positive state pursuing explicit policies of widespread intervention in the name of social justice and the public good?' (Greenleaf 1983a: 42).

The critical approaches to the BPT are also normative, identifying and advocating a competing participatory tradition in British politics (Marsh and Tant 1989; Tant 1993). In particular Tant explicitly argues from what he describes as a 'bottom up (radical democratic) perspective' (1993: 6). The normative purpose of his work is to understand how and why radical challenges to the BPT have failed to undermine the elitism of that tradition. Similarly, Evans states: 'I am an advocate of participatory rather than elite democracy, and this belief system underpins my narrative of British Constitutionalism' (2003: 11). He also acknowledges that he borrows heavily from Marxism and Elite theory in developing his critique of the BPT.

The British political tradition, the nation and identity

Despite the apparent emphasis on Britain, there is insufficient focus on the importance of a sense of national identity in discussions of the BPT. There is no discussion of the role that British nationalism and a sense of Britishness play or have played. McAnulla (2006a: 189) does refer to British nationalism as a cross-cutting set of ideas that links in with the BPT, but we should broaden the discussion to incorporate questions concerning identity, that is to say, Britishness.

Avoiding questions of identity gives rise to two problems. Firstly the absence of any consideration of the extent to which a concept of Britain forms an integral part of the BPT opens up its broader purpose with regard to both social and centre-periphery relations in the UK. It could be argued that the BPT has helped to narrate the concept of Britain and thus maintain the territorial integrity of the UK. From this perspective, we would clearly need to consider the importance of this functional aspect of the BPT to dominant economic and political groups within UK society. We might also note again the centrality of British exceptionalism to this sense of Britishness.

Relatedly the extent to which the BPT might form a component part of the political-cultural identity of Britain (Preston 2004) is underdeveloped in the literature to date. Although Beer (1965) uses the idea of a political culture, his view is theoretically underdeveloped. Oakeshott's (1962) suggestion that the BPT is rooted in the British national character is hardly persuasive. Rather a critical focus on Britishness, its sources and the BPT would help us consider broader questions concerning the purpose or function performed by that tradition in both territorial and socio-economic relations in the UK. Here, Preston's (2004) identification of the UK having a 'grand tradition', which is a key component of British political-cultural identity, is particularly relevant.

Crucially, there has been insufficient recognition that 'the different parts of the UK have, to varying extents, different political traditions and identities' (Marsh and Hall 2007: 225). The idea of a single BPT certainly underplays the significance of political traditions, identities and discourses in other parts of the UK which have diverged from those embedded at Westminster (Kenny 1999: 282). The notion that there might be different political traditions and identities in Scotland, Wales and Northern Ireland has, to date, been ignored by those advocating the existence of a distinctive BPT. Indeed these sub-national identities seem to be seen as what Preston (2004) terms 'little traditions' forming part of the broader notion of political-cultural identity. Political analysts need to allow for regional differences within the UK, in addition to highlighting the sense of Britishness and British nationalism linked to exceptionalism that has been a distinctive feature of the BPT. In particular these competing senses of national identity form part of the dynamic for change and continuity in British politics.

Conclusion

In this chapter we have focused upon those authors who have utilised the idea that there is a distinctive BPT. In explaining their respective approaches a number of criticisms of the concept and its usage to date have been identified and discussed. Of those approaches utilised, the classical view of the BPT has undoubtedly been the more influential over time. However its tendency towards Whiggish developmentalism and under-theorisation in a number of ways make it an unconvincing portrayal of the ideational features of the British political system over time.

Conversely, the critical perspective on the BPT is underdeveloped and little acknowledged in the wider literature on British politics. For example only McAnulla (2006a) among the large number of introductory texts on British politics offers any reference to, or comment on, the critical works on the BPT. The clear strength of this approach is that it seeks to expose the underlying elitism and inequalities that have fundamentally shaped the institutions and processes of British politics. However the major problem here is in the omissions or the questions left unanswered in the critical perspective rather than any substantive objection to the argument. Chapters 4 to 7 of this study build upon this and the work of Marsh and Hall (2007) to seek to develop this approach. As such, the critical perspective offers a basis for a more persuasive account of the ideas that have underpinned British politics. Consequently if developed and more fully theorised, it deserves wider recognition and application in accounts of the British political system than has previously been the case.

However it is also important to note here that wider interest in the idea of tradition has been sparked by the recent work of Bevir and Rhodes (2002; 2003; 2004; 2006a; 2006b 2008a; 2008b) and Marquand (2008). In particular the challenge presented by the former to both traditional accounts of British politics rooted in the WM and to the views of the BPT outlined above requires detailed consideration. It is to this that we will now turn.

2
Tradition or Traditions?

Introduction

In recent years, renewed interest has been sparked in the concept of political tradition and its application to the study of British politics. Various authors operating from different methodological and normative perspectives (Bevir and Rhodes 2003; 2006a; Marsh and Hall 2007; Marquand 2008) have pointed to the centrality of political traditions in British political life. The concept of political tradition is by no means a new one in political analysis[1] and it remains a contested one. However two interrelated developments have sparked renewed interest in it. Firstly, we have witnessed an increasing trend towards what Hay (2004) describes as 'the ideational turn' in Anglophone political science. In keeping with this trend those utilising political traditions as an explanatory variable focus explicitly on the ideas that underpin political practice. In doing so, they seek to remedy an oft-cited weakness of the available literature on British politics (Gamble 1990; McAnulla 2006a). Secondly the interpretivist work of Bevir and Rhodes and responses to it have re-focused attention onto the concept.

Through the publication of *Interpreting British Governance* (2003), *Governance Stories* (2006b) and various articles (2002; 2004; 2006a; 2006c; 2008a; 2008b), Bevir and Rhodes have been fundamental in sparking renewed interest in political traditions. Their rejection of the notion of a single tradition operating within British politics in favour of a variety of competing traditions provides a provocative and stimulating challenge on a number of levels. Firstly their view of multiple traditions directly challenges much of the work on the British Political Tradition (BPT). Secondly their interpretive approach focuses directly on the role of ideational factors in the development of outcomes. Thirdly and perhaps most significantly, they offer a non-essentialist, contingent approach to traditions, in which agents can and do alter the content of traditions. Thus their perspective is by definition, diachronic. In doing so, they raise issues regarding the relationship between continuity and change which remains a central concern for all social science. Such is the import of their work that, alongside the Differentiated Polity Model (DPM), Bevir and Rhodes's 'interpretivism' has begun to establish itself as the central alternative to the Westminster Model (WM) (Kerr and Kettell 2006).

In response to Bevir and Rhodes, various authors have sought to critique their approach and, in one case, offer a different concept of political traditions (Marsh and Hall 2007). For example McAnulla (2006a) has critiqued their ontological and epistemological position. Marsh and Hall (2007) have taken issue with their concept of tradition and dilemma. Smith (2008) has critiqued their misrepresentation of interpretivism and their failure to adequately address the issue of power. Finally Marsh (2008a; 2008b) has sought to highlight the link between their interpretivism and the DPM, and the limitations of both. However the use of political traditions as an explanatory variable is not confined to Bevir and Rhodes. In *The Strange Career of British Democracy* (2008) David Marquand offers another concept of political traditions. In this article, Marquand argues that 'our political culture has been shaped by an interplay between four longstanding traditions, each encapsulating a different narrative and different vision of democratic politics' (2008: 466). This chapter offers a critical appraisal of both Bevir and Rhodes's and Marquand's approach. Given the notoriety of their work in recent times, we will deal first and foremost with Bevir and Rhodes. In doing so the assessment will be situated within a broader discussion of how political analysts can and should conceptualise the relationship between continuity and change.

Bevir and Rhodes

The interpretivist approach of Bevir and Rhodes (2002; 2003; 2004; 2006a; 2006b 2006c; 2008a; 2008b) has seen a new dimension to discussions of tradition emerge which is both provocative and stimulating. Their aim is to attempt to 'bring together some philosophically derived themes about context, agency and tradition with political science research into the conduct of British governance today' (Finlayson 2004: 129). In their debate with Marsh they argue that their approach offers 'narratives of the contingent relationships in the core executive' (2008b: 733) rather than a general model of power within it.

What is Interpretivism?

Interpretivism refers to approaches that emphasise the meaningful nature of people's participation in social and cultural life. The methods and approach of the natural sciences are seen to be inappropriate for such investigations and consequently interpretivists favour qualitative over quantitative data. Social researchers working within this tradition analyse the meanings people confer upon their own and others' actions. Bevir and Rhodes state that 'Interpretive approaches begin from the insight that to understand actions, practices and institutions, we need to grasp the relevant meanings, the beliefs and preference of the people involved' (2003: 1). Two key points should be recognised concerning the interpretive approach. Firstly interpretivism suggests that individuals act on their beliefs and preferences. As such we can explain their actions by referring to these. Secondly interpretivism suggests that we cannot simply 'read off' an individual's beliefs and preferences from allegedly objective facts about them such as class, gender, ethnicity or institutional position. Consequently when seeking to develop explanations we can only point to the 'conditional and volitional links between beliefs, desires, intentions and actions' (Bevir and Rhodes 2002: 134). There is a long-running tradition in social science that emphasises 'interpretation' (Smith 2008). Indeed since the 'qualitative turn' in sociology in the 1960s it has been commonplace in social analysis. Bevir and Rhodes (2002) point to various interpretative approaches in social analysis including hermeneutics, ethnology, post-structuralism and postmodernism. However until recently this approach has had little impact upon political science (Smith 2008: 143). Indeed we should note again the tendency of much Anglophone political science towards positivism (Hay 2004).

Having defined briefly defined interpretivism we will turn to questions regarding ontology and epistemology.

Ontology and epistemology

Since the mid 1990s, political analysts have become increasingly sensitive to notions concerning ontology and epistemology. In a widely praised text, Hay (2002) defines ontology as relating to what exists in the social and political world. Norman Blaikie suggests that ontology 'refers to the claims or assumptions that a particular approach to social (or by extension, political) enquiry makes about the nature of social (or political) reality – claims about what exists, what it looks like, what units make it up and how these units interact with each other' (2007: 6).

Conversely, epistemology refers to what can be known about that reality, and 'the claims and assumptions that can be made about the ways in which it is possible to gain knowledge of reality' (Blaikie 2007: 6–7). In relation to ontology and epistemology, Hay defines methodology as 'the means by which we reflect upon the methods appropriate to realise fully our potential to acquire knowledge of that which exists' (2002: 63). Hay argues that methodological choices are informed by ontological and epistemological assumptions.

This increased interest in ontology and epistemology, and more broadly, the attempts to promote political analysis to become more reflective regarding its assumptions, has been driven in no small part by the work of Marsh and Stoker (1995; 2002) and Hay (2004). Indeed Furlong and Marsh (2007) suggest that political scientists at the University of Birmingham have been at the forefront of such attempts.

Finally before turning to Bevir and Rhodes, it should be noted that we can distinguish between positivist, realist and interpretivist approaches to these issues. Marsh and Furlong (2002) suggest the following general distinctions between these positions:

- Ontologically, positivist approaches are foundationalist in that they stress that there is a real world that exists independently of our knowledge of it. Epistemologically, positivists seek to develop theories or models and then test them by direct observation. Crucially, for positivists observers can be objective in their research.
- Realists also adopt a foundationalist view of ontology. However unlike positivists their epistemology suggests that not all social phenomena are observable. Consequently social research can only achieve 'a best explanation' rather than complete knowledge of social phenomena. More recently, critical realists (see for example Archer 1995; McAnulla 2006b) suggest that there is a real world 'out there' but that our knowledge of it is fallible/partial and that much of our understanding of that world is socially constructed.
- Interpretivism denies the idea of a real world that exists independently of our knowledge of it. Instead interpretivists suggest that social phenomena are socially or discursively constructed and consequently their ontology is anti-foundationalist. Epistemologically, interpretivists seek to identify and understand the meanings of social phenomena as it these that affect outcomes. For interpretivists, objective analysis is impossible.

Bevir and Rhodes explained

Ontologically and epistemologically Bevir and Rhodes's approach is novel when compared to the positivism of most British political science (Hay 2002). Their approach is, by their own admission, anti-foundationalist. They critique the positivism of most political science for adopting an epistemological position that 'postulate(s) given facts divorced from theoretical contexts as the basis of legitimate claims to knowledge' (2004: 132). Contra this, Bevir and Rhodes (2004: 132):

> reject explicitly the idea of given truths whether based upon pure reason or pure experience: all perceptions, and so facts, arise within the context of a prior set of beliefs or theoretical commitments. As a result, we typically look suspiciously on any claim to describe neutrally an external reality. We stress the constructed nature of our claims to knowledge.

Adopting this approach makes the work of Bevir and Rhodes a challenge to mainstream political science[2] (McAnulla 2006b).

They also critique the methodology of positivist political scientists by suggesting that:

> adherents of a positivist epistemology study political actions and institutions as atomised units, which they examine individually before assembling them into larger sets. They assemble such units into larger sets by comparing and classifying their similarities and differences. In contrast, post-foundationalism stresses that webs of beliefs informed by traditions construct political actions and institutions. (2004: 132)

Again this view offers a direct challenge to the methodology of most mainstream political science.[3]

In this post-foundationalist interpretivism Bevir and Rhodes stress the centrality of agency. This can be demonstrated through reference to Bevir's earlier work, *The Logic of the History of Ideas* (1999). He concludes that we should 'reject the possibility of pure experiences of past intentions' (1999: 171) when developing explanations. In particular he rejects the possibility of 'value-free inquiry' and positivist tendencies of much political science (McAnulla 2006b: 115). This approach is married to a belief in the importance of agents' intentions. Bevir's 'agents' are rational, conscious creatures capable of sincerity. Thus when studying the intentions of agents we can place some faith in them as indicators of what agents actually intended their actions to achieve and what their motives were. Through focusing on the intentions of agents we can develop explanations. Bevir sees no persuasive alternative to intentionalism, stating that 'unless we wish to defend either the idea that our social inheritances determines what we say or the idea that we have pure experiences, we should retain an intentionalist analysis of historical meaning' (1999: 171).

Bevir and Rhodes (2003) develop this agency-centric approach. They 'insist on the fact of agency' (2003: 32). For Bevir and Rhodes, agents are creative. They do not however suggest that agents are fully autonomous. Instead they distinguish between autonomy and agency, arguing that agents act against a background of social discourse or tradition when they reason and respond. Thus they argue for 'situated agency' (2006: 4). So, they seek to 'explain actions by the beliefs and preferences of actors' (2003: 20) and 'let interviewees explain the meanings of their actions' (2008a: 176).

By their own admission they 'are sympathetic to the historical and philosophical approach to British politics found in the work of Beer (1965) and Birch (1964)' (Bevir and Rhodes 2004: 132), discussed in Chapter 1. This is interesting in two regards. Firstly they too see the significance of ideational factors in explaining outcomes, although they conceptualise tradition somewhat differently to either Birch or Beer. Secondly like those authors they stress the role of agency, although even a cursory analysis of Birch and Beer's work highlights the importance of agency to their analyses. This can be demonstrated in two ways. Firstly both authors are idealists in that, to a lesser or greater extent, they do not fully explain the relationship between ideas and institutions. Consequently their analyses privilege agency at the expense of structure. Secondly both authors find time for protracted discussions of both individuals and group politics but offer a limited focus on the institutional.

We should also situate Bevir and Rhodes's approach alongside the rise of the governance thesis mentioned in Chapter 1. They (2003: 2004; 2006b) seek to highlight the limitations of the WM that has dominated explanations of British politics. Bevir and Rhodes define governance as 'a new process of governing, a changed condition of ordered rule or the new method by which society is governed' (2004: 132–3). Clearly this purported shift from government to governance has wide-ranging implications for the study of British politics. Here we should recognise three points. Firstly it raises major problems for the WM as mentioned in Chapter 1. Secondly in response to these changes two conflicting models of British politics have been developed, the DPM (Rhodes 1997) and the Asymmetrical Power Model (APM) (Marsh, Richards and Smith 2001; 2003; Marsh 2008a).[4] Thirdly Bevir and Rhodes's interpretive approach attempts to explain 'the rise of governance in part by reference to the beliefs embedded in the Tory, Whig, Liberal and Socialist traditions' (2003: 5). On this basis alone, the 'governance thesis' has necessitated a reappraisal of much thinking on British politics. It is as part of this process that Bevir and Rhodes's work has been developed.

Having identified a number of observations on their approach we will now turn our attention to explaining two of Bevir and Rhodes's central ideas: tradition and dilemma.

Tradition

Bevir and Rhodes explore the notion of governance through beliefs, traditions and dilemmas. Their expressed aim is to 'decentre the British political tradition into its various constituent traditions – Tory, Whig, Liberal and Socialist – in order to show how each of these traditions views 'governance' differently' (2004: 133). This will then help them to explain in part how governance has developed and continues to do so.

Bevir and Rhodes define tradition as 'a set of connected beliefs and habits that are intentionally or unintentionally passed from one generation to another at some time in the past' (2003: 33–4). Traditions are 'sets of theories, narratives and associated practices that people inherit and form a background against which they reach beliefs and perform actions' (2002: 140). Thus traditions are inherited webs of beliefs that are received during socialisation and influence the responses of actors.

Bevir and Rhodes suggest there are multiple traditions at work within British politics. They initially identified four traditions and used them to narrate both governance and Thatcherism (2003; 2006). These are the Tory, Liberal, Whig, and Socialist traditions. In their more recent work they have referred to an increasing number of traditions, a point we will return to shortly. As such, they suggest that discussing the existence of a single BPT is misleading. Rather we should recognise the existence and impact of multiple political traditions.

They reject the notion that traditions have an unchanging core idea or set of ideas. Instead they offer a non-essentialist concept of tradition, 'a decentred study of tradition, practice or institution ... (which) ... unpacks the way in which it is created, sustained or modified through the beliefs, preferences and actions of individuals in many arenas' (2003: 35).

Traditions are inherited webs of beliefs rather than fixed or essential concepts. They influence actors but are capable of adaptation as actors respond to the changing dilemmas they face. These traditions are not fixed or static. Rather it is only possible 'to identify the particular instances that compose any given tradition by tracing its appropriate historical connections back through time' (2002: 140). In this view continuity in a tradition and its influence are negated in favour of change, flexibility and diversity. In a sense a tradition only ever exists in the perceptions and responses of actors as it is constantly changing and developing. Thus agency becomes of paramount importance when explaining outcomes.

This interpretive approach to tradition is agency-centric in that 'the human capacity for agency implies change originates in the responses or decisions of individuals, rather than the inner logic of traditions' (2003: 35). Thus they seek to avoid reifying traditions and do not see them as anything other than a starting point. They argue that 'tradition is not an unavoidable influence on all we do' (2003: 33–4) or a constraint on outcomes. Rather it is something that is 'contingent, produced by the actions of individuals. The carriers of traditions bring it to life. They settle its content and variations by developing their beliefs and practices, adapting it to new circumstances, while passing it on to the next generation'. Thus they develop an agency-centred approach to traditions that emphasises the contingent and change.

They also warn of the dangers of hypostatising traditions (2003: 33). They do not believe that traditions exist independently of the actions or beliefs of individual agents. If traditions are not fixed entities then there is no possibility for suggesting that they exist beyond the individual. Indeed 'we can only identify the beliefs that make up a tradition by looking at the shared understandings and historical connections that allow us to link its exponents with one another' (2003: 33).

Bevir and Rhodes's approach is both novel and provocative. In their various works Bevir and Rhodes allege five advantages to the interpretive approach.[5] Their approach certainly raises questions for those who believe in the existence of a BPT and the impact this tradition has on outcomes. Before turning to a critical evaluation of their concept of tradition, we should focus on their usage of the concept of 'dilemma' as the contingent factor promoting change within traditions.

Dilemma

The idea of dilemma is central to Bevir and Rhodes's approach. They utilise the concept to explain how change is originated in the responses of actors to the dilemmas they are faced with. They state: 'A dilemma arises for an individual or institution when a new idea stands in opposition to existing beliefs and practices and so forces a reconsideration of these existing beliefs and traditions' (Bevir 1999: 221–64). Bevir and Rhodes define dilemmas thus:

> A dilemma is any experience or idea that conflicts with someone's beliefs and so forces them to alter what they inherit as a tradition. It combines with the tradition to explain (although not determine) the beliefs people go on to adopt and so the actions they go on to perform. Dilemmas and traditions cannot fully explain actions both because actions are informed by desires as well as beliefs and because people are agents who respond creatively to any given dilemma. (2006c: 400)

They suggest that it is through reference to the dilemmas that change in traditions and, more broadly, political outcomes can be explained. These dilemmas need not be identifiable in "allegedly objective' pressures to be found in the world but rather in ideas and views that people come to hold as true, 'irrespective of whether they reflect pressures we believe to be real' (2003: 36).

Thus the inter-subjective understandings, beliefs and ideas of actors are the cornerstone of 'dilemma'. They provide the manner in which actors assess and understand the world and the challenges they face. Dilemmas arise from the personal experiences of actors and their theoretical and moral reflections. They can also arise from an actor's external experience of the world. Within this process, consistent with their anti-foundationalist approach, there is no preference given to academic or theoretical reflections. Therefore 'the new belief that poses a dilemma can lie anywhere on an unbroken spectrum passing from views with little theoretical content to complex theoretical constructs only remotely linked to views about the real world' (2003: 36).

Dilemmas do not have agreed or fixed solutions (2003: 36). Rather resolving dilemmas is a creative process. Tradition(s) provides actors with a guide to possible courses of action but does not fix what actors must do. Instead they argue that 'traditions and practices could be fixed only if we did not encounter novel circumstances' (2003: 37).

The contrast with previous discussions of the BPT is stark in that these emphasise the essentially fixed or continuous nature of that single tradition and its largely consistent impact on outcomes over time. Contra this, even those actors that believe that in response to a particular dilemma they are: "continuing a settled tradition,...are often [in reality] developing, modifying and changing beliefs and practices" (2003: 37). Solutions to dilemmas are arrived at through actors developing their existing beliefs and accommodating new ideas within their existing beliefs. In this process it is possible to hook certain ideas onto existing beliefs to create solutions, whilst other ideas will simply not fit. Consequently traditions change over time and the impact they have on outcomes will be more diverse. Thus change becomes a continual eventuality.

Therefore it is through the process of how actors respond to the dilemmas that traditions become important in informing outcomes. Traditions are appealed to as actors solve the dilemmas they face. However two important points should be made here. Firstly 'change does not arise in the inner logic of traditions' (2003: 35) but rather in the responses of actors to dilemmas. Secondly dilemmas are only important insofar as they are narrated or constructed by agents, and these narrations are themselves constructed through the medium of traditions.

Having outlined Bevir and Rhodes's approach, we will now turn our attention to offering a critical evaluation of their interpretivism.

Evaluating Bevir and Rhodes

Bevir and Rhodes have offered a provocative and stimulating approach to explanation in British politics. However despite its burgeoning influence as a challenge to mainstream analyses their interpretive approach remains problematic.

Their view of tradition and dilemma does make a number of valuable contributions to understandings of British politics. In particular three key contributions can be identified:

- They raise the profile of political change by offering a perspective that is by definition diachronic, where a concern for contingency and change is at the forefront of the analysis. This helps focus attention away from overly synchronic views of politics and an overemphasis on continuity. Whilst recognising the importance of a diachronic approach, the narrative below characterises the relationship between change and continuity somewhat differently. Moreover such is the

significance of Bevir and Rhodes's approach to change that we will return to it later in this chapter.
- Their focus on tradition affords greater attention to the role of ideational factors in explaining outcomes than is usual in Anglophone political science (Hay 2004).
- They raise the importance of competing narratives of British government in promoting change. As Marsh and Hall (2007: 227) argue: 'Bevir and Rhodes are right that a continual process of contestation forms the backdrop against which British politics is conducted and helps shape and inform future choices'.[6]

However despite these contributions, Bevir and Rhodes's approach contains some fundamental problems that negate its value in explaining both the importance of traditions and more broadly, developments in British politics.

Critiquing the 'new interpretivism'

Prior to turning our attention to a critical evaluation of tradition and dilemma we should briefly focus on the ontological and epistemological approach of Bevir and Rhodes. We will also consider their approach to the meta-theoretical issues raised in Chapter 1.

Bevir and Rhodes's interpretivism has been widely evaluated and aspects of it have been commended. For example prior to developing a persuasive critique of their work, McAnulla notes the contribution made by Bevir and Rhodes, describing their work as: 'exceptional in offering both a considered philosophical grounding for their approach, as well as a practical analytical vocabulary which they apply in analysing a range of empirical case studies in British politics' (2006b: 113).

Bevir and Rhodes can be critiqued for neglecting ontology in favour of epistemology. McAnulla argues that in their interpretivism 'ontology became seen as coterminous with epistemology' (2006b: 118). As such Bevir and Rhodes fall into an epistemic fallacy by discussing being only in terms of knowledge and thus ignoring ontology or that which exists. McAnulla (2006b: 118) suggests that it is interesting that work informed by post-structuralist insights such as those promulgated by Bevir and Rhodes suffers from the same myopia as positivism as it only discusses the world through our apprehension of it. By conflating ontology and epistemology Bevir and Rhodes ignore the limitations of human perception and the attendant point that an agent's knowledge of the world is, at best, partial. Or to put it another way, they do not fully address the notion that: 'that which is and that which we can know' are not necessarily the same. If this insight is accepted then Bevir and Rhodes's work fails to maintain a clear distinction between ontology and epistemology.

Bevir and Rhodes argue that agents understand the world through inherited webs of beliefs or traditions. Any influence on agency derives from the impact of these traditions on agents as they face dilemmas that have emerged in their minds. Thus Bevir and Rhodes focus on epistemology or that which individuals know. They leave no room for a causal role for the context within which individuals find themselves. Rather they negate this context and the idea that structures or discourses may shape belief or agency. McAnulla argues that Bevir and Rhodes's 'advocacy of this epistemic fallacy appears quite overt – the approach is designed to generate accounts of the political world (being) through statements regarding individuals' beliefs (knowledge)' (2006b: 118–19).

That their approach privileges epistemology over ontology has important consequences for their view of key meta-theoretical debates, in particular the central debate over structure and agency. Bevir and Rhodes privilege agency and undervalue the role of structure (Marsh and Hall 2006). Indeed their usage of tradition derives directly from this approach. For example they argue that 'the concepts of episteme, language and discourses typically invoke social structures that fix individual acts and exist independently of them. In contrast, the notion of tradition implies that the relevant social context is one in which subjects are born, which then acts as the background to their later beliefs and actions without fixing them' (Bevir and Rhodes 2003: 32).

For Bevir and Rhodes focusing on context or structure leads the political scientist to then 'read off' agents' beliefs from their position within a given structure, thus negating agency. Consequently as McAnulla suggests, their view is that 'if a meaningful role for agents is to be defended then this causal notion of structure must be rejected' (2006b: 119).

Whilst they are correct to reject the idea that structure simply determines agency, Bevir and Rhodes are guilty of over privileging agency and to an extent sustaining the simplistic dualism between structure and agency evident in much political science (Hay 1995: McAnulla 2002). Whilst they reject the idea of autonomous individuals, they also reject the idea that traditions can act as structures in the sense that they can constrain or limit the beliefs of agents and therefore the options available to them. Marsh and Hall (2006) suggest three further observations in this regard. Firstly that Bevir and Rhodes (2006c) in their response to McAnulla's critique demonstrate that they believe that 'critical realists can contribute usefully to political science if they come over to the interpretive camp' (Marsh and Hall 2006). Secondly that they also incorrectly equate critical realism with positivism. This can clearly be seen in their comment that 'McAnulla holds out the intriguing prospect that critical realists might be able to rethink their position to make it post-positivist and perhaps even post-foundationalist' (Bevir and Rhodes 2006c: 398). Finally that Bevir and Rhodes's work suffers from the view that the WM is the 'other'. This leads them to undervalue and even ignore alternative viewpoints such as critical realism and the APM[7] (Marsh 2008a).

Their overemphasis on agents and their beliefs is also problematic. Bevir and Rhodes state that they seek to 'explain actions by the beliefs and preferences of actors' (2003: 20). To demonstrate the limitations of this approach we will turn again to the WM, something that Bevir and Rhodes have consistently critiqued. The details of the WM were dealt with in Chapter 1; our concern here is to critically evaluate their claim that their 'governance narrative is a valuable corrective to the traditional Westminster Model' (2003: 199). Indeed their work suggests that, in certain respects the WM is the 'other' to be challenged and moved beyond.

They see the WM as both a narrative[8] of the British political system and one that was 'an illusion masking the contested and contingent nature of British constitutionalism' (2006: 168). On these points our views bear some similarity. As explained in Chapter 1 the WM is indeed best viewed as a narrative of the British political system. The WM was/is actually a self-image rather than an accurate description of the reality of British political life. However contra Bevir and Rhodes we should seek to understand the nature and source of this inaccuracy, and also characterise it somewhat differently.

This inaccuracy however does not detract from its resonance and influence. Again, Bevir and Rhodes recognise this by suggesting that 'many political actors continue to use the language of the Westminster Model to describe the past, present and future of British politics' (2006: 169). Thus numerous actors still believe in the WM and view the political world through it 'irrespective of whether these ideas reflect real pressures, or to be precise, irrespective of whether they reflect pressures we believe to be real' (2003: 36). However they suggest that 'these beliefs do not fix practices' (2008a: 175).

They do not accept, however, that the WM narrative and its meanings have become inscribed into the institutions and processes of British government. Rather they believe it is a narrative, confined to the beliefs and interpretations of actors. Thus they depict 'a storytelling administrative and political elite with beliefs and practices rooted in the Westminster Model, confronting the dilemmas posed by both marketisation and managerialism' (2008: 176). They also suggest that politics should be viewed as a 'cultural practice' (2008a).

As such their focus is undoubtedly on agency. Here again we encounter their faith in 'situated agency' discussed earlier. This emphasis on agents and their beliefs is, upon closer scrutiny, deeply problematic. In the context of British politics it raises a number of key questions.

Firstly what if actors believe themselves to be structurally constrained? If actors believe that structural constraints exist and we are interpreting their beliefs as they offer the only sure guide to explaining outcomes, how do we account for these without reference to structures themselves? For example if actors believe that the WM exists as a structural constraint upon their choices and actions, then how do we account for the latter without reference to the institutions and processes of the WM? To do so we would have to accept that the WM narrative has been inscribed into the institutions and processes of British government, a point Bevir and Rhodes do not allow for.

Conversely might we suggest that actors are mistaken in their belief that structural constraints exist?[9] For example if political elites in the UK see themselves as operating within the structures of the WM, then these actors may simply be mistaken in that belief. To accept that they were would surely raise major concerns about using actors' beliefs as the basis for any explanation which Bevir and Rhodes's methodology requires. Alternatively they would need to adjust their ontological position to accommodate the idea that actors may hold mistaken views of the world which then act as constraints or enablers of action. This would necessitate a move away from their reliance on belief and interpretation and greater recognition of the potential impact of structure.

Secondly if the WM narrative is illusory then why have actors believed in it and why do they continue to do so? Bevir and Rhodes do not address how or why actors come to hold their beliefs. This is of fundamental importance if we are to move beyond partial explanations. For example we should highlight the link between the development of the WM narrative and the predominant political tradition in British politics, the BPT (Marsh and Hall 2007). Thus belief in the WM narrative is linked to perceptions of the success of the institutions and processes of British government over time and faith in the BPT.

Indeed the WM is best seen as both the institutional expression and legitimising narrative of that tradition. The central concepts of the WM narrative are however portrayed benignly (Kerr and Kettell 2006).

They are seen as democratic, desirable and effective in that they have served the UK well and are a superior manner of government. This helps to mask their essentially limited and elitist nature. Furthermore the 'invented traditions' (Hobsbawm 1983a) of the WM narrative act as key symbols and signifiers of the distinctiveness and superiority of the BPT.

Nor do Bevir and Rhodes explain why actors continue to see the world through the prism of the WM. Contra their 'agency-centric' approach we might consider three potentially useful 'structuralist' concepts to explain this. These accommodate the notion of some 'cultural practice' but conceptualise it more persuasively. Firstly the idea that culture helps to establish and maintain institutional hierarchies, and also embodies power relations (Bourdieu 1980) may explain how patterns of behaviour at Westminster became replicated. Secondly a culture of organised practices and attitudes, or 'governmentalities' (Dean 1999) may help ideas and institutions persist over time. Collectively these may help to inculcate and perpetuate patterns of elite dominance within the political system and outcomes that generally favour their continued dominance. Thirdly these institutions, processes and cultures may then become the context for future debates and discourses, leading to a strategically selective environment (Jessop 1990) that privileges certain ideas over others. As Judge suggests: 'UK governments become locked into common modes or trajectories, of behaviour and working routines (irrespective of party composition or the personal characteristics of leaders)' (2006: 371). Thus the WM narrative, however inaccurate, remains centrally significant for explaining the responses of actors.

Contra Bevir and Rhodes, we should recognise the importance of the pre-structured context in which current agency takes place (Archer 1995). Indeed the narratives or traditions that influence agents are part of the pre-structured context which is itself partially the result of previous agency. Consequently the positions in which agents find themselves cannot be reduced to current agency alone. Nor should we ignore the fact that this pre-structured context will generate relationships between agents such as position and role within this context and established patterns of behaviour or practice. It will also generate relationships between ideas, traditions and discourses and the broader context. In these relations some of the former are likely to be privileged vis-à-vis others. This raises two important observations. Firstly we cannot explain outcomes solely by reference to agents and their beliefs. Secondly we might properly ask what factors privilege certain ideas, traditions and discourses within our broader context. Here factors such as structured inequality and asymmetrical power relations are fundamentally important in the privileging of certain ideas, traditions or discourses over others. Thus narratives, traditions and discourses resonate in an asymmetrical fashion linked to the uneven nature of the socio-economic/political landscape agents find before them.

Such a view does not reify structure at the expense of agency. Rather it seeks to situate agents in their proper structural context. Here we should distinguish structure ontologically from agency (McAnulla 2006b). Contra Bevir and Rhodes 'agents find themselves cast into material relationships, roles or practices they did not choose but will subsequently condition their future actions'[10] (McAnulla 2006b: 121). Structures, traditions, discourses and culture, whilst being the product in part of past agency, will influence or 'act back' on present agency in a causal manner. This takes us beyond 'situated agency' and raises the real possibility of conditioning and constraint. Thus structures in both a material and ideational sense can be seen to act as constraints or enablers of agency.

Or to put it another way, if 'the Westminster model is the pervasive image shared by British politicians and civil servants' (2003: 26) and we are to take actors' beliefs seriously, then can we suggest that the WM narrative is continuing to have an impact on outcomes? If not, then how can we place any faith in the interpretation of actors' beliefs when explaining outcomes? If so, then this raises two further questions we will deal with shortly. Firstly how do we account for the ubiquity of change that Bevir and Rhodes claim? Secondly does this not suggest a degree of path dependency?

If actors continue to believe in the WM (Marsh, Richards and Smith 2001; Judge 2006) and narrate options and outcomes in relation to it, then dismissing that model and its impact in favour of the 'governance thesis' may be somewhat premature. Indeed given that Bevir and Rhodes recognise the pervasiveness of the WM narrative, might we not suggest that their *Governance Stories* would be more accurately referred to as *Westminster Model Stories*? If not they may be guilty of implying that patterns of governance act as a set of structures which have an existence external to the beliefs of actors in the political elite and thus guilty of claiming an ontological existence for their concept itself.

Therefore contra Bevir and Rhodes's agency-centric approach, the structure-agency relationship should be seen as dialectical in that is interactive and iterative (Marsh and Hall 2006: 11). In such a view the relationship between structure and agency is far more complex than

Bevir and Rhodes suggest. This dialectical approach to structure and agency offers a far more persuasive view for explaining outcomes than either intentionalism or structuralism. Bevir and Rhodes's narrow view of the relationship between structure and agency, rooted in intentionalism, can also be seen to have implications for their approach to other meta-theoretical issues.

In privileging agency, Bevir and Rhodes simplify the relationship between the material and the ideational to the simple prioritisation of one over the other. Indeed for Bevir and Rhodes it is debateable whether traditions exist in a material sense at all. They suggest that:

> post-foundationalism implies that all experiences are constructed in part by prior theories, so all beliefs are similarly constructed, which means that all actions, practices, and institutions are informed by beliefs or theories. For post-foundationalists, the entire social world thus appears infused by meanings. They are therefore sceptical of a distinction between ideational and material aspects of the social world. (2006c: 402)

On the basis of this it can be argued that they privilege the ideational over the material, seeing the latter as largely a product of the former. Through reference to their brief discussion of material-ideational relationship (2006c: 402) it is possible to identify three points. Firstly they suggest that critical realists sometimes associate the material world with the economy and/or interests, whilst post-foundationalists suggest that the economy 'is the product of actions infused with ideas, beliefs and theories...and people's interests are never simply given to them. People construct their understanding of their interests in part through their ideas, theories and beliefs' (2006c: 402).

However we might readily ask here if ideas, theories and beliefs are in part constructing interests, for example, then what else might be seen as constructing them if not the material world in an objective sense. Furthermore the material-ideational relationship is far better conceived of as dialectical (Hay 2002). This allows us to develop more complex and ultimately more persuasive explanations of outcomes. Finally their discussion of the material-ideational relationship offers the misleading impression that critical realism privileges the material over the ideational when it conceives of the relationship as dialectical (Marsh and Hall 2006: 13).

On the central relationships between ideas and institutions Bevir and Rhodes's privileging of both agency and the ideational leads them to undervalue institutions in their explanations. For example their interpretivism suggests that traditions do not exist independently of the beliefs of individuals. They argue: 'interpretive theories deny that institutions have a reified or essential nature. They challenge us to decentre institutions; that is, to analyse the ways in which they are produced, reproduced and changed through the particular and contingent beliefs, preferences and actions of individuals: (2003: 41).

From this we can make two observations. Firstly Bevir and Rhodes suggest institutions are merely products of agency. Here again a more persuasive insight into how institutions come into being is to see them as a result, in part, of past agency but ones that may themselves then come to constrain or enable current agency. Secondly Bevir and Rhodes claim institutions cannot themselves embody traditions, only the individuals operating within them can. Contra this, Marsh and Hall more persuasively suggest that 'patterns of meanings are shared, that meanings are inscribed in institutions and processes, and that both affect, but certainly do not determine, individual behaviour' (2007: 216).

Finally their approach to the structure-agency question (and the related meta-theoretical issues above) has major implications for how they conceptualise change and continuity. Such is the import of their view of change and contingency that we will return to it as a separate issue shortly.

Bevir and Rhodes's interpretivism can therefore be critiqued on a theoretical level in a number of ways. By adopting insights from Archer (1995) and McAnulla (2006b) two overall criticisms can be developed. Firstly their ontological and epistemological position is problematic in that it focuses on the latter at the expense of the former. Secondly their approach over privileges agency at the expense of structure. Consequently their views of other key meta-theoretical issues do not recognise the complexity of material-ideational and institutional-ideational relations. These relationships are far better conceived of as dialectical relationships where reciprocity is a hallmark feature.

Having critiqued the work of Bevir and Rhodes in general theoretical terms we will now turn our attention to their main concepts, traditions and dilemmas.

Traditions

One of the major strengths of Bevir and Rhodes's approach to traditions is that it has raised the possibility of multiple traditions operating within British politics. They also place continual contestation between these traditions at the core of their explanation. It should be noted here that the critical approach to the BPT described in Chapter 1 also raised the notion of two competing traditions, albeit based around different concepts of democracy. However this critical approach insufficiently theorised the development of the content and development of these traditions. Nor was the relationship between the elitist and participatory views of democracy fully explored. Whilst it was evident that these views of democracy were conflicting, it was far from clear as to how and why contestation arose at a given time or why this conflict appeared more pronounced at certain points than others.

Bevir and Rhodes's focus on continual contestation between competing traditions is helpful to the critical view of the BPT in that it acts as an underpinning or backdrop for British politics, if it is characterised somewhat differently. However Bevir and Rhodes approach to traditions is not free from criticism.

Firstly Bevir and Rhodes (2002; 2003; 2004; 2006a; 2006b 2006c) identify four political traditions operating within British politics: Whig, Conservative, Liberal, and Socialist. However it is far from clear why these traditions are chosen. The failure to explain why they are chosen leaves us with the question as to whether they are the main traditions operating in British politics or the only ones. Other authors have pointed to the existence of other political traditions operating in British politics. They have merely characterised them differently. In each instance, to a lesser or greater extent, these authors sought to explain how and why they chose to characterise the BPT as they did. With Bevir and Rhodes we are left to wonder why they choose the traditions they do, other than their comment that their 'choice of traditions is conventional' (2006b: 77). Furthermore no account is given by Bevir and Rhodes as to why they do not consider any of the other ideas offered as the putative BPT worthy of inclusion.

In their most recent offerings the range of traditions cited has expanded. They refer to the Westminster tradition, Fabian Socialism, institutionalist and communitarian social science in relation to New Labour (2008a: 175) and 'a tradition of liberal representative democracy that has dominated the Labour party as well as British politics' (2008b: 730). Again we are left to assume that the range of traditions that are important in British politics is defined merely by what issue is being addressed. Given the import that Bevir and Rhodes attach to narratives this hardly seems sufficient and is not remedied in their recent engagements with Smith (2008) and Marsh (2008a). Furthermore the lack of erudition on the development and narration of political traditions over time divorces them from their proper historical context both materially and ideationally. This leaves the reader with an essentially 'free-floating' concept of political traditions.[11]

A second criticism of Bevir and Rhodes's conceptualisation of multiple traditions concerns the notion of dominance. It appears that they have chosen these traditions because of their greater resonance with actors in British politics. However no explanation is offered concerning how or why these traditions have resonated more fully and been more widely accepted. Nor do they offer an account of how this resonance then affects outcomes. They do not consider the idea that the traditions they choose or traditions more broadly may resonate in an asymmetrical manner. Rather we are left with the impression that they resonate in a similar fashion and actors choose between them free from constraint. Contra this we must consider the notion of predominant and competing traditions. A close examination of British political history suggests that certain ideas have resonated more fully than others over time. Moreover certain ideas have resonated more fully with socio-economic and political elites over time, an idea that will be explored later in this book.

Furthermore Bevir and Rhodes suggest that 'philosophical analysis tells us only about the ineluctable nature of agency and tradition. It does not tell us about the ways in which traditions work under particular social conditions... we do not provide philosophical answers to questions about the link between power and tradition, or the dominance of some traditions' (2008: 174).

However traditions cannot be seen as divorced from the social context or conditions. Rather they are operating within, and as part of, that context. If those social conditions demonstrate inequality or asymmetry then we might properly expect certain traditions to resonate more fully than others, in that certain traditions or ideas will more neatly fit with the context. Responding to Smith (2008), they suggest that they are wary of notions concerning power and dominance because they ignore the meaningfulness of action and suggest reification and essentialism (2008a: 174). However power and dominance are essential concerns for all political analysis and not just the concern of empirical social theory as Bevir and Rhodes suggest.

Ideas do not exist in a vacuum, nor do they act in a way that is free of the context. Rather ideas can be narrations and legitimisations of power relations in the broader material context. If so, three observations follow. Firstly we may be able to identify predominant and competing traditions within the range of political traditions operating within a political system, which resonate asymmetrically in relation to that context. A close examination of British political history suggests that certain ideas have resonated more fully than others over time, and crucially, with socio-economic and political elites. We should however recognise that the degree of contestation between traditions and their resonance is not necessarily constant over time. Rather it changes in response to contingent events.

Secondly actors are likely to appeal to these traditions asymmetrically as they select those traditions or ideas that fit most neatly with the prevailing ideational, material and institutional context. Indeed actors face an uneven political landscape that privileges certain ideas over others. Finally a degree of path dependency is likely to occur, as aspects of a political system, its institutions and practices are perpetuated over time.

Nor do Bevir and Rhodes consider the significance of the political landscape when discussing traditions. They offer no discussion of the relationship between ideas and institutions. Or to put it another way they do not explore the relationship between tradition and the broader institutional and socio-economic context. Marsh and Hall suggest more persuasively that 'asymmetry is woven into the very fabric of British political life, its ideas and also, crucially, its institutions' (2007: 217).[12] Contestation between traditions is a continual feature of British political life that takes place on an uneven political landscape that privileges certain ideas over others. Furthermore the degree of contestation is itself not constant but rather changes in response to contingent events. These recognitions underpin the conceptualisation of the BPT developed in Chapters 4 and 5.

Thirdly Bevir and Rhodes's concept of tradition can be criticised for paying relatively little attention to the relationship between the traditions they identify as important. They ignore the extent to which there may be points of similarity or convergence between the traditions they use. Rather they take for granted that their traditions are divergent. However as Marsh and Hall suggest: 'those four traditions are all rooted in an elitist concept of democracy that has dominated British politics and the views of political actors' (2007: 17). Thus the traditions they identify lack the plurality they claim. Bevir and Rhodes (2006b: 83) themselves acknowledge that even the socialist tradition in the UK has strong statist and bureaucratic elements which had at its core 'a top down, command style bureaucracy based on centralised rules'. Indeed as Evans suggests, it can be argued that UK politics is dominated by an 'elitist concept of statecraft which has informed the development of the modern British state and its political institutions' (2003: 313).

Two further criticisms of their approach can be developed here. Firstly they define these four traditions as ideal types, isolated from their proper historical and institutional context (2003: 107–18). This raises an interesting conundrum for their interpretive approach. If, as Bevir and Rhodes claim, these traditions will have adapted as dilemmas arise, then the context of British politics and the peculiarities of British history will have adapted traditions away from ideal type narratives. For example in the case of the Socialist tradition we must account for the peculiarities of the British version of socialism (Miliband 1972; Wright 1996; Thorpe 2001; Cronin 2004). Tant (1993) offers insights into how the Labour party came to accept much of the prevailing ideational and institutional context of British politics in the early 20th century. However by over privileging agency and negating structure, Bevir and Rhodes reduce that context to merely the responses of actors to dilemmas. However we must include the context to explain these adaptations. In particular the peculiarities of the Labour party's approach cannot be explained without reference to the institutional context and Labour's knowledge of those institutions and processes. Consequently we need to explore the development of any tradition or narrative within its institutional and ideational context to fully understand and explain political developments.

Nor are these traditions appealed to or applied as distinctly as is suggested. Rather actors will select aspects of these traditions that best fit the pre-existing ideational and structural context. The most recent addition, liberal representative democracy, and its impact on constitutional reform (2008b: 730), illuminates this point. Actors will select aspects of these traditions that best fit the pre-existing ideational and structural context. For example on Scottish devolution the Labour party made the case by utilising a variety of traditions simultaneously rather than simply appealing to the liberal democratic tradition. They argued from a Whig perspective that devolution fitted with the UK's existing constitutional gradualism,[13] from a Conservative perspective that it would maintain the union of the UK, and from a Liberal perspective that it would remedy the democratic deficit. Thus actors were not appealing to a particular tradition, rather they were appealing to aspects of various traditions in British politics, all of which fitted to a lesser or greater extent with the pre-existing ideational and institutional framework. As such the ideational and material context constrained the choice of traditions and had an impact on outcomes. Again we see that by overstating the importance of agency, Bevir and Rhodes negate the impact of the context as a factor that can constrain or enable agency. However traditions can and do constrain or enable the choices that agents make in a strategically selective environment. This allows us to more persuasively explain change and continuity over time.

This approach does not reify tradition, as Bevir and Rhodes suggest (2008: 730). Their anti-essentialism offers a view 'where a group of ideas widely shared by several individuals although no one idea was held by them all ... or ... no single idea persisted across all generations' (2003: 33). Contra this, we should consider whether the substantive core of the traditions is being altered or whether change occurs either to peripheral aspects of the tradition, or to re-narrate core ideas within a new context. With reference to the BPT, we should not deny the possibility of change to aspects of that tradition or the actuality of adaptations. However its core discourses have remained relatively constant over time, being updated, reaffirmed, re-narrated and on occasion, adapted, for a changing context. Indeed it should be noted that the notion of predominant and competing ideas by definition involves renegotiation and readjustment and is therefore a dynamic process (Gramsci 1971).

Nor does it hypostatise tradition. Rather it counters the suggestion (2003: 33) that traditions only exist in the actions and attitudes of individuals, and recognises that traditions can and do become inscribed in institutions, structures and discourses. This allows us to account for how traditions can come to inform customs and practices over time and that whilst agents may transmit and give meaning to ideas and traditions, so do institutions, structures and discourses (Marsh and Hall 2007).

Finally their approach to tradition can be critiqued for being agency centric. They argue that agents adapt traditions as they face dilemmas. However by overplaying the importance of agency they negate the impact of tradition as a factor that can constrain or enable agency. Contra this, traditions can and do constrain or enable the choices that agents make. Here we can again refer to the idea of strategic selectivity (Jessop 1990; Kerr 2002) to more persuasively explain change and continuity over time, a point we will return to shortly.

The problem of dilemmas

Dilemma undoubtedly helps shift attention away from overly synchronic views of British political development. However due to their ontological and epistemological position dilemma is heuristically limited as a tool for explaining the development of the British political system. It is problematic in a number of ways.

Firstly it is far from clear in the work of Bevir and Rhodes as to why a particular dilemma becomes important at a particular point in time. For example when discussing changes to public service they raise a number of dilemmas including 'fragmentation, steering, accountability and management change' (2003: 131). They then discuss responses to these dilemmas in relation to the various traditions they identify, in particular the conservative and socialist traditions. However as Marsh and Hall note, this 'is justified by reference to an unpublished paper by Sir Robin Butler, then Cabinet Secretary, and to Rhodes earlier work' (2007: 219). Far greater historical erudition than this is required to explain and justify the existence of particular dilemmas.

Secondly it is not clear when a dilemma becomes a dilemma (Marsh and Hall 2007: 219). Bevir and Rhodes state that 'a dilemma arises for an individual or institution when a new idea stands in opposition to existing beliefs and practices and so forces a reconsideration of these existing beliefs and traditions'. On the surface this appears unproblematic. However in reality it leaves us with a perspective in which we are focusing on isolated moments. To put it another way, as currently narrated by Bevir and Rhodes, 'dilemma' posits change developing out of a single point in time. A dilemma arises, actors respond by searching for a solution that can be accommodated into their webs of belief and through this process the tradition is adapted and an outcome created. However it is far more persuasive to suggest that 'dilemma or even crisis is likely to be a complex and cumulative process' (Marsh and Hall 2007: 219). For example it would be very difficult to identify a single dilemma or moment when the dilemma crystallised in relation to any of Labour's recent constitutional reforms. Rather their development can more persuasively be explained via reference to a number of interrelated factors over time. For example we could identify the increasingly resonant critique of the UK's constitutional arrangements that had many dimensions such as: the party's increasingly precarious electoral position (given their loss of four successive general elections, including one they thought they'd definitely win in 1992), and: 'numerous contingent events and narratives over time' (Marsh and Hall 2007: 219).

Dilemma also focuses attention onto the significance of contingent events as triggers for change. The reliance on dilemmas and their impact leads to an emphasis on the capacity for and the actuality of change as seen when they claim the existence of 'an ever changing pattern of governance' (Bevir and Rhodes 2006a: 98). Whilst this appears initially persuasive, a closer examination suggests that greater refinement of the concept is required for it to be heuristically powerful. Contra Bevir and Rhodes, dilemmas occur in response to contingent events within the prevailing structural and ideational context. In this context two further points can be made. Firstly the context is an uneven playing field characterised by structured inequality and asymmetrical power relations. This context therefore underpins the asymmetrical resonance of ideas and traditions. Secondly this context generally privileges those ideas and traditions that most easily fit with the prevailing context (Marsh and Hall 2007).

Furthermore Bevir and Rhodes's approach to dilemmas fails to confront the resonance of dilemmas within this strategically selective context within which they are experienced (Marsh and Hall 2007: 220). This is hardly surprising given their position on the relationship between the material and the ideational. However, as a consequence, their approach leaves us with a partial explanation of outcomes. Marsh and Hall (2007: 220) correctly suggest that:

> the context is strategically selective both because it reflects the structured inequality within society and because the institutions and processes of government are inscribed with a particular view of democracy, which we call the British Political Tradition. At the same time, this view of democracy also remains the dominant, if contested, view and so is crucial in the way that dilemmas are interpreted by government.

Moreover it is Bevir and Rhodes's failure to address the asymmetry of the economic, institutional and discursive landscape that leads them to privilege change over continuity.

Finally the view that political scientists cannot predict how people will respond to a dilemma (Bevir and Rhodes 2003; 2006a 2006b) is debatable. If we accept that the crystallisation of a dilemma discussed earlier is a complex historical process shaped by pre-existing ideas, traditions and structures then we can certainly make more than informed conjectures about possible responses and outcomes.

Moreover if we allow for the process of strategic selectivity (Jessop 1990) and the impact of a predominant political tradition, this will mean a degree of path dependency alongside the potential for change. The pre-existing will act as a guide to possible future outcomes if not a prediction of them. Or to put it another way, contingent events will themselves have numerous historical antecedents. They are a product of a cumulative process that features both continuity and change. Actors will have to find out how to propose a solution to the 'dilemma' that is more or less consistent with pre-existing structures, ideas and interests. In this process alternative options and solutions are considered by agents and then strategically selected. The predominant tradition and structures will act here as only those options that can be easily accommodated are likely to be selected. Thus the range of options is limited by the pre-existing structural and ideational factors.

Dilemma as conceptualised by Bevir and Rhodes does not offer an adequate explanatory tool in its current form as it leaves us with a focus on the responses of actors to contingent events isolated from their historical development and their economic, institutional and discursive context. Having critiqued tradition and dilemma we will now turn our attention to a discussion of continuity and change.

Continuity and change

The final notable aspect of Bevir and Rhodes's work is their focus on contingency and change. Explaining continuity and change is of central significance to socio-political analysis. Indeed: 'the question of change is far from a complicating distraction – it is, in essence, the very raison d'etre of political inquiry' (Hay 2002: 138). In recent years political analysis has become more aware of the centrality of concepts of continuity and change (Kerr and Kettell 2006). Detailed consideration of the problems that explain what social and political change represents is a recent phenomenon (Sztompka 1993; Hay 1996; 2002a; Kerr 2002; Marsh 2007). It is through this more critical engagement with conceptualising change that issues regarding causality, temporality and the relationship between continuity and change have come truly to the fore (for a discussion of these see Hay 2002). The need for a conceptualisation of social and political change that can provide a satisfactory account of the nature of British politics over time is long overdue (Marsh 2007).

Hay (2002) states that all political analysis must necessarily acknowledge issues to do with continuity and change, even when it attempts to offer a purely descriptive account of the present. Despite the fact that so much of the work of political analysis is concerned with explaining substantive changes and continuities in institutions, ideas and the behaviour of agents, there has been comparatively little theoretical discussion of how to conceptualise change and continuity in politics until recently.[14]

Why change and continuity?

Explaining change and continuity is a central concern of all social science inquiry. It is also one of the most challenging for social and political analysis. Indeed focusing on 'issues of transformation and change raise some fairly fundamental questions about the scope, legitimate content, scientific status and limits of political analysis (Hay 2002: 143). As Shils argues: 'a society is a trans-temporal phenomenon. It is not constituted by its existence at single moment in time. It exists only through time. It is temporally constituted' (1981: 327).

A political analysts' ontological, epistemological and methodological approach and their normative stance is of fundamental importance for how they conceptualise change and continuity. Political analysts approach the explanation of change in differing ways. For those political scientists adopting a naturalist approach, such as rational choice theory and behaviouralism, the issue of social and political change is a complicating distraction (Hay 2002a: 137). For those who would be categorised as normative or critical political analysts, interrogating the process of social and political change is of central importance. It is through the interrogation of existing institutions, practices and ideas that alternative approaches can be identified, advocated and advanced. Conversely, political analysts of a conservative disposition (Burke 1790; Oakeshott 1962) interrogate the process of change in order to identify how best to defend the status quo. They have historically been concerned with identifying the processes through which demands for reform develop into more revolutionary demands. Consequently normative political analysts of all persuasions have to confront the issue of change and continuity over time and develop explanations that best explain the process.

Of all the meta-theoretical issues confronting social theory the relationship between change and continuity holds a special significance as it can subsume other relationships such as structure and agency or material-ideational relationships (Marsh and Hall 2006; Marsh 2007). Whenever we discuss either structure-agency and/or material-ideational relationships, we necessarily have to discuss continuity and change. However such complex relationships provide a challenge for political analysts.[15]

Attempts to develop more sophisticated approaches to continuity and change have been driven by the exigencies of the structure-agency debate and the seemingly ever-changing world we now inhabit (Hay

2002). The inadequacies of both structuralism[16] and intentionalism[17] in explaining change and continuity can readily be identified, although overcoming them presents a far greater challenge for political analysis than such a recognition implies. Indeed focusing on continuity and change highlights the need to develop more sophisticated conceptualisations of causality than those found in essentially structuralist or intentionalist accounts (Hay 2002). It is here that both the work of Bevir and Rhodes and the critical realist approach are relevant. However, of the two, critical realism offers the more persuasive alternative to key meta-theoretical questions.

Continuity and change in British politics

In the context of British politics we have already recognised the decisive influence of Whig developmentalism and the WM. Widely read works including Norton (1984) and Punnett (1987) are classical examples of this approach. Butterfield (1965) identifies a number of key characteristics of the Whig interpretation of history.[18] In particular the Whig interpretation highlights notions of gradual development over time and peaceful progression. Indeed the words 'evolution' or evolutionary development are often, somewhat incorrectly,[19] associated with the Whig view. However, despite this, the Whig interpretation of history has been the dominant concept of change and continuity in the analysis of British politics. Furthermore it also incorporates an idealist aspect: 'seeing institutions as the expression of human purpose' (Bevir and Rhodes 2002: 145).

The Whig interpretation can also be found in numerous influential studies of the British political system such as Bagehot (1867), Dicey (1885) and Jennings (1936). It also underpins classic works such as Burke (1790) and McCaulay (1848). Gamble (1990: 409–11) argues persuasively that those in the political science profession in the UK 'were largely sympathetic', 'convinced that change needed to be evolutionary' and celebrated 'the practical wisdom embodied in England's constitutional arrangements'. In analyses of British politics the WM and the Whig interpretation have been intrinsically linked, offering a view of change that is 'relatively static and incremental, unilinear tradition' (Kerr and Kettell 2006: 19). Thus mainstream accounts of Britain's political development have appealed to the WM and Whiggish developmentalism.

Beyond the mainstream there have been those who have drawn inspiration from a Marxist approach, such as Anderson (1964) Nairn (1964; 1976) and Miliband (1982). The Marxist approach to issues of change and continuity is well documented.[20] Suffice it to say here that Orthodox Marxists, adopting a 'base/superstructure' approach, attempted to explain change in the superstructure (for example social and political changes) through reference to changes in the economic base and offered a view that was associated with four 'isms' (Marsh 2002b). These were economism, determinism, materialism and structuralism. It also posited a concept of change rooted in a dialectical view that focuses on conflict and contradiction as integral to any discussion of change and continuity. Over time Marxism has developed as a theoretical approach. In particular we should take account of the work of Gramsci (1971) and Poulanztas (1978) which have been particularly influential in shifting the Marxist position to a more nuanced approach.[21] However the application of modern Marxist insights to the study of the British political system remains largely outside the mainstream, despite the fact that the approach offers much to modern social science (Marsh 1999b). Indeed Burnham (2006: 67) notes that 'a review of modern politics textbooks may lead the reader to conclude that Marxism has little, if anything, to contribute to understanding contemporary political issues in Britain'. Despite this, modern Marxist or neo-Marxist insights can offer much to the analyses of British politics. In particular Jessop (1990) and the notion of 'strategic selectivity' offers a way to developing sophisticated explanations of change and continuity (Hay 1996; Kerr 2002).

Jessop (1990: 209) states:

> strategic selectivity refers to the structurally mediated bias which means that particular forms of state privilege some strategies over others, some time horizons over others, some coalition possibilities over others. A given type of state, a given state form, a given form of regime will be more accessible to some forces than others according to the strategies they adopt to gain power. And it will be more suited to the pursuit of some types of economic and political strategy than others because of the mode of intervention and resources which characterise that system.

If we adopt this approach then we can see that agents will develop strategies within this strategically selective context. However agents will not have perfect knowledge of their context. Rather they will have ideas, amongst them, traditions, concerning their environment which informs the strategies they adopt. Given the selective bias of that context and the imperfection of knowledge outcomes will not always be what was intended by agents. It should again be noted here that these unintended consequences themselves may become very important as factors promoting further change in the future (Kerr 2002; Marsh and Hall 2007).

This is relevant here in two ways. Firstly the concept of political traditions is one explicitly concerned with issues to do with continuity and change. However it has often been seen as overly synchronic. Secondly the subsequent chapters on predominant and competing political traditions seek to deploy a more sophisticated and diachronic concept of continuity and change. Sztompka states: 'in order to understand any contemporary phenomenon we must look back to its origins and the processes that brought it about' (Sztompka 1993: xiv). Therefore to explain contemporary political developments we should focus on the process by which each change came about within the prevailing context. As such we should attempt to uncover the causal mechanisms that led to the outcomes we now see being realised. We should also consider whether, inherent in these processes, there exists the possibility for further institutional and ideational change in British politics. It is the need to explain change and continuity in British politics over time that forms the basis of the discussion below.

Focusing on continuity and change highlights the need to develop more sophisticated conceptualisations of causality than those found in either structuralist or intentionalist accounts. It is here that both the work of Bevir and Rhodes and the critical realist approach are relevant. In particular the work of Jessop (1990), Hay (1996) and Kerr (2001; 2002) offer major insights into the process by which change and continuity occur.

Critical realists start with the premise that the relationship between continuity and change is the last meta-theoretical dualism confronting social and political analysts (Marsh 2007). Most political science literature sees the relationship between the two as an oppositional one where continuity and change are mutually exclusive. Critical realists view it as dialectical in the sense that it is interactive and iterative. Utilising the latter approach we can see that some aspects of the sociopolitical context may change whilst others remain the same. This may lead to the existence of contradictions that will themselves facilitate further change be it limited or extensive, although this is not necessarily the case. It is the interplay between continuity and change in terms of balance and potential contradictions that affects outcomes at any given time. Finally path dependency forms the context in which change occurs. Prior stability, the manner in which it is narrated and the way it is experienced by agents affects the likely nature, extent and permanence of change.

Discussion of continuity and change raises another key question for all social and political analysis: time. Hay (2002) identifies three analytical strategies for dealing with the process of social and political change, the synchronic, the comparative static and the diachronic.[22] Of these the latter offers the most complete picture of change and continuity over time. This treats the developmental path, the pace and timing of change as empirical issues of import. Thus diachronic analyses will proceed historically, examining and explaining the process of change over time. Such an approach builds an empirically rich picture of change and allows us to develop and test theoretical hypotheses regarding the process of change.

Before turning to Bevir and Rhodes's approach, a brief overview of evolutionary theories of change is necessary for two reasons. Firstly because, as we have seen, the dominant view of British political development – the Whig interpretation – has often utilised the word 'evolutionary' (albeit inaccurately) to describe that development. Secondly the work of Hay (1996) and Kerr (2001; 2002) offers major insights into the process by which change and continuity should be conceptualised and explained.

Evolutionary change

Kerr (2002: 332) argues that 'evolutionary thinking has a long history in attempts by social scientists to explain institutional change'.[23] However until recently it has remained largely marginalised and discredited in social science research.[24] Kerr identifies four broad themes that characterise the concerns of evolutionary theorising in the social sciences:

- A recognition of the dynamic and temporal dimensions of change
- an emphasis on the selection of variables
- a focus on adaptive processes
- a recognition of change as both path-dependent and contingent.

(adapted from Kerr 2002)

Hay (1996) and Kerr (2001; 2002; 2003) offer two stimulating approaches to theorising change and continuity from an evolutionary perspective.

Hay (1996) offers a sophisticated attempt to explain institutional transformation and public policy in post-war Britain. Hay's evolutionary approach includes three defining components. Firstly, taking influence from Habermas's concept of 'legitimation crisis', he focuses on 'crisis' and develops the idea that 'the crisis moment is the strategic moment in the evolution of things' (Debray cited in Kerr 2002: 343). For Hay, crises are contested constructs that can and are interpreted differently by agents. Thus change develops out of moments of crisis and the responses to them. Secondly he offers the notion that change involves periodic moments of 'punctuated evolution' in which crises and the response of agents lead to an increase in the pace and extent of change. In particular he highlights the likelihood of institutional development within a period of 'punctuated evolution' whereby during a crisis, state actors will intervene in order to attempt to overcome the crisis and the inability of prevailing institutional arrangements to deal with it. Finally he uses the notion of 'paradigm shifts' to explain how ideational factors influence the process of change and will create a degree of path dependency in the political environment. A policy paradigm for Hay constitutes an ideational package that limits the range of legitimate responses and thus helps to impose a degree of continuity alongside change. Here we should note that Hay adopts the idea of strategic selectivity developed by Jessop (1990). For example Hay, echoing Jessop, argues that 'the state is a dynamic and constantly unfolding system. Its specific form at a given moment in time in particular national setting represents a crystallisation of past strategies which privileges certain strategies and actors over others' (1996: 32).

Hay uses this approach to explain the changes of the post-war period in the UK from a Keynesian, social democratic paradigm to a neo-liberal paradigm of the Thatcher period through reference to the perceived crisis of Keynesianism in the late 1960s and 1970s. Hay offers much to those attempting to explain change and continuity over time. In particular he highlights major moments of change or adaptation through his focus on the three core concepts crisis, punctuated evolution and paradigm shift. However we should note here that Hay still leaves the reader with a picture of change that is largely characterised by a binary opposition between periods of stability and then periods of change (Kerr 2001).

Kerr (2001; 2002; 2003) offers a slightly different concept of evolutionary theorising and one that offers much if utilised. He suggests that 'a useful starting point for evolutionary concept of political change is to begin with the very essence of politics, that is to say political and ideological contestation' (Kerr 2002: 353). For Kerr: 'it is the continual struggle for survival between competing sets of ideas and political strategies which provides the key dynamic for political change' (Kerr

2002: 353). Here it should be noted that he offers a view that incorporates agency in that the strategic conduct of actors acts to generate changes in institutions and policies. However Kerr does not offer an intentionalist analysis, rather he adopts the dialectical approach to structure and agency argued for earlier, and insights from critical realism. He argues that ideational contestations occur: 'within institutional, contextual and discursive environments which are the products of past struggles and ideas; the embeddedness of which impose a selective bias in favour of some over others' (Kerr 2002: 354).

The influence of Jessop (1990) and the notion of strategic selectivity can again be identified. For Kerr, adopting the critical evolutionary approach involves a focus on the constant interaction between agents and their context or environment. He argues that 'we must acknowledge that selection mechanisms work at both levels; whilst the institutional and discursive environment exerts selective pressures for particular types of political strategy, so agents continuously reflect upon their own strategic conduct thereby ordering and filtering their strategic objectives on order to negotiate environmental constraints' (Kerr 2002: 354).

This approach highlights the notion of path dependency. Kerr has been criticised by Kay (2003) and Curry (2003). However his critical evolutionary approach offers a multi-layered and dynamic approach for explaining the process of change and continuity over time. In particular it offers a view that focuses on the continual dialectical relationship between change and continuity. As such it overcomes the tendency to characterise British politics in terms of a binary opposition between periods of change and periods of continuity (Kerr and Kettell 2006).

Bevir and Rhodes on change

Bevir and Rhodes raise questions concerning overly synchronic views of British politics. Their view of change warrants brief repetition here. Their use of tradition, and particularly dilemma, places both contingency and change at the centre of explanations. They offer 'an analysis of change rooted in the beliefs and action of situated agents' (2006a: 169). For them change is driven by agents responding to dilemmas and therefore their view of change is agency centric. Furthermore they suggest both contingency and change are ubiquitous. However their approach fails to grasp the complexity of the relationship between change and continuity.

Firstly Bevir and Rhodes emphasise the existence of 'an ever changing pattern of governance' (2006a: 98). This is problematic on various levels. Firstly it fails to fully explain continuity. On a basic level if change is ubiquitous then what place continuity? Their approach is almost exclusively concerned with explaining change and struggles to account for continuity (Marsh and Hall 2006; Marsh 2008a). Indeed they maintain a simplistic dualism between change and continuity instead of developing a convincing view of the complex relationship between the two. This occurs as a direct consequence of their privileging of agency over structure and the ideational over the material.

Further problems for Bevir and Rhodes's agency-centric approach to change can be readily identified. To demonstrate this we will return to the WM. If belief in the WM narrative or tradition is as pervasive as they suggest and actors use it to respond to dilemmas, then how do we account for the ubiquity of change that they claim? Whilst change and adaptation may be evident, to suggest that it is ubiquitous is to either ignore the demonstrable continuities in the British political system or to suggest that actors' beliefs are not as important in informing outcomes as they claim.

Contra Bevir and Rhodes, there are numerous constraints and enablers acting upon agents, including traditions and discourses. Institutions and material factors can also constrain or enable agency. Recognising these allows us to explain both change and continuity more satisfactorily. If we allow for the process of strategic selectivity emanating from a widespread belief in WM, this will mean a degree of path dependency alongside the potential for change. The pre-existing context will act as a guide to possible future outcomes if not a prediction of them. Contingent events have numerous historical antecedents. They are a product of a cumulative process which features both continuity and change. Actors will have to find how to propose a solution to the 'dilemma' that is more or less consistent with pre-existing structures, ideas and interests. In this process alternative options and solutions are considered by agents and then strategically selected. Predominant narratives or traditions and structures will act here as those options that can be easily accommodated are more likely to be selected. Thus the range of options is limited by the pre-existing structural and ideational context.

Furthermore the resonance of dilemmas themselves is affected by the strategically selective context within which they are experienced. For example if we take the issue of constitutional reform used by Bevir and Rhodes (2008b), there were various well known aspects to this 'dilemma' including concerns over the erosion of rights, the democratic deficit and the dangers of an overly mighty executive at the centre. The importance attached to these aspects was undoubtedly affected by the pre-existing ideational and structural context and an actor's views. Thus their knowledge of the dilemma was conditioned by that which already existed, the context, and how this and the dilemma itself were viewed.

In this instance New Labour's underlying faith in the BPT was crucial. Their prioritisation of constitutional reform and their actual reforms were conditioned by their views of the constitution, its central ideas and their efficacy.[25] Whilst New Labour sought to tackle these 'dilemmas', they did so in such a way as to preserve those aspects of the pre-existing context that they revered such as parliamentary sovereignty and the union. Indeed they shied away from reforms that would endanger these, such as codification and federalism.

Moreover if we accept that the WM narrative is still informing actors' views to a great extent, then does this not suggest a degree path dependency in outcomes? Bevir and Rhodes pay little attention to the notion of path dependency. Indeed they roundly dismiss it, arguing:

> our interpretive approach to British governance does not read off actions from allegedly objective social facts about institutions or people. Rather it leads us to explore historical and contingent patterns of belief that inform current governmental practices in Britain. So, instead of describing reified institutions with alleged path dependency, we decentred the relevant traditions and explored how they were modified in response to dilemmas. (2006b: 195)

They argue that those who advocate path dependency adopt a position that privileges structure over agency, the material over the ideational and institutions over ideas. They believe that a focus of path dependency also privileges continuity over change. However stressing the interactive and iterative relationship between change and continuity does not privilege either. Rather it allows us to consider the relationship between the two. In particular utilising insights from Jessop (1990), Hay (1996) and Kerr (2002) allows the highlighting of both the path- dependent and contingent aspects of ideas, institutions and practices. Such an approach offers the opportunity to consider temporality, causality and the direction of change more thoroughly. Thus a multifaceted approach to change and continuity can be offered rather than Bevir and Rhodes's unpersuasive suggestions regarding agency and the ubiquity of change.

This approach also recognises that the context is an uneven playing field and that this underpins the asymmetrical resonance of narratives and traditions. This context generally privileges those ideas and traditions that most easily fit with it. Such a concept of change and continuity offers a multi-causal/multi-directional approach to the problem in which the conflict between competing sets of ideas results in both continuity and change over time (Kerr 2002). By focusing on the process by which change and adaptation develop at both a macro and micro level we can 'direct our attention to what is not likely to occur' (Kerr 2002: 334), alongside what is likely to occur. This allows us to comment fully on both the temporality of change and crucially, on any path dependency. It is through the latter in particular that we can highlight continuities with the past in ideas, in institutions, and in practices, as well as make informed conjectures about possible responses and outcomes. Thus contra Bevir and Rhodes, by recognising the dialectical relationship between continuity and change (and other meta-theoretical relationships) we develop a far more persuasive view of political developments over time. Doing so moves us beyond both the Whiggish developmentalism of the WM narrative and Bevir and Rhodes's agency-centric interpretivism, both of which offer an ultimately unsatisfactory view of the development of the British political system.

Having dealt critically with various aspects of Bevir and Rhodes's view of political traditions, we will now turn our attention to the most recent conceptualisation, that promulgated by David Marquand.

Marquand

More recently, eminent political scientist and commentator David Marquand has offered his view of political traditions. He (2008) also stresses the importance of four political traditions, arguing that the interplay between these political traditions has been fundamental to Britain's political culture. Significantly, Marquand recognises that 'the democratisation of Britain was a slow, fiercely contested process spread over more than 350 years, and its results have always been in dispute' (2008: 466).

He notes that these traditions do not fit easily into the conventional categories of left and right or liberal, conservative and socialist. The four key political traditions identified by Marquand are: Whig Imperialist, Tory Nationalist, Democratic Collectivist and Democratic Republican. On each, Marquand gives a sketch of their ideational development before concluding that they are alive and well in contemporary British politics.

The Whig Imperialist tradition was shaped by and is most associated with the ideas of Burke. Marquand suggests that this tradition is the most pervasive of all. Burke's views will be dealt with in greater depth in Chapter 4; meanwhile, we note the key facets as identified by Marquand: 'a spirit of preservation and improvement' (2008: 468) and gradual, 'evolutionary' change. In relation to identity, the Whig Imperialist tradition stressed the notion that Britain, via its empire, was spreading freedom around the globe. Marquand notes that this was largely, though not entirely 'humbug'.

The Tory Nationalist tradition is, according to Marquand, more pessimistic in tone than the Whig Imperialist. However, like the latter, its primary concern 'was to defend and sustain authority, social and political' (2008: 468). Unlike the Whig Imperialist tradition, the Tory Nationalist sought to change only to 'restore a lost golden age of order, discipline and respect for tradition' (2008: 468). Marquand notes how the resonance of the Tory Nationalist tradition was contingent in that it depended on the extent of 'calm' or 'trouble' occurring socially and politically.

Contra Whig Imperialist optimism and Tory Nationalist pessimism, the Democratic Collectivist tradition focused on 'the ineluctable advance towards a better future' (2008: 469). Democratic Collectivists were also largely content with the structure of the British state but viewed it as the agent of social transformation in line with Fabian gradualist socialism. For the likes of 'the Webbs' it was 'science, reason and their own grasp of the dynamics of historical change' (2008: 469) that would deliver progress to a less wasteful, more equitable society.

Finally advocates of the Democratic Republican tradition were, according to Marquand 'the awkward squad of British democracy' (2008: 470). This tradition also emphasised equality but focused on 'fellowship and dignity more than economic equality' (2008: 470) and stressed 'the self-liberating potential of ordinary citizens' (2008: 470). Despite repeated defeats across the course of British history this tradition has re-emerged to continue to press its case via the work of G. D. H. Cole and R. H. Tawney.

Marquand then uses his four traditions and the interplay between them to narrate Britain's political history since the advent of universal suffrage in 1928. Two interesting points can be made here. Firstly he does not see these four political traditions as mutually exclusive. Rather he argues that 'the frontiers between them are hazy and porous, and sometimes run within the divided souls of their adherents as well as between them' (2008: 466). Secondly he notes the extent to which three of his political traditions have been influential on governments whilst the Democratic Republican tradition has 'had a great influence on certain civil associations but except for brief periods governments have shied away from it' (2008: 473).

Like Bevir and Rhodes's approach, Marquand's conceptualisation of political traditions has a number of merits:

- He recognises the importance of ideational contestation and conflict in shaping British political life over time.
- He also recognises that actors may appeal to or draw from various political traditions in their political views.
- In recognising the continued resonance of Whig ideas and the centrality of Burke, Marquand goes some way towards pointing to its significance. Indeed he states that 'Whig Imperialist tradition has enjoyed a kind of hegemony; and Burkeian themes have sounded again and again' (2008: 467) and he stresses the importance of this tradition in shaping 'our political culture, the iconography of our Parliament and the understandings of our political class' (2008: 467).

However as with Bevir and Rhodes, there are a number of weaknesses with his analysis which limit its heuristic value and it is to these that we will now turn.

Firstly whilst Marquand is correct about the importance of Whiggish ideas emanating from Burke, by suggesting they are the 'most pervasive' (2008: 467) he falls short of affording them the dominant position they undoubtedly deserve. Nor does he explain how or why this 'pervasiveness' may have occurred or remained the case. As with Bevir and Rhodes, notions such as power, dominance and asymmetrical resonance are absent from Marquand's approach. Furthermore he does not explain how or why the Whig tradition has adapted or developed over time in relation to contingent events such as the extension of democracy and the rise of the party system.[26]

Secondly Marquand does not relate the traditions he identifies directly to the institutions and processes of British government historically. Whilst other authors have highlighted the Whiggish element to the WM (Gamble 1990; Kerr and Kettell 2006), Marquand's analysis leaves us to speculate about the precise relationship between ideas (in this case political traditions) and institutions and processes. Indeed the institutions and processes of British politics are largely absent from the piece, with these four political traditions and British democracy outlined devoid of institutional or procedural context. The reader is left to wonder what precisely is the relationship between the ideas described and what we see find at Westminster, Whitehall and beyond.

Thirdly Marquand downplays the similarities that exist between the political traditions in the UK in favour of diversity and difference. Like Bevir and Rhodes, he fails to recognise that three of his political traditions operate within the confines of two elitist discourses concerning democracy, and two further discourses concerning change and national distinctiveness. It is this that explains why these three traditions have been largely convinced of the role of the state as Marquand suggests. Unlike Bevir and Rhodes, he does note one point of similarity between the Whig Imperialist, Tory Nationalist and Democratic Collectivist Traditions when he suggests that all three are paternalistic. However the ideational and material basis of this paternalism is left both unexplored and unexplained. Here we should recognise the elitist attitudes that pervaded the socio-economic and intellectual elites in the UK in the 18th and 19th centuries as being integral to this paternalism. In essence, one common facet in the views of Edmund Burke, Robert Cecil and Sidney Webb was that each (in their own way) thought that they 'knew best'. Furthermore in the case of the Whig Imperialist and Tory Nationalist, we find a deep hostility towards notions such as popular sovereignty and participatory ideas concerning democracy.

Fourthly Marquand pays little, if any, attention to the meta-theoretical issues discussed in detail above. We have already noted that he offers little insight into the relationship between institutions and ideas. Furthermore this approach to political traditions offers an insufficient conceptualisation of change and continuity. Indeed by stating his traditions and then applying them to post-1928 British politics he leaves the impression of a largely static view of the traditions themselves in which their content has remained fixed for the last a hundred years or so. Thus he offers a somewhat reified view of political traditions. Nor does he adequately explain why the tradition(s) adopted by the government of the day change, other than pointing to the reactionary nature of the Tory Nationalist tradition in the face of challenges from various movements including the Women's Movement, Trade Unionists, the young, homosexual and environmental activists, and nationalists to name but a few. The reader is also left to wonder which, if any, of Marquand's four traditions, these groups advocate or appeal to. This weakness is particularly telling in the case of the nationalists given the changes to British politics emanating from these groups via demands for devolution and its creation post 1997. Indeed to explain the increased demands for constitutional reform since the 1970s we have to focus on the influence of political traditions rooted in competing concepts of democracy and territorial politics in the UK.

Nor does Marquand explain why actors such as those he cites come to believe in and advocate the political traditions they do. He thus ignores crucial questions regarding the relationship between structure and agency, and the material and ideational. As such there is no discussion as to why certain political traditions have resonated more fully than others over time. Like Bevir and Rhodes, Marquand fails to take into account the significance of the context in relation to the resonance of traditions. Nor, to use Marquand's own terminology, is it explained why actors at the centre have tended to avoid the 'democratic republican tradition'. To answer this we must consider both the importance of material conditions, in particular socio-economic factors and notions such as structure.

Finally like Bevir and Rhodes and those who have advocated the existence of a BPT, Marquand does not theorise or offer reflection on either the concept of tradition, or more specifically, political tradition. In this he falls into an oft-found problem in social analysis of treating the concept of tradition as a given, a point we will return to in Chapter 3.

Conclusion

Both Bevir and Rhodes, and Marquand have made contributions to the concept of political tradition, and through these contributions, to the study of British politics more broadly. Both approaches offer a focus on the role traditions play in explaining political developments and they highlight a process of continual competition between traditions as central to explaining outcomes in British politics.

However both approaches, in their own specific ways, offer an ultimately unsatisfactory view of the development of British politics over time. Furthermore a number of common problems can be identified with both. These can be summarised thus:

- Both conceptualisations of political tradition are unpersuasive. In particular neither recognises the existence and importance of predominant and competing traditions. Nor do they recognise the structured inequalities and asymmetries of power that have characterised UK society. As such they both downplay or ignore the asymmetrical resonance of political traditions in UK politics.
- On the key meta-theoretical issues both conceptualisations are unpersuasive. Bevir and Rhodes privilege agency over structure, the

ideational over the material, ideas over institutions. As such they continue to support dualisms with regard to these important issues. Marquand, for his part, fails to deal with such issues.
- Neither perspective offers a convincing view of change and continuity in British politics. Bevir and Rhodes's view tends towards the privileging of change over continuity. Marquand's approach insufficiently addresses this concern.
- Finally neither approach seeks to theorise the concepts of tradition, or political tradition.

Having dealt with the work of Bevir and Rhodes, and Marquand, we can now turn to considering the last of these common problems: the lack of detailed reflection on the concept of tradition itself.

3
Exploring Tradition

Introduction

As we saw in the preceding chapters, political tradition is a concept that has been applied to British politics by a diverse range of authors from various methodological and normative perspectives. What unites these authors is a desire to focus on the ideas that underpin the institutions and processes of British government. In doing so, they attempt to offer a more ideationally driven interpretation of the development of the British political system over time. This, as suggested earlier, would remedy a weakness in the analyses of British politics that has been increasingly identified (Greenleaf 1983a; McAnulla 2006a; Kerr and Kettell 2006). Despite this, perspectives utilising political tradition have all too often been ignored in mainstream analyses of British politics. Instead the majority of authors have favoured either explicitly or implicitly the Westminster Model (WM) as an explanatory framework, without considering how the institutions and processes it narrates came into being or, crucially, what ideas and views of democracy underpin them.

Of the criticisms that can be levelled at authors examining political tradition thus far, one major flaw of this approach has been that none of these authors discuss or theorise the concept of tradition itself. Rather it is usually treated as a given in the literature on political tradition and, indeed more broadly in social theory (Shils 1981; McAnulla 2007). Clearly, it is somewhat surprising that authors who have appealed to the significance of political traditions have spent little, if any, time considering how the notion of a tradition may be conceptualised or why we should consider it as a significant factor in explaining political development.

For this reason, we will now turn to the concept of tradition itself, as to adequately consider the role that political traditions have played in shaping the British political system we must begin by establishing a putative understanding of tradition.

What is tradition?

In many ways 'tradition' is a common-sense term in that it is often appealed to, but rarely defined, in political explanations. On a basic level, tradition can be defined simply as 'the way we do stuff' (Finlayson 2003: 664). The word 'tradition' derives from the Latin word *tradere*, meaning to transmit, deliver or hand down (Williams 1983a). When discussing tradition, we are considering the heritage of the past or that which 'has been delivered to us by our forebears' (Finlayson 2003: 664). Therefore tradition, in its most basic sense, can be defined as 'simply a traditum; it is anything which is transmitted or handed down from the past to the present' (Shils 1981: 1).

McAnulla (2007: 7) identifies various definitions within academic inquiry of the word 'tradition', with many of them focusing on tradition as something that remains of the past. For example Raymond Williams defines tradition as 'the surviving past' (1977: 115), whilst Michael Young sees it as 'crystallisations of the past which remain in the present' (1988: 142). Other scholars have sought to define tradition in a more 'active' sense, as something that involves 'the active re-enactment of associations with the past' (McAnulla 2007: 7). For example Halpin, Power and Fitz view tradition as 'customs and ceremonials by means of which the past speaks to the present' (1997: 1). Therefore tradition has been seen as either fragments, or entire aspects, of the past nature of society existing in the present, or as those aspects of the past that are still utilised by actors.

In popular vernacular the word 'tradition' is often used interchangeably with words such as 'custom' and 'habit'. However Hobsbawm (1983a: 2), in his influential study of 'invented traditions',[1] suggests that we should distinguish between these notions. For Hobsbawm, tradition can be distinguished from custom by its invariance. He states that:

> the past, real or invented, to which they (traditions) refer, imposes fixed (normally formalized) practices, such as repetition. Custom in traditional societies has the double function of motor and fly wheel. It does not preclude innovation and change up to a point, though evidently the requirement that it must appear compatible

or identical with precedent imposes substantial limitations on it. (1983a: 3)

He distinguishes between tradition and routine, convention or habit, suggesting that it has no significant symbolic or ritualistic function, although it may acquire it incidentally. Young (1988) also seeks to distinguish between tradition, custom and habit, suggesting that the latter is in reality a personal attribute and that customs do not contain the 'extra measure of inertia' (1988: 96) which tradition implies.

From this brief overview it can be seen that there is a degree of dispute concerning the notion of 'tradition'. Moreover the discussion and theorisation of tradition has been sporadic in social analysis, with very few attempts to fully theorise the concept.[2] Undoubtedly, society, politics and culture are constituted of aspects of the past, and thus have traditions within them. These can be found everywhere. We can identify them in the relationships that pervade society or in the institutions that are all around us. We find traditions in theories, beliefs and attitudes that persist over time. We can see them in practices, pastimes and behavioural norms.

However there is no agreed definition of the substance of traditions. Nor do distinctions between material, ideational and cultural examples of traditions do justice to the concept. Rather they overly simplify the complex and interwoven nature of traditions in society. Such distinctions do, however help to illuminate the all-pervasiveness of tradition. In essence, we can identify traditions in all aspects of human existence. They are woven into the very fabric of human society and are thus inescapable. Tradition is therefore, by definition, of central concern to socio-political analysis, given the latter's aim to understand and explain human society.

In socio-political analysis tradition is sometimes seen as tacit knowledge that creates predispositions towards continuity with the past and the necessity of retaining connections with the past for the good of the present. Conservatives such as Oakeshott (1962) argue this point. Tradition is also sometimes viewed as arguments or positions within debates in society. For example Popper (1989) claims that traditions can be found throughout society and are the context within which people think and act.

Tradition has also been seen as wisdom via repetition, its significance lying in the wisdom that is believed to be incorporated within a traditional idea or practice (Giddens 1994). In this view the accuracy or usefulness of tradition is not as important as its repeated usage. Traditions perform functions by helping to legitimise actions, institutions and/ or ideas (Hobsbawm 1983a). Indeed this repetition can help traditions to develop an almost common-sense status. This in turn can help to perpetuate institutions, ideas and practices over time. It can also help actors to overcome the crises they face and legitimise the decisions they take.

Furthermore traditions are often linked to change and continuity. Sztompka (1993) suggests that traditions are often transmitted by the sheer force of habit or inertia, that is to say, subconsciously. Importantly, they can act as powerful constraints on choice by suggesting to actors that 'ready-made' solutions exist. However they can also spur actors to adopt change and challenge the status quo. He claims that traditions are transmitted via both the material and the ideal and that they are appealed to or modified by actors, points that we will return to shortly.

Alongside these assertions we could see tradition as an integral part of the wider notion of culture. Defining what is meant by culture is notoriously difficult. Williams (1983a: 87) argues that:

> culture is one of the two or three most complicated words in the English language. This is partly so because of its intricate historical development, in several European languages, but mainly because it has now come to be used for important concepts in several distinct intellectual disciplines and in several distinct and incompatible systems of thought.

However if we accept the broad definition offered by Jenks that culture is 'all which is symbolic: the learned, ideational aspects of human society' (1993: 8), then this raises two possibilities. Firstly this suggests that tradition forms an integral part of culture. Williams argues that the theory of culture is defined as 'the study of relationships between elements of the whole way of life' (1965: 63). For Williams, culture is constituted by the meanings generated by ordinary people, by their lived experiences, by their attitudes, and by their attitudes and the practices they engage in during the course of their lives. Using this definition, we can suggest that tradition, in its many guises, is part of culture. Secondly a broad definition of culture suggests that we should see the ideational as integral to the cultural (Bottomore 1987). Traditions can be seen as acting as symbols and rituals that transfer ideas, values and meaning in institutions, in social relations, in systems of belief and in material life more broadly.

The notion that traditions, ideas and culture are linked raises a couple of further possibilities. Firstly we can consider the relationship between tradition and two broader notions: identity and power. Secondly we can develop a more sophisticated concept of the key meta-theoretical issue of the relationship between structure and agency, through the work of Archer (1995; 2000) and its discussion in McAnulla (2002; 2006b).

Discussions of culture in social theory often intersect with those concerning major issues such as identity and power relations in society. On the issue of identity, a diverse range of social theorists have seen culture as integral to the formation and maintenance of identity.[3] As Frosch states:

> Recent sociological and psychological theory has stressed that a person's identity is in fact something multiple and potentially fluid, constructed through experience and linguistically coded. In developing their identities people draw upon culturally available resources in their immediate social networks and in society as a whole. The process of identity construction is therefore one upon which the contradiction and disposition of the surrounding socio-cultural environment have a profound impact. (in Bullock and Trombley 1999: 413)[4]

Thus traditions, as part of the societal environment, should undoubtedly be considered when considering identity construction, including 'political identity'.

Culture is also often seen as intrinsically linked to the notion of power and domination. Again, Marxists and neo-Marxists have focused on the relationship between culture and power. In particular the latter, influenced by the work of Gramsci (1971), have offered insights into the importance of culture in the maintenance of patterns of power and dominance. They have focused on the notion of cultural hegemony to explain how dominant and subordinate cultures emerge and are inculcated and maintained over time. Predominant and subordinate or competing cultures or aspects of culture such as traditions are fundamental to the replication of patterns of dominance and asymmetrical power relations more broadly. The strength of this approach is to suggest a link between culture and the structured inequalities found in capitalist society.

Other theorists have also considered the relationship between culture and power. For example Swartz notes that Bourdieu uses culture to consider 'how stratified social systems of hierarchy and domination persist and reproduce intergenerationality without powerful resistance and without the conscious recognition of their members... [C]ultural resources, processes and institutions hold individuals and groups in competitive and self-perpetuating hierarchies of domination' (1997: 6). Bourdieu develops the concept of 'habitus' to help answer this question. He defines the concept of 'habitus' as:

> the conditioning associated with a particular class of conditions produce conditions of existence, produce habitus, systems of durable, transposable, structuring structures predisposed to function as structuring structures, that is, as principles which generate and organise practices and representations that can objectively be adapted to their outcomes without presupposing a conscious aiming at ends or an express mastery of the operations necessary in order to attain them. (1980: 53)

Habitus is not a consciously held set of beliefs but rather a disposition or set of dispositions that actors experience within a specific set of social structures. Bourdieu suggests that struggles amongst actors serve 'primarily to reproduce the existing structure of the fields rather than transform them' (1980: 53), although this is not always the outcome.

The idea that culture is both the ground for human interaction and a source of domination which helps establish and maintain social and institutional hierarchies, as well as embody power relationships, is a useful one. Using this insight, we can ask important questions concerning the relationship between tradition and culture and the existing power relations in any given society. In particular tradition should be considered in relation to the creation, maintenance and reproduction of asymmetrical power relations.

Culture has therefore been of major concern in the social sciences. If we accept that culture and tradition are linked in the sense that traditions form an integral part of the wider notion of culture, then we can ask what role traditions play in the formation and the maintenance of both identity and power relations. The significance of the idea that tradition can be seen to form part of a wider notion of culture is evident in the work of Preston and the idea of political-cultural identity (1997; 2004).[5] Indeed we could argue that the idea of tradition and political tradition discussed in subsequent chapters forms an integral part of the wider notion of a sense of political-cultural identity.

The most thorough attempt to theorise tradition can be found in Shils's *Tradition* (1981). As we saw earlier, Shils suggests that tradition is everything that is handed down from the past (1981: 12). Tradition plays a key role in social life because it involves: attachment to the past, convenience, accumulated wisdom and experience, and a desire for connections with, or even a reinstatement of, the past. Despite charges of essentialism,[6] Shils attempts to move beyond simple conservative accounts of tradition and their preoccupation with continuity by discussing change within traditions. Here, he sees the opportunity for correction within a tradition as anomalies or contradictions are identified and overcome over time. Changes can also occur in the content of a tradition, as certain aspects of that tradition receive greater emphasis or are re-conceptualised. Shils does not, however, adequately account for what might allow certain aspects of a tradition or traditions open to change at any given time, whilst other characteristics remain essential. This is clearly of central significance for both those discussing tradition and change.

Before turning to the usage of tradition in political analysis, we should briefly consider how traditions are passed on or down as this will be relevant to the later discussion of political traditions. Knowledge of the 'traditional' will be passed down through both practical and discursive means. The practical transmission of the traditional is active and arises out of actors' interactions and engagements with the 'material world'. It is therefore learned by 'doing' and does not end with the acquisition of language. Alongside this, traditions are transmitted discursively via actors' meaningful communications. Archer (2000: 173–6) argues that it is through 'discursive knowledge' that we develop and maintain ideational commitments to theories, doctrines and ideological positions. Furthermore discursive knowledge is developed and transmitted via scholarship and the teaching of propositions and meanings. In the process of transmission of 'the traditional', the practical and discursive are not mutually exclusive. Rather the relationship between them is reciprocal and reinforcing. Furthermore this reciprocity allows for the adaptation of traditions over time, as either developments in practical or discursive knowledge may lead to adaptations in both the content and usage of tradition.

Having offered a brief discussion of what is meant by the word tradition in social analysis, our attention must now turn to an explanation of why the discussion of tradition is important for those attempting to explain social and political phenomena.

Political analysis and tradition

The centrality of tradition to human society has often been recognised but it is usually underdeveloped. Shils explains the centrality of tradition to human society by stating that 'a society is a trans-temporal phenomenon. It is not constituted by its existence at a single moment in time. It exists only through time. It is temporally constituted' (1981: 327). For Shils, the temporal nature of all societies means that recognition of the importance of tradition is essential. However as we shall see below, detailed theoretical discussion of tradition has been less than widespread in political analysis, particularly with regard to the British political system.

Discussion of tradition in the existing literature in political analysis is neither uniform nor thorough. Whilst widely mentioned in political analysis, particularly by conservatives such as Burke (1790), Oakeshott (1962) and Gilmour (1978), tradition and its role are all too often left under-theorised and underdeveloped. Conservatives tend to only go as far as the contention that society is a partnership between 'those who are living, those who are dead and those who are to be born' (Burke 1790: xix), thus asserting the central significance of that which is passed down from previous generations. Tradition is, in this perspective, the accumulated wisdom of the past. On the basis of this assertion, they then argue that the traditional has value afforded by its longevity, in a quasi-Darwinian sense, because it has stood the test of time. In the conservative use of tradition, the length of time an institution, custom or practice has been in existence is the defining criteria by which its continued utility should be judged. For the conservative, tradition is important because it offers the surest guide for action by those in the present when confronting a 'boundless and bottomless sea' (Oakeshott 1962: 60). For conservatives, the virtues of the traditional are such that broader critical reflection upon tradition is unwarranted. In fact, Oakeshott (1962) dismisses the idea that traditions are anything other than concrete social realities that are embodied in the behaviour of actors and established practices (McAnulla 2007). For Oakeshott, traditions are 'real' in every sense of the word.

We should note in passing here the influence of the conservative concept of tradition in traditional explanations of the British political system, such as the WM. That particular model and its adherents frequently make reference to the survival of traditional practices such as 'ministerial responsibility' and the ability of the UK's uncodified constitutional relations to embody traditional institutions and practices. Furthermore as Tant (1993: 57) observes, these traditional behaviours and practices have often come to be seen as 'natural' British characteristics, conferring legitimacy and a degree of timelessness to them. Bevir (2000) correctly notes that conservatives often seek to promote a concept of tradition that attempts to naturalise certain social practices when they are, in fact, the product of social interactions and struggles in the past.

Although this is not the place to develop a detailed explanation of the relative neglect afforded to tradition in socio-political analysis, scholars schooled in rationalist thinking have tended to downplay or undervalue tradition in their explanations. Instead, they have focused upon concepts that can be linked to notions of progressive social change. Indeed the assumption has been that there is something fundamentally irrational about tradition and appeals to it. Shils (1981) also suggests that scholars have tended to focus their attention elsewhere, believing, it seems, that the notion of tradition has little, if anything, to offer to an explanation. Therefore we should consider why focusing on tradition has heuristic value for those of a non-conservative persuasion.

For non-conservatives, tradition was, until recently, all too often simply seen as the legacy of the past and left largely under-theorised or ignored. This is particularly true of critical political analysts who often ignore, or undervalue, its explanatory potential (See for example Hay 2002a; Miliband 2004). Until recently, the only widely held approach that offered no detailed comment on, or analysis of, tradition was Marxism. Indeed historically, Marxists have seemed to have neglected the role of tradition and its importance. They have left consideration of tradition to their conservative counterparts such as Oakeshott (1962) and Shils (1981).[7] Marxists and neo-Marxists have readily discussed culture[8] (see, for example Williams 1983b; Nelson and Grossberg 1988; Jameson 1991), but apart from a few notable exceptions, they have not explicitly considered tradition. Marx's famous observation that 'the tradition of all dead generations weighs like a nightmare on the brains of the living' (Marx 1851, cited in McLellan 1977: 300) suggests that tradition should be a central concern for those attempting to explain and critique contemporary capitalist society. However historically, orthodox Marxists have paid scant explicit attention to it. Focusing on the centrality of economic relationships often led to an underappreciation of the role of ideational and cultural factors in shaping social and political life (Marsh 2002b). Indeed Williams (1977: 115) argues that Marxist thought has 'radically neglected' the concept of tradition. The extent to which this may be the case can be shown in a simple sense. *The Dictionary of Marxist Thought* (Bottomore 1983) contains no reference to tradition or a Marxist approach to the concept. As such, Marxists have ignored a potentially fruitful avenue for explaining the continued existence of the capitalist system and the institutions and practices that support it. More recently, the influence of Gramsci (1971) has led to an appreciation of the manner in which ideas function as part of the capitalist system. Hegemonic ideas and practices help to secure consent for capitalism in the sense that they become 'common-sense' notions that are appealed to in an uncritical manner and are utilised to justify the continued existence of institutions, relationships and practices that perpetuate the capitalist system (Gramsci 1971; Boggs 1976). In this sense, a Marxist or neo-Marxist appreciation of tradition becomes a potentially fruitful avenue of analysis.

Some Marxists, notably Williams (1977), Hobsbawm and Ranger (1983), and Miliband (1991; 2004), have, in recent times, discussed tradition and have offered persuasive insights about the role it plays in capitalist society. Williams argues that tradition 'is in practice the most evident expression of the dominant and hegemonic pressures and limits' (1977: 115) and hence is worthy of Marxist analysis and critique. Hobsbawm (1983a) discusses the invented nature of tradition and the functions it performs. If these insights are applied to the British political system, we can trace the manner in which certain aspects of British democracy have been inculcated over time to the point where they have achieved an almost unquestionable or 'common-sense' status. More broadly, this would help explain the continued existence of the capitalist system and the perpetuation of patterns of asymmetrical power and structured inequality.

Miliband (2004) advocates the idea that there will be multiple traditions at work within capitalist society. Such an insight is persuasive and will be returned to throughout the subsequent chapters. He contends that 'tradition is not a monolith. On the contrary, it always consists of a large and diverse accumulation of customary ways of thought and action. In other words, there is not in any society one tradition but many; some may be more congruent with other, some less' (2004: 46).

Therefore in any society, according to Miliband, there will exist both a tradition of conformity and a tradition of dissent, or indeed several of each. Such an insight offers political analysts the opportunity to recognise the existence of various predominant and competing traditions working within any social and political system, a point which forms a central tenet of this analysis. It also helps to explain both change and continuity over time.

However despite its potential explanatory value when considering the continued dominance of capitalism and capitalist ideas in Western societies, Miliband (2004) argues that the polymorphous nature of tradition is not particularly helpful to Marxism because none of these traditions will prove particularly useful to the Marxist revolutionary project, given 'the Marxist notion of the most radical rupture with traditional ideas' (2004: 46). However this recognition does not negate the potential heuristic value of analysing tradition and its function from a Marxist perspective, if the project is to secure radical change itself. Contra Miliband, a Marxist or neo-Marxist approach necessitates a focus on the role and function that tradition plays in maintaining established relationships and patterns of behaviour in capitalist society. Only through understanding how political systems in capitalist economies have functioned and have been legitimised, can a method for challenging them be identified. Given the centrality of tradition to social life, a Marxist appreciation of tradition would seem to be far more important than Miliband suggests.

Finally we should in passing recognise the importance of studying traditions for political analysis more broadly. Finlayson (2003) correctly argues that political analysts must consider 'tradition' if they are to be self-reflective. All political analysis and theorising is itself the product of one or more traditions. As such, reflection on tradition can form an important part of academic enquiry generally. Such a view suggests that the approach to tradition advocated by MacIntyre (1984) and described above is 'tradition as argument'. Indeed the view of tradition offered by an author can tell us much about their broader views. For example Norton's (1984) view of the British constitution clearly demonstrates the influence of the conservative tradition. The point here is twofold. Firstly when approaching concepts of tradition, much can be learned about the author's normative assumptions from how they conceptualise the concept. Secondly self-reflection on how our own research is informed and influenced by intellectuals and academic traditions can be of benefit when developing analyses and explanations.

Why consider tradition?

If tradition is a fundamental part of the fabric of human society, then those who seek to criticise that society, and advocate alternatives, must focus attention on how the current nature of society is maintained through, at least in part, tradition. It is here that detailed theoretical and empirical consideration of tradition becomes valuable. The study of tradition is intrinsic to political analysis and theorising, as much of the latter focuses on attempting to explain, and defend, the status quo or critiquing the manner in which things are presently done, and on proffering alternatives (Finlayson 2003: 664). It is this that leads us to consider the impact of tradition on present and future developments.

Tradition also forms a key facet of the political-cultural identity (Preston 2004) of a nation and, as such, should be considered by those assessing ideas concerning national identity.

In any contemporary society or political system traces of the past can be detected. These elements may have a causal impact on present and future developments. As Shils stresses, 'the connection that binds a society to its past can never die out completely; it is inherent in the nature of society' (1981: 328). Thus whatever aspect of society is studied, we will find the residue of the past inscribed into the structures, practices and attitudes of that society. Attempts to offer alternative ways in which politics should be conducted will need to consider the actual existing traditions in a political system and whether their alternative can be easily accommodated into existing or traditional institutions and practices. Even perspectives that offer a radical rupture with the past, such as Marxism, must consider the role of tradition, if only to identify the impact it has had on the perpetuation of the status quo, and to assess how to move beyond it (Hobsbawm and Ranger 1983).

If it is accepted that fragments or features of the past exist in the present in the form of traditional ideas, practices, institutions and norms of behaviour, then we should consider the basis on which these fragments have survived and what functions they perform in that society. Such an approach will need to consider the dimensions of these fragments and also the extent to which they resonate in society. Social analysts should also consider their potential causal impact on the future development of that society (Sztompka 1993). Indeed the notion of 'wisdom through repetition' (Hobsbawm 1983a) and the quasi-Darwinian aspect to appeals to tradition are of particular significance in attempting to explain change and continuity over time.

Stzompka (1993) suggests that we should consider the potential causal impact of traditions in a material and an ideal (ideational) sense. In doing this, we should view traditions as both objective and subjective. Traditions can be seen in the physical environment that surrounds us, including the institutions themselves. For example we can easily identify the traditional institutions of the British political system by visiting central London and seeing the Westminster Parliament or government departments in Whitehall. We may also identify key symbols or practices in the British political system that act as signifiers of tradition. The State Opening of Parliament or the Speaker's procession, whilst performing practical functions, also serve to reinforce perceptions of the British political system and its historical development and basis. These signifiers invariably help to sustain a sense of 'otherness'.[9] Such notions are often appealed to with regard to the British political system in relation to other political systems, in particular those in the EU or the USA.

However alongside the material manifestations of tradition we must also consider its ideal and subjective aspects – ideas, beliefs, practices and memories, be they shared or individual. These all facilitate the process of historical continuity and change based on an appeal to, or a negation of, tradition. For example in political analysis we often find reference to tradition in relation to sets of ideas or ideologies, such as the conservative tradition or the socialist tradition (see, for example Bevir and Rhodes 2003; 2006a). We also often find reference to traditions of thought, such as the radical tradition (Derry 1967; Vallance 2009). Indeed we can also refer to the notion of tradition in relation to views of democracy in both theory and practice (Marsh and Hall 2007). The idea of a political tradition will be dealt with more fully later in this chapter. However, one key point should be recognised here. In each of these instances, political analysis should consider the process by which these have developed and been inculcated over time. Indeed this is one of the most important tasks for a critical approach to 'tradition'. The manner in which traditions have been passed from generation, be it discursively or in the form of customary patterns of behaviour, in the form of institutions or ideas, can tell us much about how a present-day political system functions and may develop in the future.

Tradition functions as one of the major sources of authority in society (Weber 1958). Institutions and practices can be, and are, powerfully justified in society through appeals to tradition (Burke 1790). For example institutions, such as the monarchy or the House of Lords, are more often than not justified with some reference to their status as traditional institutions. Their authority and legitimacy is seen as being rooted in their historical basis (Norton 1984; Hanson and Walles 1990). Indeed it is here that conservative usages of tradition have been most prominent, justifying the continued existence of institutions and practices through reference to tradition and history (Burke 1790; Gilmour 1978). Indeed appeals to tradition have proven to be a key facet of the perpetuation of long-established patterns of rule, power relations and inequality.[10]

Moreover critical political analysis should also consider the role that tradition plays in the wider context of structured inequality and power-structured relationships that exist within society. Despite the shift to governance and the role played by policy networks, it must be remembered that inequalities of power remain a fundamental part of all contemporary societies (Miliband 1991; Marsh 2002a). As Marsh, Richards and Smith (2001: 250) suggest, 'British politics may be characterised by plurality, but it does not reflect a pluralist power structure'. It is in relation to these asymmetries of power that, for a non-conservative, tradition could be seen to play a fundamental role, given that traditional relationships or practices may assist in the perpetuation of asymmetries of power and the socio-economic inequality that underpins them.

In relation to structured inequality and asymmetrical power relations, we may also suggest that traditions themselves resonate in an asymmetrical manner. Asymmetrical resonance simply means that ideas and patterns of behaviour, in this instance, traditions, have resonated to different degrees over time. To explain why a particular tradition has resonated in a political system, we would need to analyse pre-existing and existing structures and institutions, power relationships, material interests and cultural factors. Therefore this asymmetrical resonance occurs in relation to the environment within which traditions operate. That is to say, some traditions will resonate more fully within the environment because they fit better with, or support, the asymmetrical nature of that environment, its structure and relations. Indeed the idea of asymmetrical resonance is linked to, and supports, the idea that we can find predominant and competing traditions in society will be discussed later.

Traditions embody key ideas and discourses. They also embody practices and behavioural norms. Their replication in the institutions and relationships that exist in society is indeed observable. Actors within the core executive and beyond may also subscribe to the tradition, be it consciously or subconsciously. For those in the core executive we can suggest, as do Marsh, Richards and Smith (2001), that they appeal to tradition because 'it legitimises their authority and power'. For those actors outside the core executive who seek influence, we need to consider the process of political socialisation and how the rules of the game are inculcated into their ideas and actions. For example Tant (1993) offers insight into how the Labour party was quickly 'constitutionalised'[11] as it became a serious contender for power in the early part of the 20th century.

Similarly, the ways in which the traditional ideas and values of a nation's political system have been transmitted to the public should be considered. This will help us to better understand the perpetuation of aspects of that system over time, as well as the challenges to it. For example when assessing the British political system we should attempt to identify both the traditional ideas and views that have shaped it and crucially, how these have been narrated over time. This brings us back to considering the role of the prevailing narrative of the British political system and its allegedly superior mode of development (Norton 1984; Punnett 1987) which has been a hallmark feature of much of the discourse regarding the British political system.

Finally we should consider the manner in which tradition forms an integral part of a wider notion of political-cultural identity (Preston 2004) mentioned earlier. According to Preston, both tradition and nostalgia, and common-sense thinking play an integral part in the construction and maintenance of British political-cultural identity (Preston 2004: 95–6). In the light of the points made previously, we might ask a range of questions in relation to the political-cultural identity of Britain. Of paramount importance amongst these is the extent to which the development of British political-cultural identity can be seen to link to the broader structured inequalities in UK society. Or, to put it another way: how did the development of a distinctive British political-cultural identity help to maintain the position of the socio-economic and political elite over time? Relatedly we might ask how the development of a distinctive British political-cultural identity might link to the asymmetries of power we find in British society. Indeed we could ask how the development of a British political-cultural identity was facilitated by notions such as the asymmetrical resonance of traditions and ideas generally, within a strategically selective environment. Finally we should undoubtedly ask how the development of a British political-cultural identity was assisted by the inculcation of distinctive tradition(s), including political ones, into the populace throughout modern British history.

Analysis of the process by which a tradition develops and is inculcated will also need to address the potential construction or invention of that tradition (Hobsbawm and Ranger 1983). Indeed it is on this idea that critical political analysts have developed some of their most interesting and persuasive insights into the manner in which a sense of nationhood and national identity was invented, and to what end (Hobsbawm and Ranger 1983; Anderson 1983). This contrived or imagined past need not be accurate. Rather it will perform functions in both a historical and contemporary sense. Hobsbawm (1983a) suggests that tradition performs three functions. Firstly it can symbolise and express social cohesion and unity. Secondly it can legitimise institutions, values and ideas, thus conferring authority. Finally it can socialise certain ideas, practices, norms and rules of behaviour within society, a point we will return to shortly.

Such a recognition of the role of tradition will undoubtedly help the political analyst explain a great deal. Miliband (1991: 142) puts in succinctly when he states that:

> tradition is something that is indeed 'invented', used, manipulated, and that it serves ideological and political purposes, and that where it does not exist it is contrived and affirmed by ceremonies, rituals, codes of behaviour, costumes, language, all of which are intended in one way or another to encourage the worship of what Aneurin Bevan once called, 'the most conservative of all religions' ancestor worship.

Therefore through an appreciation of the potentially constructed nature of tradition (Hobsbawm and Ranger 1983) we can develop an understanding of the role that tradition plays in explaining the sociopolitical relationships we encounter, as well as any developments that may occur. In particular it will also help us explain aspects of the development of broader notions concerning political-cultural identity.

The value of such an approach can be demonstrated through reference to British political development. Miliband suggests that we should consider tradition in the context of 'the need felt by dominant classes to use it as one or more response to the rise of labour movements in the second half of the 19th century and the dangers that were thought to arise from the extension of suffrage to the working class' (1991: 142).

Hobsbawm notes that 'the widespread progress of electoral democracy and the consequent emergence of mass politics...dominated the invention of official traditions in the period 1870–1914' (1983b: 267–8). Therefore 'tradition' was a key facet of the response of rulers or dominant groups to questions of 'how to maintain or even establish the obedience, loyalty and co-operation of its subjects or member, or its own legitimacy in their eyes' (Hobsbawm 1983b: 265). More broadly, we should note the extent to which the emphasis on developing distinctive British traditions, including a political one, could be linked to the range of problems faced by the political, social and economic elites in the 18th and 19th centuries (Colley 1993; Preston 2004).

In the context of a discussion of political traditions and UK politics, the above arguments of two Marxist scholars are both interesting and useful. Firstly both imply the need for a historically informed approach to the development of the British political system and, crucially, one that recognises the broader socio-economic relationships that informed that development. Indeed focusing on how the latter influenced the actions and intentions of socio-economic and political elites explains how the British political system and those who run state and other institutions of power, have proven remarkably successful at achieving 'the containment and reduction of popular pressure' (Miliband 1982: 1). Tradition has been fundamental to this endeavour, as whilst 'deliberate management' is often responsible for continuity of existing power structures and the thwarting of challenges, so to are 'habits, traditions and constraints, which make for inertia and acceptance rather than for pressure and conflict' (Miliband 1982: 2).

Therefore it is also essential to consider the impact that a tradition or the perception of a tradition may have on agency and outcomes. We can make a number of basic observations about the interaction between traditions and the actions of actors. Firstly the attitude or orientation taken by contemporary actors towards the past is of great significance for explanations of contemporary political outcomes. Secondly if a tradition supports or legitimises the power and authority of those in power, then they are likely to support or defend it (Hobsbawm 1983b; Miliband 1991; Marsh and Hall 2007). Finally if a tradition is treated with reverence or awe, this may have an impact on options and potential outcomes when decisions have to be made. This brings us back to the idea of 'strategic selectivity' (Jessop 1990).

The importance of tradition is not, however, confined to those with power and influence. Tradition has an impact upon actors outside the political and socio-economic elite. Here, we can make two basic observations. Firstly no matter how widespread the support for the predominant tradition is, it will never be total. As Gramsci (1971) suggests, hegemony is a dynamic process that is constantly re-narrated, reaffirmed and renegotiated over time. Indeed this dynamic process occurs in part because some actors may have come to believe in, or have adopted, competing traditions or practices to those held by those in power. These competing traditions will, in most instances, offer a critique of, and an alternative to, the predominant tradition. Such a view opens up the idea of contestation between political traditions as a key driver of change. It also raises questions regarding their resonance over time and across society and it brings to the fore the idea that contestation and competition between traditions is both possible and likely within society.

Secondly the broader impact of tradition on the populace at large must be considered. The extent to which the public accept, and adopt, traditional ideas and practices is of significance if we are to explain the continuation of certain institutions, ideas and practices. In addition, if a tradition has been successfully inculcated, then we might ask why this has been the case and what sustains its resonance. Here again, an example will help to illustrate the point. The extent to which the British public accepted the British political system as democratic is important for any explanation of how the traditional institutions and practices of British government have persisted over time. If British citizens believe that the British political system is democratic, they are likely to act as though it is and thus help to perpetuate it. However the fact that they believe it to be democratic does not mean that it is, or that they have conceptualised the nature of that democracy correctly. Rather they have come to accept that it is, in part at least, because it has been narrated as such. Indeed Beer (1965) argues that the BPT has found widespread support amongst the populace and Norton (1989: 10) states that the British constitution 'used to be a subject of praise but little discussion', suggesting the successful inculcation of a political tradition in the UK. That is not to say that the predominant political tradition in Britain has been uncontested, but, rather to suggest that it has resonated more fully and widely with the populace than its competitor.

We should also note here that the notion of predominant and competing traditions could be applied more widely to debates concerning political-cultural identity. This might work in two ways. Firstly the predominant and competing traditions themselves could form part of wider notions of identity within a nation. For example it could be argued that the notion of British political-cultural identity has, operating within it, the predominant political tradition. When making such a suggestion, it is obviously important to recognise the extent to which the predominant tradition has been articulated and advanced by elite groups. Preston (2004) sees the development of Britishness as intrinsically linked to the needs and interests of the ruling elite in British society.

Relatedly we may identify competing senses of political-cultural identity existing within a nation. These may incorporate, or appeal to, differing traditions and, consequently may be rooted in a sense of distinctiveness or otherness. For example in the UK, we can find various national identities in existence linked to the constituent parts of the UK. We might reasonably ask how notions concerning a British political-cultural identity and a sense of Scottishness or Welshness have co-existed and interacted over time. In particular in the light of recent developments we should consider the extent to which competing senses of political-cultural, and even national, identity within the UK have influenced competing political traditions over time.

As has been suggested, critical political analysis can benefit greatly from a recognition of the importance of tradition. Two further points are important here. Firstly we should note the functional aspect of tradition. Sztomkpa (1993: 64) identifies the functions performed by traditions:[12]

- They place the beliefs, norms, values and objects created in the past within easy grasp of those in the present. In this sense, as conservatives have stressed that which is seen to be worthwhile from the past can easily be accessed by actors in the present.
- They give legitimation to existing ways of life, institutions, ideas and practices. Here we can identify the idea that because something has always been it should continue to be so.
- They provide persuasive symbols of collective identity and strengthen a sense of togetherness on a group, community or national level.
- They can provide an escape route from grievances or dissatisfaction with the contemporary. Tradition can be appealed to in times of crisis and as Shils (1981: 207) suggests, 'the past is a haven to the spirit which is not at ease in the present'.

However Sztompka also stresses the potentially dysfunctional consequences of traditions:

- Traditions may, as a result of their content, be dysfunctional or even harmful, in that negative aspects of the past are appealed to and are recreated in the present.
- Traditions may, independent of their content, prevent or restrain creativeness or innovation via the provision of apparent ready-made solutions to the problems that actors face.
- There may be a tendency to place trust in the traditional when none is required or deserved. This can lead to inertia, ineffectiveness and ultimately, failure. Indeed we might note that at times faith or trust in a tradition can develop into what Sztompka refers to as the 'fetishization of tradition' (1993: 65).
- Traditions can be retained, not by conscious choice, but by the subconscious and, in a sense, by a level of habit or inertia. In such instances it is not fondness for the tradition that leads to its retention but rather convenience.

Hobsbawm (1983a) also suggests another function of tradition. He believes that we should recognise the relationship between 'traditions' and the prevailing economic, social and political context and its elite. It is in the context of structured economic and social inequalities and the attendant asymmetries of power and influence that 'invented traditions' function. 'Invented traditions' help to mask or distort reality and can therefore assist in the maintenance of existing power relationships and inequalities in society. Certain ideas or practices may be afforded special status, whilst others are downgraded or even pilloried. As such, 'invented traditions' also resonate in relation to the asymmetry of the environment which itself is indicative of the broader socio-economic inequalities in a capitalist society. Undoubtedly the process by which this may occur needs examination if the causal impact of tradition is to be better understood. However this is a far broader project than our present one. Discussion of a predominant political tradition and its impact on UK politics forms merely one aspect of this broader project. In the context of the British politics, we should consider the way that this potentially false or distorted picture of the British political system has been developed and how it has been sustained over time. Suffice to say here, in the British political system we can identify the existence of a contrived past or self-image. This has been based upon the perceived development of an increasingly democratic and representative system that has found expression and narration in relation to the WM and notions regarding British exceptionalism (Norton 1984; Punnett 1987).

Traditions and change

Finally we should briefly address the process by which a tradition can be challenged, changed, adapted or even removed over time. Indeed this is of central significance for normative political analysis as one of its central concerns is how to effect or prevent change. Furthermore in attempting to understand how change and continuity occur in society, we must confront the role of tradition as a potential enabler or constraint upon change. Again, Sztompka (1993) offers useful insight, contending that change in any tradition is agency-driven. He suggests that 'sooner or later, any tradition starts to be questioned, doubted, re-examined and at the same time new fragments of the past are being discovered and validated as tradition' (1993: 62). If a tradition clashes with reality, and is shown to be flawed or it no longer satisfies the social reality or circumstances, then, according to Sztompka, it will be questioned. Sztompka is right to emphasise the importance of agents in the process of contestation of tradition. However it should also be noted here that actors are operating within the prevailing institutional structures and ideational context in which tradition(s) form a part. Crucially, actors are also influenced by pre-existing cultural and behavioural norms in which tradition(s) play a fundamental role.

Here, we encounter again the structure-agency debate whose importance has been increasingly recognised in political analysis in recent years (Hay 1995; 2002a). McAnulla (2002: 271) defines the structure-agency debate as fundamentally concerning:

> the issue of to what extent we as actors have the ability to shape our destiny as against the extent to which our lives are structured in ways out of our control; the degree to which our fate is determined by external forces. Agency refers to individual or group abilities (intentional or otherwise) to affect their environment. Structure usually refers to context: to the material conditions which define the range of actions available to actors.

The centrality of this debate to social analysis leads us to consider whether adaptations to traditions are the result of the actions (intentional or otherwise) of agents or the product of structure, that is, changes in the material context or environment. The ability of agents to change traditions is a recurring theme throughout discussions of tradition. It also formed a substantial facet of the earlier analysis of the existing literature on the BPT and review of the recent work of Bevir and Rhodes (2003; 2006a) and Marquand (2008) on political traditions. For the moment however we should merely note that whilst agency is undoubtedly of importance when explaining political change and, more broadly, political outcomes, such a recognition does not undermine or negate the importance of the context.[13] Indeed as Marsh, Richards and Smith (2001) suggest, a more nuanced perspective regarding the ability of agents to affect outcomes can be advanced by avoiding a simplistic dualism and adopting a dialectical approach to the structure-agency question. As they state, 'agents operate within structured contexts that constrain or facilitate their actions' (2001: 10). Therefore the relationship between structure and agency is best seen as interactive and iterative.

On this, the strategic-relational approach developed by Jessop (1990) and Hay (1996) and the morphogenetic approach of Archer (1995), offer major insights into how change can and does occur. They also offer insights into the role of ideas within this process. Furthermore the evolutionary approach advocated by Kerr (2001; 2002) builds upon these views, offering persuasive insights for those attempting to explain how change and continuity occur. The strategic-relational approach suggests that 'action only takes place within a pre-existing structural context which is strategically selective, that is to say it favours certain strategies over others' (McAnulla 2002: 280). Archer (1995) suggests that the context in which action takes places is of paramount concern, even allowing for the role of agency. Structures are the context within which agents act and thus they can constrain or enable action. From this, we can make two further points. Firstly certain actions fit with the context better than other. Secondly if this is the case then a degree of 'path dependency' will be discernible whenever change occurs. Indeed change is most likely when its proponents can demonstrate a degree of continuity with the pre-existing environment, as stated by Kerr: 'institutional, contextual and discursive environments which are the product of past struggles and ideas... impose a selective bias in favour of some over others' (2002: 354). Therefore structures, be they institutional, procedural or cultural, are not unchanging or unchangeable. Whilst agents may not control the structured context or environment or be able to act independently of it, 'they do interpret it and it is as mediated through that interpretation that the structural context affects the strategic calculations of actors' (Marsh, Richards and Smith 2001: 10).

Therefore to return to the consideration of how change may occur in traditions, although actors can and do adapt or change the traditions they find before them, they do not do so free from constraint. Rather the traditions themselves and the broader structural context act as powerful enablers or constraints on their actions and ability to effect change. These constraints privilege certain adaptations over others and help to make evident both change and continuity within the traditions and the broader context over time. Thus the process of contestation and adaptation or affirmation of traditions is a complex and continual one. In this process, change, be it macro or micro, is often, but not always, the result. Alongside this there will undoubtedly be major continuities within traditions and more broadly tradition(s) contributing to institutional and ideational continuities. Furthermore tradition(s) can and do contribute to continuity in the structured inequalities we find in capitalist society. However they may also challenge it too.

If the idea that every tradition will be subject to challenge and potential adaptation or negation is accepted, then why this would occur must be considered. Traditions may be increasingly contested for a variety of reasons. Undoubtedly, questioning will be linked to growing criticism of that tradition and/or the increased resonance of a competing tradition or traditions. Thus we must recognise again the significance of the existence of predominant and competing traditions. This is fundamental to explaining the process of change and continuity in the British political system. However the idea that the resonance of traditions is linked inexorably to contingent events is crucial here. A greater questioning of a traditional idea, institution or practice can and will be promoted by contingent factors. The recent work of Bevir and Rhodes (2003; 2006b) on traditions has received a great deal of attention. Central to their concept of traditions is the notion of dilemmas. It is through facing dilemmas that traditions are adapted by actors. Their work focuses upon and explains the capacity for change in traditions in an interesting manner because it highlights the importance of the contingent. However their approach is unpersuasive because, amongst other failings, they do not address notions such as power, dominance and asymmetry.

Two points that were dealt with earlier should again be noted here. Firstly the impact of contingent events occurs within a prevailing institutional and ideational context that generally privileges the predominant tradition (Marsh and Hall 2007: 220). Secondly change in the substance or content of a tradition does not necessarily imply that the tradition will be entirely abandoned, or even adapted. Rather it is to say that it will undergo reappraisal and examination and aspects of it will potentially change as a consequence of this contestation. Conversely they may become re-entrenched or re-narrated in this process. In this sense, change in a tradition may be either macro or micro, substantive or minimal.

We should also recognise that this process of contestation and re-examination may occur through their interaction with competing traditions on various levels, that is to say local, national or global. Traditions may be compared to others beyond the boundaries of the community or nation of which they form a part. For example aspects of the British political system that are considered traditional, such as the British constitution (Norton 1984), are often compared to those found elsewhere in the world. Norton (1984) draws direct comparison between the US Constitution, which is codified, and a British constitution that 'is admired by Britons for reflecting the wisdom of past generations, as the product of experience – in short a constitution that stipulates what should be on the basis of what has proved to work rather than on abstract principles' (1984: 59–60).

The above statement is interesting on a number of levels. Firstly it displays both Norton's conservatism and the Oakeshottian anti-rationalism of this approach. Secondly whether knowledge of the workings of the British constitution and revulsion for abstract principles has permeated into the populace to the extent that Norton and other conservatives believe, is and highly questionable. However the UK constitution is still compared favourably to the US Constitution. Conversely, we might note here that advocates of constitutional reform, such as Charter 88, often based their critique of the UK's traditional constitutional relationships on unfavourable comparisons with codified arrangements to be found elsewhere in the world.

Therefore contestation and conflict in both a material and ideational sense can lead to a questioning of tradition. However this only takes us so far. Political analysis must also address two further questions if adequate concepts of change and continuity are to be developed: Is the re-examination of traditions a continual process (Kerr 2002)? Is it merely a punctuated moment in an otherwise long-running pattern of stability (Hay 1996)? We must explain and account for the outcomes of this re-examination of a tradition. On this latter point, a number of questions suggest themselves, which we will return to later: Is the tradition changed to any degree or alternatively left untouched as part of this process? Are any adaptations that occur partial or extensive? Or to put it another way, has change occurred at the macro or micro level? What is the broader impact of this re-examination of a tradition on political institutions, behaviour and outcomes generally?

To answer such questions we must return to the relationship between structure and agency discussed earlier. The notion that contestation of tradition(s) leads to the re-examination and re-evaluation of traditions and their efficacy and, crucially, to the potential for change, clearly views agents as key actors within this process, as Sztompka (1993) suggests. However traditions are both the context within which actors act and part of the broader structural and cultural context of society. This brings us full circle to the need for a more nuanced approach to explaining change and continuity and the need to move beyond a simplistic dualism (Marsh 2007). Only by adopting the strategic-relational approach (Jessop 1990; Hay 1996; Kerr 2002) can an adequate explanation of this process of contestation and re-examination and its outcome be developed. Here, another earlier point warrants repetition. To adequately explain contestation and the re-examination of traditions, we must also once again address the resonance and relative strength of different traditions. The status of a tradition and the extent of its articulation and pervasiveness in society are all relevant in this context. We must also consider the support that a tradition has from powerful groups and institutions in society and the extent to which it underpins the overriding nature of that society. Only then will we be able to fully account for the persistence of certain ideas and institutions over time.

Having considered the concept of tradition and why we should see tradition as a central concern for socio-political analysis, we should now consider what we mean by a political tradition.

Political traditions

Like the concept of tradition, the term 'political tradition' is often found in socio-political analysis. It appears in the title of major academic works such as Richard Hofstadter's *The American Political Tradition and the Men Who Made It* (1948) and W. H. Greenleaf's three- volume opus, *The British Political Tradition* (1983a; 1983b; 1987). However these two authors conceptualise the notion of a political tradition differently. Hofstadter, focusing on the ideas that underpinned the various political views prevalent in American politics, defines the American Political Tradition as based upon 'a shared belief in the rights of property, the philosophy of individualism, the value of competition...They (its advocates) have accepted the economic virtues of capitalist culture as necessary qualities of man' (Hofstadter 1948: xxxvii).

He sees the American Political Tradition as rooted in a consensus concerning key ideas. In a sense, it could be argued that Hofstadter's view presents a monolithic approach to political tradition, whereas Greenleaf sees the BPT as involving conflict between competing sets of ideas, rather than an underlying consensus or monolith. One important conclusion follows from this brief comparison. As with tradition, the concept of a 'political tradition' is defined and utilised in a variety of ways in political analysis, each of which claim both descriptive and explanatory purchase. This can be seen by focusing briefly on its varying usage in political analysis.

Most frequently, political tradition is used to refer to an ideology. Indeed the words ideology and tradition are often used interchangeably in socio-political analysis. For example we can find much reference to the Marxist tradition or the conservative tradition. Sometimes we find that the phrase 'political tradition' is used to describe a set of interrelated ideologies or interlinked 'families of ideas'. For example we find reference to notions such as the 'radical tradition' (Bullock and Deakin 1964; Derry 1967; Vallance 2009) that span ideological positions such as liberalism and socialism in both historical and contemporary accounts. Again, in this context tradition is used interchangeably with 'ideology', denoting a relatively coherent set of political ideas. Popular textbooks such as Jones et al. (2004) use the concept of tradition in this way. Kingdom (2003) places various ideological viewpoints within a wider

Exploring Tradition 117

framework, 'the Western tradition', which he sees developing from the break with the past, as found in the Renaissance, the Reformation and the Enlightenment (Kingdom 2003: 25–5). Whilst this usage of political tradition is prominent, we should recognise that this is not the only conceptualisation that is utilised.

In explanations of British political life, the concept 'political tradition' is used in various other ways by political commentators:

- Greenleaf (1983a; 1983b; 1987) uses the concept to refer to a defining clash between ideas that have dominated politics over time. He focuses upon the conflict between libertarianism and collectivism as constituting the BPT.
- Beer (1965) uses the concept to refer to a political culture or set of beliefs that is widely held in society.
- A number of authors use the term political tradition to refer to sets of ideas and practices that remain relatively constant over time. Examples of this approach can be found in the work of Birch (1964) and Marsh and Tant (1989), as well as work informed by them (Tant 1993; Evans 1995; 2003; Marsh, Richards and Smith 2001; 2003). The critical view of the BPT emphasises the centrality of an elitist concept of democracy.
- Marquand (2008) also stresses the importance of four political traditions. He notes that these traditions do not fit easily into the conventional categories of left and right or liberal, conservative and socialist. Rather he argues, as we saw in Chapter 2, the four key political traditions in the UK are: Whig Imperialist, Tory Nationalist, Democratic Collectivist, and Democratic Republican.
- Bevir and Rhodes (2003; 2006b) use political tradition to refer to inherited webs of beliefs that actors appeal to when facing dilemmas. However in their conceptualisation of tradition they make two crucial points. Firstly they point to the existence of multiple traditions operating with British politics. Therefore we should discuss the notion of political traditions(s) rather than a single BPT. Secondly they reject the notion that there is any essentialist element to traditions, thus suggesting that actors can and do adapt traditions.

Through focusing on explanations of British politics alone we can clearly see that political tradition is used in a variety of ways, all of which may offer some explanatory value. In the subsequent chapters political tradition is viewed as a set of ideas, discourses and cultural practices that persist over time and that inform institutions, processes, and the attitudes and responses of actors. One point should be made clear. For this conceptualisation of political tradition to have true heuristic value, we need to move beyond the idea that there is a single political tradition. For example whilst Hofstadter (1948) may be correct to suggest that there has been a degree of consensus between the major political groupings in the US over the underlying ideas and values upon which the US should be built, these have not gone uncontested. There have been competing traditions or views at different times in American life, such as the socialist tradition that existed in the 19th and early 20th centuries. As such, rather than discussing a monolithic concept of the American Political Tradition we should recognise the existence of predominant and competing traditions and attempt to explain their asymmetrical resonance over time. Of course, this observation constitutes a major critique of much of the work on the BPT dealt with in Chapter 1.

Rather than there being a single political tradition, there are multiple traditions operating at any given time in the UK (Bullock and Deakin 1964; Bevir and Rhodes 2003; Marsh and Hall 2007; Marquand 2008). However these traditions are unlikely to be of equal weight or import within the political system as the political landscape is an uneven playing field (Marsh, Richards and Smith 2003). Therefore just as we might expect to find predominant and competing traditions in other areas of society, we may identify the existence of predominant and competing political traditions.

The predominant political tradition can be defined as the generally accepted ideas, beliefs, assumptions, discourses, customs and practices within a nation and its political system. These ideas will be found in, and influence, existing institutional structures and relationships, as well as the views and behaviour of actors (Marsh and Hall 2007). The predominant tradition will be institutionally embedded and will reflect established political practice. Through its dominance, it will also inform the parameters for debates and discourses regarding the political system. It will also condition how actors view existing arrangements and alternatives to established practices. Norms of political behaviour will be established and passed through the predominant political tradition and these help to shape the manner in which a political system functions and develops.

Over time, predominant political traditions come to function as 'common understandings' of the political system that are widely appealed to by both politicians and scholars alike, even if their actual nature goes unexplored.[14] Political traditions, like traditions more broadly, are articulated/communicated discursively over time through various 'texts'. Texts, be they written documents, speeches, symbols, artwork, buildings and other artefacts, will convey meaning and an understanding of a political tradition and its core tenets, which are then 'learned'. These will help to form and maintain 'common understandings' of how a political system works, its key principles, and the roles of actors within its institutions. In this process discourses function in both the formation of political traditions and their transmission over time. For example a focus on what might be referred to as the 'scholarly spine' of British politics[15] demonstrates promulgation of aspects of the predominant political tradition.

Political traditions will also be promulgated textually via institutional and procedural norms as well as by the attitudes and assumptions of actors therein. These will also transmit and establish their meanings over time. Indeed we have already noted the extent to which institutions and practices in Westminster and Whitehall flow from and reinforce the predominant ideas about the British political system. Texts therefore act as sources of information and interpretation which actors use when seeking to understand the world. As such they may be viewed as a source of promulgation of a political tradition.

Texts are important in that they are reflections or echoes of the material/ideational world, which, in turn help to inform and shape understanding of that world as well as to inform future debates and developments. Thus the relationship between text and context is a reciprocal one. Such texts (and political traditions generally) contribute to the formation of a 'mindset' or mentality that conditions the understandings, behaviour and outlook of actors as they respond to contingent events. They do this by narrating and thus by establishing, meanings, norms, assumptions and the parameters for debate and further consideration. They also inform procedures and practices over time, to the extent that they are written into the very fabric of British political life. These 'common understandings', 'standard operating procedures', assumptive worlds of actors, and inherited commitments of the pre-existing environment then impose a degree of selectivity, as Kerr (2002) suggests.

Furthermore predominant traditions will resonate with those with power and influence and with the public, and will establish themselves as the 'norm' for generations of politicians and public alike. The predominant tradition, in turn, will be influenced by these and may develop or become entrenched over time. However political traditions, even predominant ones, are not static or time-bound. This immediately suggests that we should adopt a diachronic approach to studying political tradition, rather than the synchronic approach to be found in much of their discussion.

Competing political traditions offer alternative views of how politics should be conducted and they are often advocated by those seeking to challenge and change the nature of politics and even social organisation within a nation state. They may be advocated by those seeking power and influence from within, as well as those outside, the political system. For example groups such as Charter 88 advocated a competing political tradition that draws from a more participatory concept of democracy. This tradition will be dealt with in Chapter 6.

Political traditions can also appeal to competing senses of national identity and nationhood.[16] For example we can identify the existence of different identities and political traditions in the different parts of the UK (Kenny 1999: 282). For such traditions, the target has been the notions of centralisation of power and the unionism, via critique of the unitary state and the notion of Britain itself. This tradition will be considered in Chapter 7.

Three further observations on competing political traditions should be made here. Firstly as with predominant traditions, competing traditions are likely to have historical antecedents in the sense that their contemporary incarnation is itself part of broader historical tradition. For example contemporary critics of the British political system, such as Unlock Democracy, are the heirs to a tradition of dissent and demands for reform that can be traced back into the 19th century and beyond.[17] Secondly competing political traditions may also be partial or comprehensive critiques of the nature of politics and the political system. For example Charter 88 offered a wholesale critique of the British political system,[18] whereas CFOI or ERS target only aspects of it. Thirdly we should be wary of drawing the distinction between competing political traditions too sharply. For example demands for changes to UK territorial politics often draw influence from both the participatory tradition and the national tradition, conceptualising issues regarding democratic practice in the UK with distinctly nationalist flavours. This suggests the influence of various competing traditions and emphasises.

Ideational conflict has been, and remains, a hallmark of human society. This occurs at both a micro or macro level in the sense of challenging either aspects of the political system or its entirety. Similarly, these contestations can account for change at both a macro and micro level. Moreover contestation between traditions is fundamental for explaining change within, and beyond, traditions. Predominant and competing traditions will interact and come into conflict with each other in an interactive and iterative relationship (Marsh 2003; Marsh and Hall 2007). Through this process of contestation between predominant and competing traditions, both change and continuity will occur. Here again, we should recognise the importance of the idea of a strategically selective environment that privileges certain adaptations or developments over others (Jessop 1990; Kerr 2002). Political traditions can both constrain and enable change. It is within such an environment that political traditions operate and it is through reference to conflict within such an environment that explanation of change and continuity over time can be most fully developed.

One final point can be made about the concept of 'political tradition'. Political traditions form an integral part of the wider notion of political-cultural identity developed by Preston (1997; 2004). His dichotomy between a 'great tradition' and 'little tradition(s)' offers those discussing political traditions an interesting and potentially fruitful avenue. The predominant political tradition could be conceptualised as the 'great tradition', in the sense that it forms the 'overarching set of ideas expressed in particular concrete institutional arrangements and carried by the distinctive patterns of the life of the elite that legitimate and order extant social patterns' (Preston 2004: 82). This opens up the linkage between the predominant political tradition and the development of a distinctive sense of national identity. In the case of Britain, therefore, we should explore the linkage between a predominant political tradition and the notion of Britishness or British national identity. Or, to put it another way, we should consider the extent to which that tradition forms an integral part of the political-cultural identity of Britain.

Having recognised the diverse conceptualisation of the term 'political tradition', we will now return to the predominant political tradition in the UK historically, the British Political Tradition.

4
The British Political Tradition Revisited

Introduction

In the preceding chapters we have seen how a range of authors from varying methodological and normative perspectives appeal to the notion of political tradition as a key facet of political life in the UK. We began with those authors who advocated the existence of a distinctive British Political Tradition (BPT) before turning to the challenge presented by the recent work by Bevir and Rhodes (2003; 2006a) and Marquand (2008). We then focused on observations of the concepts of tradition and, more specifically, political traditions. Despite the range of criticisms of the existing usages of political tradition, the concept offers heuristic value if characterised differently.

In Chapters 4 and 5 we will focus on the predominant political tradition in UK politics, the BPT. Understanding this tradition assists in explaining the manner in which British politics has developed and continues to do so. These chapters build upon and extend the critical concept of the BPT dealt with in Chapter 1 and in the work of Marsh and Hall (2007). This perspective offers many insights into the workings the British political system over time. However, its potential has not been fully realised or developed.

The approach below also builds upon insights from critical realism, which suggests that we should conceive of the relationship between structure and agency, continuity and change, the material and the ideational, and institutions and ideas as dialectical (Marsh and Hall 2006). That is to say we should offer complex explanations deriving from the interactive and iterative, reciprocal relations between these notions. For example if we view the relationship between institutions and ideas dialectically, then the following observation can be made. Political traditions shape the institutions and practices of British government. Simultaneously these institutions and practices are the context within which ideas are interpreted, experienced and adapted over time. In this process the predominant political tradition has had a greater, but not total or uncontested, impact. Furthermore the relationship between the material and the ideational is also a dialectical one. Consequently we should seek to uncover the socio-economic dimensions of the BPT by highlighting the relationship between dominant socio-economic interests and predominant sets of ideas.

Finally the role of conflict and contestation in promoting change and continuity over time must be recognised. Conflict between both ideas and interests is of central significance for explanations of change and continuity (Kerr 2001; 2002; 2003). Focusing on this process of conflict and contestation between predominant and competing traditions aids the development of detailed explanations of the nature and development of British political life.

The predominant political tradition

The predominant political tradition is the generally accepted ideas, beliefs, assumptions, discourses, customs and practices within a nation and its political system. Over time, predominant political traditions are both inscribed into the institutions and processes of governance, and function as 'common understandings' of the political system that are widely appealed to.

In developing a critical concept of the BPT, three observations from the classical approach to the BPT can be utilised. However in each case we should characterise the observations somewhat differently to its original form.

- Firstly we should focus on ideas concerning representation and responsibility as the core of narratives of the British political system (Birch 1964). Key debates concerning who should rule and what role citizens or subjects should play were as crucial in shaping the nature of British political life as they were abroad.[1] Equally important was consideration of the manner and extent to which the government should be responsible to its citizens
- Secondly we should view the BPT as a set of ideas that is inscribed into the institutions and processes of UK government (Greenleaf 1983a). This in part, explains the continued importance of the BPT over time. Were the BPT merely confined to the debates of the 18th

and 19th centuries then we would be less likely to detect its impact since. The products of those debates came to underpin the institutions and processes of British government.
- Finally the BPT is a body of beliefs held within British society (Beer 1965). Its permeation into the ideas, attitudes and political values of both the elite and the populace is a key facet of the BPT's resonance and impact. However here culture is viewed as a field of both human interaction and a source of domination, which helps to establish and maintain social and institutional hierarchies and power relations (Bourdieu 1980). The BPT is therefore a set of cultural tendencies (McAnulla 2006a) that informs the ideas, attitudes and subsequent actions of various actors, be it consciously or sub-consciously. These help to perpetuate patterns of dominance over time. In this process the establishment and promulgation of 'common understandings' is centrally significant.

It is from these insights that the interpretation below develops. We will now turn our attention to explaining in greater detail the development of the central ideas that form the BPT.

The development of the predominant political tradition

Since the late 18th century the BPT developed into the dominant view of political practice in the United Kingdom. Analysing the development of British politics since that time we can identify two predominant discourses concerning democracy and how it should operate in the UK, and two related discourses concerning change and national distinctiveness. These are as follows:

- A discourse that stresses a limited liberal notion of representation and the elitist view that politicians are best suited to make decisions on behalf of the populace. Politicians have come to view themselves as the guardians and executors of the national interest and are willing to act against the expressed will of the public or in the face of substantial public opposition.[2]
- A discourse that stresses a conservative notion of responsibility and the view that strong, decisive government is the most effective, efficient and desirable form of government. This can be seen in the belief in the virtue of centralisation of power through the notions of parliamentary sovereignty, the unitary state and unionism.
- A discourse about change which emphasises the virtues of continuity, gradualism, flexibility and stability. The British developmental

path is seen as setting Britain apart from other Western democracies and is emblematic of a superior approach.
- A discourse concerning a sense of British distinctiveness and superiority politically (Colley 2003). This emphasis on British exceptionalism is associated with the view mentioned above.

These discourses emerged from various 18th and 19th century debates and discussions[3] as Britain faced a period of dramatic socio-economic and political upheaval (Royle 2000). The elites were concerned with the retention of their power, privilege and socio-economic dominance (Gash 1979; Anderson 1987; Garrard 2002) and it was their interests and attitudes that most obviously shaped this emerging political tradition. Appeals to the ideas of Hobbes (1651), and Burke (1790) were hugely significant, but ideationally some of their arguments could be traced back much further. Over time, these discourses were inculcated into the institutions, processes and practices of the British political system. From their earliest expressions, these discourses have also been promulgated in some of the canonic texts of British politics.[4] Through these material and discursive media they have come to form 'common understandings' or assumptions concerning British political life, widely believed and appealed to by politicians and public alike. Thus the BPT established the ideational, institutional and cultural parameters within which actors operate and change and continuity occur.

We must, however, recognise that political traditions do not necessarily remain unchanged over time. Rather new ideas or aspects may be included, emphasised or even downplayed. These discursive developments occur in relation to changes in the broader context. However when such developments occur, they do so on terms that are largely consistent with the prevailing ideational and discursive context, as that context generally privileges pre-existing ideas and discourses. This point can readily be seen in New Labour's constitutional reform programme (Marsh and Hall 2007). For example Scottish devolution developed in a discursive environment that stressed the importance of parliamentary sovereignty and the union. This shaped the eventual settlement found in the Scotland Act 1998 (Hall 2009).

A discourse concerning representation

Tracing the development of the BPT, we should begin with debates from the late 18th and 19th centuries between the Tories and the Whigs. These were crucial in shaping how representation was viewed in the UK. The Tory discourse was rooted in a feudal/organic view of society where the monarch was both the representative and symbol of the national community. The 'divine right of kings' underpinned monarchical rule throughout feudalism and resulted in the monarch being the key actor within policy-making.[5] This Tory discourse was challenged during the British Revolution of the 1640s and the Whig notion of a balanced constitution became the predominant view of constitution and government in Britain over time. However elements of the Tory discourse remained. For example post 1660, the idea that the king should make policy whilst the MPs merely expressed their constituents' grievances at Westminster remained part of the debates regarding Parliament, as did the emphasis on hierarchy and order. For example the position of the House of Lords as the more important Parliamentary chamber retained a primary role for the aristocracy.

Contra the Tory view, the Whig discourse stressed that the unreformed Parliament had a fundamental role to play in two senses. Firstly MPs were to express the various interests and attitudes found in British society. This 'virtual representation' (Pitkin 1967) meant that MPs required neither popular election nor to be resident in their constituency. Secondly Parliament was to reconcile these in order to advance the best interests of the nation. Here the notion of the 'balanced constitution' dominated. The king remained but was subordinate to the legislature. Parliament's role was to govern by formulating and initiating policy on behalf of the people. Authority was therefore divided between the newly constrained monarch and the Westminster Parliament. Two notions were important here. Firstly that Parliament, and the government drawn from it, knew what was in the national interest. Secondly that the majority of the populace were politically incompetent and potentially dangerous. Consequently Parliament, and the Executive governed on behalf of the people, without much recourse to them.

Crucially, despite their differences, both the Whigs and the Tories shared an outright revulsion for popular sovereignty and democracy. Both groupings reflected and reinforced an elitism that stressed the legitimate power and dominance of those drawn from or supported by the socio-economic elite[6] (Garrard 2002). This can be most readily seen in the Whig discourse on representation developed by Edmund Burke, the pre-eminent Whig theorist of the time. It was his work in a context of socio-economic and political upheaval that helped secure its eventual dominance.[7]

Burke advocated a view of representation where MPs acted according to their consciences and were not bound by the views of the electorate.

This view was famously articulated during his campaigns in Bristol. In 1774 he described the ideal form of representation:

> it ought to be the happiness and glory of the representative to live in the strictest union...with his constituents. Their wishes ought to have great weight with him; their opinion high respect...It is his duty to sacrifice his repose...his satisfaction to theirs...But his unbiased opinion, his mature judgment, his enlightened conscience he ought not to sacrifice...to any man living. (Burke in B. W. Hill 1975: 157)

Burke's view of representation or 'trusteeship' was built upon the idea that an MP possessed greater knowledge and understanding than the electorate. Thus the MP's judgment was deemed to be superior. This view is commensurate with Burke's suggestion that the majority of the populace were politically incompetent.[8] As such his belief that the political elite were to govern on behalf of the nation can be seen as a classic early expression of the elitist concept of democracy which has shaped British politics.

Burke argued that a representative should be 'close' to the wishes of his constituents in the sense that their wishes should carry great weight with him. However he believed government should involve judgment and thus 'your representative owes you, not his industry only but his judgment; and he betrays, instead of serving you, if he sacrifices it to your opinion' (Burke in B. W. Hill 1975: 157).

To Burke, the representative was a political expert who was to debate and discuss with other 'experts', before offering decisions based upon the wider interests of the nation, rather than the narrow wishes of his constituents (Conniff 1994). He also suggested that 'Parliament is not a congress of ambassadors from different and hostile interests...but a deliberative assembly of one nation, with one interest, that of the whole...where not local prejudices ought to guide, but the general good, resulting from the general reason of the whole' (Burke in B. W. Hill 1975: 158).

Burke's view of 'trusteeship' was centrally significant to the development of a common understanding of the notion of representation. Burke saw 'the parliamentary representative, whether it is the hereditary member of the House of Lords or the elected member of the House of Commons, as in some sense, an agent of the people' (Conniff 1994: 137).

He argued that the MP should be removable by the people if he failed the popular trust. However he qualified his view of accountability in two ways. Firstly he suggested a largely defensive view of trusteeship in which the job of the MP was to protect the people against the misrule of others rather than to enact the will of the people. Secondly Burke developed a view of 'virtual representation' as opposed to 'actual representation', in which popular election was not required as long as interests, primarily economic ones, were represented (Pitkin 1967; Judge 1999a). This view was informed both by the electoral practices current in Burke's time and the attitudes of the elites towards the political competence of the populace.

It should be recognised that Burke allowed for the influence of the electorate in a limited or restricted form. Burke does not suggest, as O'Gorman (1973: 61) argues, that the representative should not be controlled by the people. Instead some more limited form of accountability was essential to ensure that the Commons acted as a check on misgovernment. Therefore Burke was not suggesting that MPs should be totally free from control. Rather he suggested that MPs should make their own judgments and be held accountable at the next election. This can clearly be seen in 1780, when he sought to defend his parliamentary record. Burke argued that the entirety of his record should be considered, stating: 'most certainly it is our duty to examine; it is our interest too; but it must be with discretion; with attention to all the circumstances, and to all the motives...look gentlemen, to the whole tenor of your members' conduct' (Burke cited in Conniff 1994: 143).

Burke suggested that over the course of time he had repeatedly been shown to be correct on controversial issues such as Irish Trade, because he was more informed than the voter (Conniff 1994).

Thus Burke argued that although the voter's opinions should weigh on the representative, they should not necessarily be followed in decision-making. At the heart of this, notions concerning superiority and inferiority in relation to political capabilities are stressed. Indeed we might view it as 'aristocratic trusteeship' (O'Gorman 1973: 54) as Burke utilised what amounts to a typology of 'political fitness and unfitness'. To Burke, some people are born with superior intelligence and abilities, and society is naturally hierarchical. However Burke's description of aristocracy in the *Appeal* (1791) highlights that to him, aristocrats or rulers are made as much as they are born. This occurs through a process of education, training and the acquisition of experience, all of which were at the time reflections of socio-economic position. From this two points follow. Firstly to make political decisions requires a degree of education, training and experience and thus the most desirable politicians are specialists or experts. On this Burke was neither original nor alone.[9] Secondly as at the time the majority of society did not have the material position or opportunity to acquire the pre-requisites for participation in decision-making, they were politically unfit and thus should be excluded from the vote, and political influence more broadly, if possible. It is also interesting to note that under Burke's view of trusteeship accountability and participation was reduced to voting in periodic elections. As a consequence of notions concerning political competence, the electorates' role was to give periodic legitimisation of elite rule. Indeed trusteeship had implications for the long-term development of representation in the UK.[10]

This elitist view of political competence was to be found in the electoral practices of the day. At the time less than 5 per cent of the adult population could vote. The franchise qualification utilised various property qualifications and excluded all women on the basis of their gender and alleged inferiority. That said, the absence of the vote was not a total bar on political influence in the 18th and 19th centuries (O'Gorman 1989; Vernon 1993). Non-voters were frequently both politically aware and engaged. MPs and their patrons often participated in lively debate and the control exercised by both the great landowners and the Crown was: 'exercised at great cost, with great care, with great difficulty, with much effort, and sometimes for no very great return' (O'Gorman 1989: 384). However we should recognise that whilst the MP or their patron needed to take account of the views of their constituents, they were not compelled to do so equally or at all times. Structured inequality and asymmetrical power relationships were woven into the very fabric of UK society and these undoubtedly had an impact on outcomes in Hanoverian Britain.

Burke himself accepted wide-ranging limitations on the right to vote and opposed the extension of the franchise. He supported the ability of Peers to control elections for the House of Commons (Conniff 1994), qualifications based upon property and gender, and the traditional constituency allocations. For Burke democracy, with its notions of political equality, was essentially tyranny (Judge 1999a) and echoing Hobbes (1651) he suggested that anarchy ensues when government breaks down. Consequently the political elite, drawn from the aristocracy, would govern not in their material interests, but for those of the nation (Pitkin 1967). This can be seen as an early expression of the mantra: 'Westminster and Whitehall know best'. Judge (1999a) notes that two notions coalesce in Burke's view of representation: judgment and nation. Thus he offers not only a view of representation but also one that prescribes a notion of legitimate government (Judge 2005: 42). This can be linked to the development of a discourse concerning responsibility discussed shortly.

However we should note at this point that this Whig discourse did not go unchallenged. For example the idea of delegation or 'spokespersonship' could find supporters amongst both the Tories and the Radicals (Garrard 2002). Before Burke, some MPs had seen themselves as merely the articulator of the views of those that elected or selected them, as Andrew Marvell, the playwright and MP for Hull between 1660 and 1678, did (Radice, Vallance and Willis 1987). The Tories could advocate delegation as it fitted with their idea that the representative was simply a petitioner for the grievances of voters. The Radicals could argue for it because it offered the possibility of a more democratic approach to both representation and governance. There was also the Tory discourse mentioned earlier. Why this Whig discourse developed into a limited liberal discourse on representation during the late 19th and early 20th centuries is of central significance and will be dealt with below.

Reflecting and reinforcing the structured inequality of the time and the attitudes and fears of the socio-economic elites, Burke's most famous work *Reflections on the Revolution in France* (1790) highlighted what he believed to be the inherent dangers of popular sovereignty. Amongst its famous passages, we find an attack on both democracy and radical change. Burke's view: 'along with its natural protectors and guardians, learning will be cast into the mire and trodden down under the hoofs of a swinish multitude' (Burke 1790: 79) can be linked to his typology of political fitness/unfitness. Burke highlighted what he believed to be the inherent dangers of popular rule and he equated democracy with mob rule. Popular sovereignty was something to be feared and resisted wherever possible. It would lead inexorably to tyranny and the rule of the mob as well as the destruction of valued traditional institutions and practices.[11]

In *Reflections*, Burke again built upon the views of earlier writers such as Plato, Aristotle and Hume (Conniff 1994: 225–6). Furthermore his assumptions both reflected and reinforced many of the prevailing attitudes of the socio-economic and political elite of the day (Garrard 2002). What gave Burke's work greater force over time were |the most terrible events of the revolution – the September massacres. The Terror, the executions of the King and Queen – all lay in the future when the Reflections was written and published' (O'Brien 2002: 215). This increased the impact that the text and its discourse had upon those with wealth and power in the UK. Radical change would always be accompanied by chaos, and this in turn would lead to tyranny and international conflict. Revolutions inevitably led to chaos and destruction. In placing the blame for the emergence of the Revolution on both the radicals and the failures of the French government, he would influence the attitudes and responses of both the Whigs, and later the Tories, to parliamentary reform and change.

As mentioned earlier, the loose affiliations known as the Whigs and the Tories were drawn from a largely similar socio-economic background (Garrard 2002). They viewed moves towards popular sovereignty with hostility, fearing the socio-economic and political consequences of change. The debates of the late 18th and early 19th centuries were dominated by members of the socio-economic elite of the time, the aristocracy or the land-owning class. Ownership of the land equated to knowledge, wealth and power in Britain at this time (Anderson 1964; Gash 1979) and this can clearly be seen through a cursory examination of the aristocracy's position in Westminster and Whitehall. For example in the 1826 general election no fewer than 165 MPs were members of the aristocracy, with estimates suggesting that around 200 seats in the House of Commons were controlled by peers during the first 30 years of the 19th century. There is little doubt that this group dominated the institutions and process of British government. As Garrard notes 'the rise of industrial business enterprise notwithstanding, the landed classes dominated the nation's governmental, parliamentary and administrative elite until at least the 1880s' (2002: 86).

Members of the land-owning class dominated the House of Lords and occupied the majority of cabinet posts and parliamentary seats. Given this prevalent position and the background of the Whigs and Tories, the debates of the late 18th and early 19th centuries were dominated by the socio-economic and political elite. Moreover these elites were primarily concerned with the maintenance of their dominant position in society and thus the continuation of existing institutions and practices. This was particularly important given the changes emanating from the advent of early industrial capitalism and the upheavals brought about by the French Revolution. Burke's ideas regarding the desirability of continuity and the maintenance of the established order reflected and reinforced these concerns.

That is not to say that those from outside this social grouping were without a voice (Thompson 1980) or influence (O'Gorman 1989). Rather there was an asymmetrical power relationship expressed in these debates rooted in the structured inequality of UK society and the attendant knowledge of, and access to, the institutions and process of government. Nor is it to deny the existence of a radical voice within Parliament.[12] Rather it is to suggest that views emanating from outside the elite had not yet developed into a wholesale critique or alternative. Nor had they gathered sufficiently widespread support amongst the populace.[13] The deference of the lower classes should also be recognised here. Belief in the alleged superiority of the aristocracy, as evidenced by the widespread view that they were the natural rulers of society, can clearly be found amongst a significant portion of the lower classes at the time.[14] Given this widespread deference, acceptance of elitism amongst the lower classes was instrumental in perpetuating the dominance of the socio-economic and political elite in the UK. Garrard (2002: 86) argues that 'British, particularly English, society was highly susceptible to elite influence. In 1800 it was strongly hierarchical and deferential'. Consequently socio-economic and political inequality, and asymmetrical power relations, influenced the debates concerning parliamentary reform.

From initially being one of a number of views on representation, Burke's view would have a lasting impact upon British political life, as a consequence of the context of the structured inequalities of UK society and the upheavals that threatened the dominance of the socio-economic elites in the late 18th and 19th centuries. Over time, this Whig discourse would undergo adaptation in response to contingent events and would come to form a central discourse of the predominant political tradition in the UK. Before turning to this adaptation, we should consider the development of a discourse concerning change.

A discourse concerning change

Equally important for the development of the British political system was Burke's conceptualisation of change. For Burke 'a state without the means of some change is without the means of its own conservation' (1790: 21).

It was the refusal of the Ancien Regime to change that had led to its eventual destruction and the advent of popular rule. Thus states and their elites must be willing to adopt minimalistic change where necessary in order to preserve the continued dominance of those best equipped to rule and to ensure that traditional institutions continued to exist. Consequently Burke (1790) both defended the existing order and argued for how best to achieve the continued dominance of the elite.

Contra this view, the Tory discourse suggested that change should be resisted and that repression was often the best way to ensure this. Toryism had, as Bentley suggests, 'developed a language of Pittite resistance against the enemy within, enriched with a strong flavour of soil tenantry and aggressive churchmanship' (1999: 9). The infamous Peterloo Massacre of August 1919 and the Tory government's response to it highlighted their antipathy towards demands for political reform. The views of Lord Wellington in November 1830 are indicative of this.[15] Wellington confidently asserted the ability of the elites to resist popular demands for change in 1831 when he stated: 'We have instances, even lately, of resistance to the law of the largest masses of men who commenced their resistance under the most advantageous circumstances, but they soon found themselves powerless against the power of government and of the law united.'

Thus the Tory discourse concerning change was one of hostility towards the very notion and a wholehearted resistance towards any changes to the socio-economic or political order of the day.

It was these two discourses that informed much of the debates between the Whigs and Tories at Westminster c.1830–32 over the extension of the franchise. The triumph of the Burkeian view was decisively stated in both the 1832 Reform Act. As Hanham states: 'everything possible was done (in 1832) to preserve the continuity of the great landed interests, which dominated British politics since the 17th century' (1969: 12). With Peel's acceptance of this approach in the 1834 Tamworth Manifesto, the Tories themselves began to accept the Whig discourse. Furthermore its dominance was firmly established in how it influenced later approaches to reform and was decisively important in shaping the debates concerning the British political system throughout the 19th century. Indeed the idea of incremental development and minimal reform as both a virtue and a necessity became inscribed into the attitudes of the political elite over time and was reflected in the piecemeal changes to the institutions and process of British government evident in the later 19th century. As such, Burke's approach is the basis for the discourse concerning change.

The dominance of the socio-economic and political elites allowed the development and promulgation of a discourse concerning change that stressed the virtue of continuity, gradualism, flexibility and stability. This view of change was most obviously expressed in the Whig interpretation of history mentioned earlier. This suggested that the 1688 Glorious Revolution had delivered a set of flexible and balanced institutions and that Grey and the Whigs had built upon this in

1832. This portrayal of Britain's political development was one where a prudent approach to political reform would dominate. Britain had developed a stable and secure democracy over time, avoiding the upheaval and turmoil found elsewhere. Indeed the wise governance and cautious approach of the political elite had allowed for the emergence of a parliamentary democracy without revolution. For example Erskine May wrote in 1861: 'no law since the Bill of Rights is to be compared with it in importance – it conferred immortal honour on the statesmen who had the wisdom to conceive it' (cited in Canon 1973: 254).

To the socio-economic and political elite, the Reform Crisis 1830–32 and the Reform Act itself confirmed both the value of elitism and the dangers of popular sovereignty. Crucially it also maintained their dominant position in UK society, which they believed to be both legitimate and based upon their superiority. Furthermore this approach was viewed as peculiarly British and undoubtedly superior, suggesting a sense of national distinctiveness that will be dealt with shortly. Institutionally, this view underpinned the institutions and processes described by the WM narrative (Gamble 1990; Kerr and Kettell 2006). Textually, it was promulgated in the work of McCaulay (1848), Bagehot (1867), Trevelyan (1922), Jennings (1941), as well as more recent explanations such as Norton (1984) and Punnett (1987). Notions such as the gradual 'evolution' of the British political system and the organicism often associated with its constitutional development highlight this.[16]

Having outlined the discourse concerning change, we will now return to the development of the discourse concerning representation in the 19th century.

The extension of the franchise in the 19th century

Politically, the 19th century in the UK was characterised by periodic discussion and debate concerning the extension of the franchise. These debates resulted in both continuity and change in the political process, in line with the approach to change advocated by Burke. Whilst the debate regarding the franchise burned at differing intensities in different periods for varying reasons, it was a hallmark feature of 19th century politics. The debates between advocates and opponents of parliamentary reform were often rancorous and occasionally riotous.[17] In Parliament a small minority of MPs favoured the extension of the franchise, with most MPs adopting the antipathy towards popular sovereignty advocated by Burke.[18] Outside of Parliament, groups such as the Chartists in the late 1830s and 1840s, or the Reform Union and Reform League c.1866 adopted the more participatory concept of democracy, discussed in Chapter 6.

Over time a gradual extension of the franchise occurred in 1832, 1867 and then, 1884. Each time, the political elite sought to enfranchise those that they felt were no longer politically dangerous and at a time they thought would be advantageous to them electorally.[19] This would prove to be crucial in transforming the Whig discourse into a limited liberal one and thus influence the nature of representation favoured in the BPT. However the idea of political fitness/unfitness remained. The middle classes could demonstrate their political fitness by virtue of their ownership of property.[20] However there still existed the widespread belief amongst the socio-economic elite that most of populace were, by dint of their inferior socio-economic position, politically unfit and frankly, rather dangerous. As such elite rule was to be preserved and change resisted where possible, because it was a way of avoiding the dangers of democracy and the direct, unfettered input of the politically undesirable.[21] Once established, this aspect of the Whig discourse on representation acted as an 'agenda fixing gateway' (Garrard 2002: 93).[22] Over time elements of the male working class came to conform to the views of the elites by abandoning Chartism and disorder generally and adopting key ideas such as rationality, self-improvement, self-help and thrift via participation in savings banks, retail co-ops and friendly societies, all features primarily associated with the 'labour aristocracy' (Hobsbawm 1967). Conformity to these types of behaviour required acceptance of a political and socio-economic system that was asymmetrical and unequal. Thus 'political fitness', to a large degree, involved accepting the existing socio-economic hierarchy and power relations.

These views were themselves the product of the elites' dominant position, prejudices and, crucially, interests. Furthermore conformity required acceptance of a political and socio-economic system which was asymmetrical and unequal. As such the role of the elites and their view of limited political participation and influence was an essential ingredient in the extension of the franchise. Once again a negative view of the lower sections of society can also be detected here. It was not just that the lower classes were not fit to rule (Burke 1790) but that they were unfit in a broader sense as they had failed to demonstrate 'merit'. Here the doctrine of 'self-help' associated with Samuel Smiles (1859) dominated. The elite groups believed that they occupied that position by virtue of their superiority and this was demonstrated by their greater material wealth. Given their superiority they knew what was best for society and should be allowed to govern. They believed that to be allowed to have even a limited say, conformity to their ideas was necessary.

Once 'political fitness' was demonstrated, politicians such as Gladstone adjusted their view to include some of the previously dangerous or incapable.[23] Moreover in calling for the inclusion of artisans like Bagehot (1867), Gladstone was suggesting that they were now to be deemed politically fit. As Garrard (2002: 93) suggests even those most famous of political opponents – Disraeli and Gladstone – could agree that 'after as before 1867: voting was 'a popular privilege' and what had been created was not democracy'.[24] Therefore the political elite sought to enfranchise those that they felt were no longer politically dangerous, in that they had accepted the broader tenets of elite rule.

Two further points should be recognised here. Firstly the extension of the franchise was not the result of, nor did it lead to, a dramatic shift in the predominant ideas that underpinned politics in the UK. The franchise was extended but the debate over the extent of representation that was necessary or indeed desirable was never broadened, at least not amongst the elites. Indeed as Birch notes, even to the liberals: 'the member of the legislature was not a delegate sent merely to reflect the will of the people, he was a representative charged with deliberation on the common good' (1964: 33).

Deliberating on the common good allowed the possibility of limited influence, even for those without the vote (O'Gorman 1989; Vernon 1993). However it did not guarantee it. Here again the significance of the ideas of Burke can be detected. Parliament was representative because it was elected in free and fair elections.[25] Both individual MPs and the government that is formed from them should then be free to act as they see fit in order to further the national interest. The MP, once elected, should be free to take decisions based upon their own deliberations and conscience because they were better equipped to do so than the electorate themselves. Accountability to the electorate was to be largely confined to periodic elections. As Birch states: 'No serious politician has suggested that representatives should be bound by specific instructions from their constituents and subject to recall if they did not follow these instructions' (1964: 227).

Indeed by the mid 19th century there was a general acceptance amongst both the political and socio-economic elite that the proper role of Parliament and its Members was as Burke had described. J. S. Mill (1861) highlighted the deliberative role of representatives and as Judge states, whilst there were differences in how they viewed political responsibility: 'Burke and Mill were agreed that representatives should not be bound by instructions from the represented. Equally they agreed that the best interests of the nation could be established and promoted through parliamentary deliberation' (2005: 42).

Furthermore to the elite the Burkeian approach to change had proven itself to be 'successful'. Parliamentary reform, which had eventually occurred in 1832, had avoided the upheavals seen in French Revolution and, crucially, preserved the power and position of the elites. Trevelyan would later laud both the substance of these developments and the manner in which they occurred, stating: 'the sovereignty of the people had been established in fact, if not in law' (1922: 242).

This process of continuity and change was most clearly narrated in the mid 19th century in Bagehot's *The English Constitution* (1867). In this canonic text he suggested that 'doubtless...there is tacit reference to probable public opinion; but certainly also there is much free will in the judgment of the Commons. The House not only goes where it thinks in the end the nation will follow; but it takes the chance of the nation following or not following; it assumes the initiative, and acts upon its own discretion and caprice' (1867: 151).

Bagehot, like Burke, opposed the idea of universal suffrage,[26] stating that it was incompatible with a parliamentary government made up of moderate men. In particular he suggested that the 'the working classes contribute almost nothing to our corporate public opinion' (1867: 176) and defended the disproportionate role of the landed classes in Parliament.

There are a number of notable features of Bagehot's narration of representation that highlight continuity. Again we find reference to the importance of judgment and in Bagehot's terms, 'moderation'. Politicians should be free and willing to act contra the expressed wishes of the electorate and act in an initiatory fashion in the national interest. Furthermore the typology of political fitness/unfitness seeps through his commentary (Bagehot 1867: 161–72). He stated that 'certain persons are by common consent agreed to be wiser than others, and their opinion is, by common consent, to rank from much more than its numerical value' (Bagehot 1867: 171).

Again by linking knowledge and understanding, and thus political competence, to wealth and social position Bagehot both reflected and reinforced the prevalent attitudes amongst the elites.[27] He also made frequent reference to notions concerning national identity through reference to the national character of the English[28] and favourably compared Britain's constitutional arrangements with those in the US. This is a notable feature of much of the literature on the British political system (see for example Norton 1984) and one that can be linked to the alleged superior developmental path of the UK which we will return to later.

A limited liberal discourse on representation

As a consequence of the electoral changes of 1867 and 1884/85 the Whig discourse concerning representation underwent slight revision. Where once it had stressed 'virtual representation', now 'actual representation' was deemed to be desirable. This linked the idea of representation to the notion of constituency more clearly by more fully emphasising the importance of individual constituents' preferences. These would be expressed in periodic elections and a representative had to be mindful of them, if only to get re-elected. However this did not see the abandonment of all tenets of the Whig discourse. The numbers of people voting and the nature of constituencies were changed to reflect the growing influence of liberal ideas of individual representation and popular election (Norton 2005). However it was not a fully liberal view as Norton (2005) suggests. Rather it extended the numbers of people whose opinions a representative now had to consider. The notions of limited participation and the superiority of politicians remained. Thus this new discourse amounted to a limited liberal view of representation.

Even when stressing more liberal notions, politicians were able to retain a role for themselves as the arbiters of varying interests. Essentially they would remain those with a concern for the national interest. Whilst individual voters may only see their specific interest, politicians remained those with the ability to deliver what was best for all in the 'long duree'. To achieve this, they had to retain the ability to ignore the expressed wishes of the voters. Thus to a large degree, elitism was retained.

Furthermore the notion that the wishes of the electorate should be followed rather than simply be considered remained firmly outside the discourse. The franchise was extended; however accountability to the electorate was not. Indeed it was in some ways downgraded. Burke had suggested, somewhat vaguely, that the wishes of the electorate should carry great weight with the MP, although his own judgment remained more significant. O'Gorman (1989) demonstrates that this was often the case, as political influence was not merely confined to those with the vote. However once the franchise was extended to the point where working class men became the largest single group in the electorate, the elitism of the predominant political tradition seems to have hardened. From the late 19th century onwards, undoubtedly the role of voters was to periodically legitimise elite rule in general elections. Their wishes would be important in the context of re-election rather than frequency of participation, policy formulation or import generally. As Miliband notes: 'if democracy is defined in terms of popular participation in the determination of policy and popular control over the conduct of affairs, then the British political system is far from democratic' (1982: 1).

The retention of elitist and undemocratic assumptions within the discourse on representation demonstrates substantial continuity. Furthermore it was hardly surprising given the views of those with power in the late 19th century and the persistence of socio-economic inequality in 19th and early 20th century British society (Anderson 1987; Garrard 2002). Indeed this inequality both informed and supported their continued resonance. For many in the elite, the growth of a limited liberal discourse on representation was part of a superior model of political practice, in which the prudent approach of the political elite was paramount. The success of this had been proven empirically by the British mode of development. That this approach to politics maintained their dominant position in UK society, and their faith in the legitimacy of their position should not be underestimated.

Despite their differences, the two parties of government, the Liberals and the Conservatives, operated within the confines of a limited liberal discourse concerning representation. Their faith in this was rooted in the material context of the time and the debate, a product and expression of the elitism that characterised Britain. It was also driven in part by contestation from rival political discourses. The context for the debate was the socio-economic inequality evident in British society and the asymmetrical power relations that had developed from that inequality. Subsequently these dominant ideas came to both reinforce it and ensure that inequality and asymmetry developed further. Garrard (2002: 86–7) notes that:

> in conjunction with wealthy business families with whom they were merging to produce a 'generalised upper class', they (the Aristocracy)

remained centrally important until 1914. The elites' role was underpinned by the fact that landowners remained the wealthiest social group until at least the Agricultural depression (of the 1880s). They retained significant patronage powers. Land dominated the exclusive London Circle, and subsidiary county circles, until the 1880s. In numerous rural localities where landholdings were large and owners resident, they dominated local administrative, social, political and economic life – commanding dependency, deference, patronage and social admission.

The emergent BPT was both a product and reinforcement of socio-economic inequality to be found in UK society, where those with wealth and knowledge wielded political power in their interest. The political system they dominated and the ideas that underpinned it both reflected and reinforced this.

Having established a 'common understanding' of the most acceptable form of representation by the mid 19th century, the Whig discourse had the impact of imposing a discursive selectivity which accounts, in part, for the continuation of elitism and the limiting of the liberal aspects of the discourse concerning representation. Once constructed, this discourse informed the development and subsequent operation of the British political system. Since the end of the 19th century it has been narrated by numerous authors and has undergone some further adaptation. For example in Jennings's *The British Constitution* (1941) we see some common themes recurring. He (1941: 14) argues that:

> to represent Coventry is no doubt an honour, but the member's primary purpose is not to represent Coventry but to vote according to his conscience, his party, or his chances of getting re-elected. As Lord Coke said more than 300 years ago, though he is elected for his constituency he serveth for the whole realm. He helps decide national policies on national grounds; he is not the representative of a community, supporting local interests or a local patriotism; he does not take instructions from his constituents though he runs the risk of losing their support if he disagrees with them too thoroughly.

Here the limited liberal discourse on representation is narrated as before but is positioned alongside party. This can be attributed to the impact of universal suffrage which was introduced in 1928. However like Burke and Bagehot before him, Jennings suggests that the MP's own judgment was paramount and that the role of the populace in UK democracy was to be limited to voting in periodic elections. Once again, this suggests that the judgment of the politicians is superior to those of the populace and that 'Westminster and Whitehall know best.'[29]

The incremental extension of the franchise in the 19th and 20th centuries saw political parties, in a modern sense, develop (Ingle 1999). This led to tighter party discipline at Westminster and the emergence of the idea that the representative was very much a party representative (Judge 1999a; Norton 2005). This would have an impact upon the manner in which representatives conducted themselves at Westminster, thus presenting a new tension for MPs and, to a lesser extent, Lords. It would have an impact upon narrations of the representation found in the iconic texts of British politics (see for example Jennings 1941; Birch 1964; Beer 1965), and thus the 'common understandings' of British politics. However stressing the importance of party does not guarantee involvement for constituency views or interests, as many MPs see these as congruent anyway (Norton 2005). Nor does stressing the need for re-election move too far beyond Burke's idea that only accountability at the next election was needed, because 'the natural ties of interest and affection in a hierarchical social order would insure that the leaders would look after others' (Conniff 1994: 157). Political parties with claims to class-based identity and interest representation (Ingle 2000) could now claim to fulfil the notion of 'the natural ties of interest', allowing politicians to continue to act according to their own allegedly superior judgments.

Nor does a greater role for political parties necessarily equate to a greater role for the population via membership of those parties. For example the Conservatives operated, until recently, as a highly hierarchical, centralised party (Garner and Kelly 1998). Conversely the Labour party management has been dominated by a struggle between a leadership which sought policy independence, in line with the BPT, and a wider party which sought greater involvement and control over policy-making (Coates 1975; Minkin 1980). Indeed Miliband (1962: 104) notes how the desire to demonstrate a concern for the national interest underpinned the leaderships' pre-war desire for freedom from extra-parliamentary control by the wider party. As such even those who joined one of the two main parties in the 20th century were not necessarily guaranteed a greater role in decision-making.

The enfranchisement of the working classes did witness the development of a much larger constituency for the emergent social democratic tradition in the UK. This would quickly give rise to the formation of the Labour Representation Committee in 1900. In this party there was a strong element who favoured a more participatory concept of democracy. Not only would this cause tension within the Labour party over time (Tant 1993) but it would also provide one source of potential contestation of the BPT in the 20th century. Thus conflict between the predominant tradition and competing traditions continued and was somewhat intensified by the unintended consequences of the extension of the franchise. However we should also recognise that when it finally secured an overall majority in 1945, it did so in a form that more easily fitted with the BPT, a point we will return to.

The BPT and its adherents were therefore not left unscathed by the debates of the 19th century. Adaptations and accommodations to these challenges can be seen in both the extension of the franchise and the social democratic policies of the post-war period (Kerr 2001). However the essential elitism and resistance to radicalism and participatory notions was retained at the core of the British political system.[30] Alongside political change, a degree of path dependency can be detected, as those in power developed solutions that fitted neatly with the prevailing institutional, contextual and discursive environment which was itself the result of past struggles and ideas (Kerr 2002; 2003). Thus in many ways, the BPT still held sway.

In summary, the version of representation that developed during the 19th century in the UK was a limited one. Throughout the debates between Tories, Whigs and then Liberals and Conservatives, a common thread can be detected. All four positions shared a belief that the representative role of Parliament was to give voice to various views and interests, but also to deliberate and develop policy without much recourse to the public at large. The political elites were the supreme arbiters or judges of the national interest, not the public itself. This limited view of representation was rooted in the broader inequalities and asymmetries found in British society. By the 1930s universal suffrage had been introduced incrementally and this occurred in part due to the unforeseen consequences of earlier extensions of the vote and the impact of both contingent events such as the First World War. As with previous electoral changes, the influence of competing political traditions which stressed notions concerning political and in some cases, social equality, should also be recognised. However the discourse concerning change had a decisive impact on the manner in which the extension of the franchise developed. This limited the extent of change evident as representative government developed, contributing to the development of a limited liberal view of representation by helping to thwart more radical moves towards popular sovereignty.

The advent of universal suffrage did not lead to wider democratic participation in decision-making or a fundamental change in the relationship between representative and constituents. The numerical size of the electorate was increased, but the parameters within which they operated were left, to a substantial degree, unscathed. There was a possibility for influence, but this occurred on an uneven political landscape that favoured the ideas and interest of those with wealth, knowledge and power. Moreover 'Westminster and Whitehall knows best' remained the mantra upon which parliamentary democracy in the UK operated. That is not to say that post 1928 it has gone uncontested. However in the dominant discourse the populace was to participate primarily through voting in periodic elections.[31]

A discourse concerning responsibility

Alongside debates about representation, a discourse concerning responsibility can also be seen. As Marsh and Hall (2007: 222) argue, these 'ideas about responsibility were always implicit, and sometimes explicit, in Tory, Whig and liberal views about representation'. By the late 19th century the debate concerning responsibility was increasingly prominent. As the franchise was extended most politicians came to accept the increasing authority of the House of Commons. This led to a debate about the House of Lords, which would culminate in the constitutional crisis of 1909–11 and the Parliament Act.[32] Indeed the debate concerning the proper role and composition of the House of Lords persists to date.[33] The failure to achieve democratisation of the second chamber should be seen in the light of the impact of the four discourses of the BPT. The retention of an undemocratic second chamber fits neatly with discourses that stress an elitist concept of democracy: slow, minimalistic change and British distinctiveness. Crucially the focus of debates concerning the British political system by the late 19th century shifted to the role of government vis-à-vis Parliament.

Within these discussions two views can be identified. The Liberal view stressed the doctrines of parliamentary sovereignty, ministerial responsibility and executive accountability to Parliament. Here the key narrator was Dicey (1885). He described parliamentary sovereignty as 'the dominant characteristic of our political institutions, the very key stone of the law of the constitution' (1885: 64). As we saw in Chapter 1, parliamentary sovereignty suggests that Parliament is the supreme legislative body within the UK and that no body or individual had the right to overrule or set aside Parliament's decisions. Dicey traced the development of this notion back to the Norman Conquest and suggested that 'royal supremacy' had passed into the supremacy of Parliament. In Dicey's view the executive was and should be accountable to Parliament via the doctrine of ministerial responsibility.[34]

The conservative view was rooted in the belief that only a strong, centralised executive could ensure effective and efficient government. The emphasis for the Conservatives was thus responsible government rather than responsive government. The Conservative emphasis on hierarchy was predominant here as was the idea of a natural political or governing class. Only this class could provide the leadership which was required to deliver wise governance in the interests of the nation and stability. The influence of Hobbes (1651) should be noted here. Notions such as Tory Democracy[35] stressed the need to balance the interests within society in order to preserve its traditional structure and institutions (Smith 1996). In order to achieve this, the government required the freedom to act responsibly, in the national interest. In this view the focus lies on the strength and stability of the government, rather than its accountability to Parliament. In the conservative view therefore 'a British government is an independent body which on taking office assumes the responsibility of leading and directing Parliament and the nation with its own judgement and convictions' (Amery cited in Beer 1982: 96). In these debates, despite the centrality of Dicey to the Westminster Model (WM) narrative, the Conservative view won out. The executive would largely dominate Parliament and its business, and would wield, de facto, its legislative power.

A number of observations on the debates concerning responsibility can be made here. Firstly whilst the Liberal and Conservative views were different, the difference centred on the extent to which the executive should be primarily responsible or accountable to Parliament. Thus Parliament's centrality was now assured, and as we have seen, the role of Members of Parliament had come to be informed by a limited liberal discourse concerning representation. Neither view expressed the idea that the executive should be primarily responsible to the population. Both operated within a narrow elitist concept of democracy whereby the populace was to be governed by a political elite who would act on their behalf. Even for Liberals, the executive should be accountable to Parliament, which in turn represented the nation. Indeed the absence of participatory notions of democracy and their frequent dismissal as 'utopian folly' can be seen in the development of a discourse concerning responsibility that emphasises executive dominance.

Secondly a discourse which stresses the need for a centralised, initiatory authority dovetails neatly with the elitism of the limited liberal discourse concerning representation. If the politicians at Westminster, from whom the executive is drawn, could legitimately claim to 'know best' then their power to legislate for the entirety of the UK should be unrivalled. The reality of parliamentary sovereignty in action, particularly after the 1911 Parliament Act, was that a government that could command a majority in the House of Commons and control its backbenchers could wield that legislative power as it saw fit. Thus executive-legislative relations in the British polity were informed by elitism and the need for wise governance by a political elite in the national interest. Moreover the political elite consistently sought to minimise change and thwart pressure for more democratic reform and social change in order to protect the prevailing socio-economic structure and the interests of dominant socio-economic elites.

Furthermore the importance of centralisation to this view of responsibility must be recognised. It has been a fundamental idea in the establishment of institutions and processes in the UK political system. Executive dominance both informed, and fitted neatly with, the largely centralised approach to territorial politics that developed in the 18th and 19th centuries. The conservative discourse on responsibility dovetailed with the institutions and processes of governing this new nation-state. Centralisation of power in the hands of the executive was likely to ensure no small measure of continuity and stability across the four nations of the UK. This was of paramount importance to a socio-economic and political elite concerned primarily with the preservation of its dominant position in society.

British government became characterised by the equation of effectiveness and efficiency with the ideas of strong, centralised government. In the BPT 'responsible government' means that government acts as the guardians of national interest and pursues policies that are 'wise', even if policies do not meet with immediate approval from the electorate. The willingness of British governments to risk unpopularity by taking decisions in the national interest is often invoked to illustrate governments acting responsibly. In effect, the BPT equates 'responsible government' with leadership and prudence. Responsible government is essentially strong government (Judge 2006: 368); initiatory and decisive government is seen as effective and efficient government. Indeed the idea of effective government in the UK has been conceived of and functions as a means of legitimating executive power. The BPT emphasises the idea that the most efficient form of government is a government that is free to govern as it sees fit because it understands how best to fulfil the national interest. Thus executive dominance became a central tenet of the BPT via its discourse concerning responsibility.

Having raised the issue of territorial politics we will now turn attention to the final discourse of the BPT

A discourse concerning national distinctiveness

A sense of British national distinctiveness was also central to the development of the BPT.[36] Part of the context for the debates concerning democracy was the formation of Britain as a nation-state during the 18th and early 19th centuries. It should be recognised that there were a number of facets to this sense of British national identity that developed during this time. In particular unionism and the concept of British exceptionalism were crucial. The pursuit and acquisition of an empire during the 18th and 19th centuries was another key facet of this process.

The development of the 'imagined community' (Anderson 1983) of Britain was a major, yet often subterranean feature of the politics of the time. The creation of a distinctive sense of British national identity helped to secure a degree of homogeneity within an emergent social and political unit that contained a range of identities across and within the regions of the UK. This process began with the Union of the Crowns in 1603 and more fully following the 1707 Act of Union between England and Scotland (Gamble and Wright 2009). This saw what Colley (2003: xvii) refers to as Britain's 'invention as a unitary state and would be nation'. It was continued with the formalisation of English, now British, rule over Ireland with the Act of Union in 1800. The need for unity was undoubtedly magnified in the face of the upheavals caused by the advent of industrial capitalism.

A sense of Britishness was promoted in various ways (Colley 2003). Firstly it was developed via the promotion of what it meant to be British, or at the very least part of the union. Institutions such as the monarchy and Parliament were deified, particularly following the upheavals in France in 1789. Here the Whig narration of the British political system was fundamental. Reference to the notion that Westminster was 'the mother of all Parliaments' became increasingly commonplace in the second half of the 19th century.[37] The idea that Britain's mode of development was both exceptional and superior to that found elsewhere was fundamental in the creation of a distinctive sense of British political-cultural identity (Nairn 1981; Preston 2004).

This sense of British exceptionalism was centrally significant in the development of a sense of Britishness and, more broadly, the BPT. In the work of Burke (1790) and in the attitudes of those involved in the debates of the time was a belief that the British mode of development was superior. Indeed this formed a key part of the Whig view of history popularised by the likes of McCaulay (1848) and Bagehot (1867). For the majority of British politicians the BPT offered a superior model of politics and this had been proved empirically by the British mode of development. Indeed we should also recognise here that attempts to naturalise certain social and political practices as 'British' forms a key part of the discourse concerning national distinctiveness. This helps to explain how dominant groups maintained their position over time and secured the acquiescence of subordinate groups in society through the development of powerful 'indigenous' traditions.

Britishness was also promoted by the demonisation of a non-British element or elements. Here the centrality of difference or 'the other' should be considered. The construction of a distinctive British identity occurred relationally (Cohen 1994; Colley 2003). Both 'Protestantism' and 'Francophobia' were of central significance in giving Britain a sense of difference to the largely Catholic Europe. This was particularly important given the religious dimension to the wars with France between 1689 and 1815. The loss of the North American colonies in the late 18th century then saw the political and socio-economic elite re-invent themselves by turning outwards, stressing the need for overseas trade and the acquisition of a global empire (Colley 2003). This new expansionist view was undoubtedly 'British' as opposed to 'English'. The union with Scotland was forged, despite differences of identity, by two patrician classes pursuing economic and political gains (Brown, McCrone and Paterson 1996: 3–7). Therefore 'the political-cultural project of Britain took shape in the late eighteenth and early nineteenth centuries' (Preston 2004: 49) and can readily be identified. Indeed Preston notes that 'throughout the nineteenth century the project flourished on the back of military success, economic innovation and political repression' (2004: 53). In this the notion of British exceptionalism and superiority were confirmed and re-established by each success.

The approach to politics and change developed in the UK was portrayed as distinctly British. This was felt across the social classes, for as McKibbon notes: 'it is hard to escape the conclusion that a sense of being British was widely and positively felt in the working classes' (1990: 24). The growing popularity of this view can also be seen across the nations of the UK from the mid 18th century onwards. For example as a consequence of material prosperity and the forging of a sense of collective identity, many from Scotland, Wales and even Ireland, like their English counterparts, came to believe in the virtues of a political system imbued with elitism. In the developing BPT, a belief in the virtue of unionism and centralisation of power were to be fundamental as was the alleged success of Britain's peculiar mode of political development. These in turn came to play a fundamental role in informing the institutions and processes of British government over time.

In accounting for this process, we turn again to the role and interests of the socio-economic and political elites (Nairn 1983; Colley 2003; Preston 2004). The development of a sense of Britishness was led by these groups. It also performed the function of more fully integrating the elite groups from the former nations of the UK into a British upper class (Colley 2003). That is not to say that differences did not remain (Brown, McCrone and Paterson 1996), but rather to suggest that the development and promotion of Britishness helped to unify, to a degree, previously disparate elements. It also played a part in securing the economic, social and political dominance of the elites during a period of upheaval and potential threat. The BPT was therefore essential to the maintenance of a pattern of elite dominance during the 18th and 19th centuries.

The inculcation of a sense of British exceptionalism was a fundamental facet of the development of the BPT. Key symbols and signifiers of the British political system such as the State Opening of Parliament or key narratives and mythologies such as 'Westminster is the mother of all Parliaments' are examples of this. Phrases such as 'an Englishman's home is his castle', 'the rights of a free-born Englishman' and 'British justice' were stock phrases in the vernacular of the mid to late 19th century, and suggested a sense of British uniqueness politically. In particular Britain's political tradition was shown to be markedly different to the political traditions developing in continental Europe and the USA and characterised as superior. Taken together these helped to inculcate into actors a belief in both the peculiarity and superiority of the British political system vis-à-vis other systems. This belief helped mask the true nature of socio-economic and political relations in the UK.

In this process the emphasis on British exceptionalism and superiority in political terms stood in stark contrast to the actual nature of the political system.[38] Indeed through the invention of traditions (Hobsbawm 1983a), a stark contrast between the image conveyed and the reality of the British political system was promulgated. Its function was, as Miliband suggests, 'linked to the need of the dominant classes to use it as a response to the rise of the labour movements in the second half of the nineteenth century, and the dangers that were thought to arise from the extension of the suffrage to the working class' (1989: 142). Drawing on this insight it can be seen that the development of the discourse concerning national distinctiveness performed the function of assisting in the perpetuation of the dominance of the socio-economic and political elite of the 18th and 19th centuries. Throughout this period the elite sought to stave off potential threats to their dominant position through the development and inculcation of traditions that deified aspects of the British political system. As part of this the virtue of continuity with the past was highlighted through the Whig interpretation of history and the dangers of alternative modes of development, particularly those found in Europe.

As we have seen, changes in the British political system can certainly be identified. However such changes did so in a manner that fitted relatively neatly with the prevailing ideational and institutional parameters. These changes were narrated as confirmation of the exceptionalism of the BPT and the British mode of development. Thus they helped to reinforce and further develop that tradition and acceptance of it, both amongst and beyond the elites. Despite the extension of the franchise, an elitist view of democracy rooted in socio-economic inequalities and asymmetries of power can still be seen, suggesting that this process was largely, if not entirely, successful.

The BPT and the rise of the Labour party

The birth of the Labour party at the turn of the 20th century was partly an unintended consequence of the extension of the franchise and contestation of the predominant tradition. Tant (1993) pays attention to the emergence of Labour and to how the party, with its vastly different origins to the Liberals and the Conservatives, came to become convinced of the virtues of the BPT. Rather than emerging from elite groupings as the two existing parties had done, the Labour party was established with the expressed intention of representing the interests of extra-parliamentary groupings such as the trade unions, the Fabians and various socialist societies. Initially the ideas of the Labour party stood in stark contrast to established views of democracy and the purpose of government generally. From its formation the party adopted a structure that was based upon a more participatory view of democracy (Tant 1993). Crucially the various interests in the party were given a major voice with the party conference being created as the supreme policy-making forum for the party, rather than the Parliamentary Labour Party (PLP) itself. However as the Labour party became an increasingly serious contender for power it came to embrace the BPT.

Tant (1993) describes this process as 'the constitutionalization of the Labour party'. The PLP quickly asserted its control over policy-making and intra-party discipline at Westminster came to resemble that of the other parties. However the more participatory democratic tradition continued to play a role in Labour party politics and this has been a source of tension within the party throughout the rest of the 20th century. The party conference and the National Executive Committee between conferences were, constitutionally the main policy-making forum, existing alongside the PLP leadership's control of policy-making. This has been the source of major tensions within the Labour party, particularly when in opposition.[39] The management of the Labour party has been a more problematic task than that of managing their main rival, the Conservative party (Marsh and Hall 2007). Whilst the Conservative party was convinced of the virtue of elitism generally and more specifically the elitist view of democracy, the Labour party contained an internal tension between those who favoured the BPT and those who appealed to a more participatory tradition. Throughout the 20th century, however, the party's leadership at Westminster remained the dominant force within the party, and they and the majority of the PLP were convinced of the virtue of strong leadership and tight party discipline. These views went hand in hand with a belief that the executive should be allowed to govern and Parliament, as the representatives of the people, should hold the Executive to account. In this way Labour, like the Liberals and the Conservatives, came to be a party of the BPT. In this instance the BPT came to negate much of a potential challenge to it. In particular the need for the Labour party to compete for power within a system whose institutions, processes and practices were informed by the BPT, fundamentally affected the view of the party at its senior levels. Moreover, in relation to constitutional reform, their faith in the BPT informed their constitutional conservatism (Dorey 2008). However as noted earlier, the social democratic tradition did seek to challenge some of the inequalities in UK society via the policies of the Attlee, Wilson and Callaghan governments of the post-war period.

Conclusion

In this chapter we have focused on the predominant political tradition operating in the UK, the BPT. As the British political system developed across the course of over 200 years it did so with a political tradition comprised of four interrelated discourses at its core. Two of these focused on the notions of representation and responsibility, coalescing in an elitist concept of democracy which suggests that 'Westminster and Whitehall knows best'.[40] The other two contained references to continuity, gradualism and a sense of Britishness rooted in a belief in British distinctiveness and superiority. When combined, these four discourses form the predominant political tradition in the UK. That tradition has helped to shape British political life over time.

Of course that is not to say that change and adaptations to the British political system cannot be identified; nor has the predominant tradition gone uncontested.[41] Rather it is to suggest that those changes that did occur did so within the parameters established by the BPT and did not fundamentally alter the underlying inequalities and asymmetrical power relations found in UK society. Moreover the institutions and process of British government that developed during this period helped to reinforce and re-narrate the BPT in an interactive and iterative manner.

Furthermore a clear relationship between the material position of the socio-economic elites and the development of the BPT can be detected. The development of the BPT helped to preserve the dominant position of the socio-economic and political elites throughout the 18th and 19th centuries by perpetuating ideas and practices that favoured them and their position. Undoubtedly they believed that more participatory notions of democracy were to be avoided at all costs. In the BPT popular sovereignty was reduced to periodic involvement through elections. Birch's view of the British approach to government as being characterised by 'first consistency, second accountability to Parliament, and third, responsiveness to public opinions and demands' (1964: 245) is prescient; however it should be characterised differently. UK democracy is best described as an elitist democracy in which the ideas and interests of dominant socio-economic groups have fundamentally shaped the ideas, institutions and processes of British political life.

Having explained the development of the central tenets of the predominant political tradition, we will now turn our attention to further exploring the relationship between the BPT and British political life.

5
The British Political Tradition and Political Life in the UK

Introduction

The British Political Tradition (BPT) is, as we have seen, the predominant political tradition in the UK. It comprises four interrelated discourses which have underpinned and informed political practice in the UK. These discourses developed across the 18th and 19th centuries, reflecting and reinforcing the dominant position and attitudes of socio-economic elites at a time of dramatic social-economic and political upheaval.

In this chapter we will turn attention to two key aspects of British political life. Firstly we will consider the impact the BPT has had on the institutions and processes of British government. Secondly we will consider the relationship between dominant socio-economic groups and the predominant political tradition.

The British Political Tradition and the institutions and processes of British government

The BPT has both informed and been inscribed into the institutions and processes of the British political system.[1] However this influence has not gone uncontested.[2] Nor have those institutions and processes remained unchanged.[3] Adaptations in response to challenges and contingent events have occurred. However they do so more often than not in a manner that fits neatly with pre-existing ideational, institutional and cultural norms.

In Chapter 1 we saw that there had been little comment on the relationship between the BPT and the WM. There has been a tendency to homogenise the two concepts without exploring the manner in which one has shaped, informed and/or supported the other. Consequently we will now turn to a brief discussion of the link between the BPT and the WM.

The British Political Tradition and the Westminster Model

As we saw in Chapter 1, the WM has been and remains the central organising perspective in British politics. However it has been increasingly criticised.[4] The observation that the WM offers an inaccurate or falsified view of British politics fits well with the notion of a difference between image and reality operating within the British political system. In reality, the WM is a legitimising narrative or self-image rather than an accurate description of the reality of British political life. However as Judge argues, the WM's 'usefulness is not in its factual accuracy. It is a set of norms, values and meanings prescribing legitimate government' (2006: 25).[5]

Official descriptions of the British political system continue to highlight the WM and the notion of its success.[6] The central tenets of the WM narrative were outlined earlier. Crucially it offers a very narrow view of 'the political' and portrays a 'largely static and fundamentally benign impression of Britain's central political institutions and processes' (Kerr and Kettell 2006: 7). In this a clear linkage between the institutions and processes described (albeit inaccurately) in the WM and the discourse concerning national distinctiveness exists. The point here is a simple one. The WM highlights key aspects of the British political system such as strong, centralised government but characterises them in a benign, self-congratulatory and ultimately unsatisfactory manner. It does so due to a failure to accurately recognise, perhaps unsurprisingly, the ideational and material roots of these institutions and processes. Or to put it another way, there is no attempt made by adherents of the WM to uncover the ideas and interests that shaped those institutions over time. Nor is there an attempt to see those institutions as the context within which ideas and interests develop. Furthermore the institutions and processes developed at Westminster act as key symbols and signifiers of the distinctiveness and superiority of the British political system and the BPT.

Moreover the institutions and practices described in the WM narrative are underpinned by the BPT. Central ideas such as parliamentary sovereignty and the unitary state are in reality expressions of the limited Liberal view of representation and the Conservative view of responsibility discussed above. For example the idea of the unitary state highlights the centralisation of sovereignty in 'Westminster and Whitehall' and the dominance of the Executive over all other forms of government. Indeed it suggests that all other forms of governance such as local or regional government exist only at the behest the centre. As such the idea of dominance by the centre was inculcated into understandings of territorial relations in the UK, despite the fact that the unitary state, in its crude form, did not fully capture the actual nature of those relations (Rokkan and Urwin 1982; Bulpitt 1983; Mitchell 2002).

Two points should be recognised. Firstly the description offered in the WM failed to capture the true nature of this centralisation and its elitist connotations. Rather territorial relations were portrayed as essentially democratic, undeniably desirable and the most efficient form of managing the UK. Contra this description, the dominance of the centre over the periphery historically can be better explained by reference to the idea that the UK was a 'dual polity' (Bulpitt 1983), as mentioned earlier. The potential for Executive dominance is central to the idea of a dual polity, even if this was not always or consistently actualised. Centre–periphery relations existed in the UK and the centre dominated via the control of key policy areas. Indeed it is worth noting that the centre had control of the policy areas that define the nation-state and thus could – and did – assert both its dominance and a sense of 'Britishness' through this. Notions such as the unitary state and parliamentary sovereignty were essential to achieve this, even if, in reality, some pre-union institutions in Scotland were left untouched, which in turn, kept a sense of Scottish political identity, albeit a limited one, alive.[7] Furthermore the administration of low politics by the periphery occurred within parameters set by the centre, Westminster, in most areas. Indeed as was mentioned in Chapter 1, the centre governed as it saw fit, with lower levels of governance mainly ensuring integration wherever possible (Mitchell 2001). Through this 'Westminster has enjoyed economic, political and ideological hegemony over the periphery' (Evans 2003: 223) historically.

Secondly these institutions and processes were themselves the context within which debates concerning UK territorial relations have then developed, with that context privileging certain ideas/solutions over others. That the unitary state never fully described the reality of territorial relations in the UK has in no way detracted from its impact. Key actors within and outside the British state have believed in the unitary state and continue to do so, despite this. Indeed Labour politicians have been conditioned, as much as Conservatives, to 'a simple and unmediated perspective of the Westminster Model' (Judge 2006: 368).[8]

The focus on politics at the centre and the dominance of the Executive at Westminster also highlights the extent to which the political role of the populace across the UK was to be limited to periodic participation via voting in elections. Government was to be primarily conducted by the political elite at the centre and the notion of parliamentary sovereignty would ensure that their dominance remained difficult to challenge. Indeed the strong, majoritarian government, which is a hallmark feature of the WM's narrative of the British political system, can easily be linked to elitism and the purported virtue of Executive dominance. If 'Westminster and Whitehall knows best' then it should be free to govern and the institutions and processes of British government should deliver this. Thus notions such as parliamentary sovereignty and strong, centralised government are essentially limited and elitist in terms of democracy.

On the influence of the BPT over the institutions and process of British government two further points can be made. Firstly Bourdieu's (1980) suggestion that culture helps to establish and maintain institutional hierarchies and that it embodies power relations is useful for explaining how patterns of behaviour at Westminster became replicated. The BPT established a set of institutions and practices that were informed by an elitist concept of democracy and the idea that 'Westminster and Whitehall knows best'. These then helped to inculcate and perpetuate patterns of elite dominance within the political system and outcomes that generally favoured their continued dominance. In particular institutions and processes developed that allowed this, as did cultural tendencies within and beyond these institutions. In turn these became the context for future debates and discourses, leading to a strategically selective environment that privileges certain ideas over others.

Secondly the institutions and processes described in the WM fitted neatly with the interests and ideas of socio-economic and political elites. Preston argues that 'The Westminster Model suited the British nineteenth century liberal market very well; a global trading system was run by the oligarchy most directly involved. Reforms and redistributions of power were available on the basis of success within the global system' (2004: 85).

These institutions helped them maintain their control of the political process in a period of economic upheaval and social change as we have seen. Again the convergence between the ideas and interests of the socio-economic and political elites and the political tradition they gave birth to can be detected. The institutions and processes of British government became the institutional expression of this.

To illustrate this point, we will turn briefly to two key processes to highlight how the BPT informs the institutions and processes of British government. Firstly the use of the Simple Plurality System (SPS) for Westminster elections is informed by and upholds the BPT and is one of the central tenets of its discourse concerning responsibility: 'Executive dominance'. The major attraction of SPS is that it invariably produces single-party governments that command a majority in the House of Commons (Marsh and Hall 2007). Since 1945 SPS has only failed to deliver a government with majority support in the House of Commons in February 1974 and May 2010 when the Conservatives won 306 seats, 20 short of an overall majority. Indeed the protracted negotiations following the 2010 election were somewhat uncharted waters in the recent history of Westminster politics as the Conservatives sought to build a coalition deal with the Liberal Democrats following their failure to secure an overall majority. Even governments with a slim majority are a rarity. Indeed since 1979 the smallest overall majority was that secured by John Major in 1992. With a majority of only 22, Major was still, for the most part, able to govern comfortably. At no point did he need to form an agreement with those outside of his party.

Majority support is generally seen as a prerequisite for strong government and is used as one of the primary arguments for the retention of SPS, despite it flaws. Although since 1997 more proportional systems such as AMS have been introduced elsewhere in the UK,[9] to date Westminster elections continue to be conducted using SPS. The equation of single-party governance with strength and coalition governance with weakness, has achieved an almost 'common-sense' status within debates regarding SPS. The emergence of stable Lab-Lib coalition governance in Scotland between 1999 and 2007 does not seen to have undermined this view. It remains to be seen whether the Conservative-Liberal Democrat coalition will last and even if it does there is no guarantee that it will affect the predominant view of coalition governance in the UK.

Furthermore debates concerning the retention or reform of SPS are conducted within an environment whose parameters have been shaped by the BPT. For example the terms of reference given to the Jenkins Commission highlights this trend. The commission was charged with ensuring that any reform guaranteed the continuance of strong government (Marsh and Hall 2007: 232). The emergence of the Conservative-Liberal Democrat coalition in May 2010 has raised the possibility of electoral reform for Westminster again. The Conservative leadership, whilst negotiating the coalition, relaxed their hostility to a referendum on electoral reform in order to gain power.[10] The Liberal Democrats, for their part, relaxed their demands for STV and accepted a referendum on the Alternative Vote (AV).[11] That AV is a non-proportional system which retains a clear constituency link and if utilised would, in many instances, result in single-party majoritarian government going forward, again suggests the imposition of a discursive selectivity on the perceived permissibility of options for reform. Moreover we should recognise that sizeable numbers of MPs from both the Conservative and Labour parties oppose change here, again suggesting the impact of pre-existing practices and procedures.

Secondly the secrecy that has cloaked the UK political system historically has also been informed by the BPT (Tant 1993; Batters 2005). For most of its existence the UK's democracy was one of the few democracies to operate without a statutory right to know. Other liberal democracies such as the USA and Sweden had such instruments from 1966 and, remarkably, 1766 respectively. In the UK, however, the idea prevailed that the government was the supreme arbiter of the national interest. Therefore if the government felt secrecy was needed, then that secrecy was in the national interest. This secrecy stems from the BPT and could be seen to be the apogee of the notion 'Westminster and Whitehall knows best'. Other liberal democracies, operating with more participatory or consensus concepts of democracy (Lipjhart 1999) in their political traditions, developed a statutory 'right to know' because maximising the information available on the government was a prerequisite for more frequent and meaningful participation beyond periodic elections. The recent attempt to tackle secrecy in the British political system through the introduction of Freedom of Information legislation operated within institutional and ideational parameters established by the BPT. Indeed the de-radicalisation of these proposals can be explained through use of the BPT concept (Batters 2005; Marsh and Hall 2007).

In summary, the argument here is simple. Underpinning the institutions and processes of the British political system was characterised as: an elitist concept of democracy, a faith in gradual, minimalistic change, a sense of national distinctiveness and superiority, and a belief in the virtue of these approaches. These institutions were themselves the context within which ideas were interpreted, experienced and developed over time. The WM narrative describes an image of the British political system rather than its reality because it ignores the structured inequality, asymmetrical power relations and elitism evident in British economic, social and political life. Key ideas such as parliamentary sovereignty and the unitary state can only be properly understood if situated alongside the political tradition they seek to narrate.

The nature of the link between the BPT and the institutions and process of British government is important given the purported shift to governance. Bevir and Rhodes argue: 'the governance narrative claims to capture recent changes in British government in the way the Westminster Model cannot' (2003: 54). On the surface the criticisms of the WM and 'the formal supplanting of the WM with that of the governance thesis and the Differentiated Polity Model, as the dominant organising perspective within the field of British politics' (Kerr and Kettell 2006: 13) would seem to lead to an inevitable conclusion. If the WM is no longer relevant and the BPT and the WM were in any way linked, then discussion of the BPT is no longer relevant. However to suggest this is to both misconceive the nature of the relationship between the two and the continued impact of the BPT on actors' attitudes.

The WM narrative described institutions and processes which were informed by the BPT. However it never accurately articulated them. Rather it gave a limited, benign and somewhat self-congratulatory description of the British political system. That the failings of the WM have been exposed is long overdue; however this does not detract from the existence of influence of the BPT and its elitism. Instead it suggests that those institutions and processes need to be examined more thoroughly in relation to their ideational and material roots. The WM narrative does remain important in one regard as was suggested earlier. The WM narrative continues to influence the attitudes and responses of actors within the British political system. As it legitimises elite rule, the WM's continued resonance with actors suggests that elitism and thus, the BPT, remain significant in shaping outcomes.[12]

Having outlined the relationship between the institutions and processes of UK government and the BPT, our attention will now turn to the relationship between the BPT and the views of actors in British politics.

The British Political Tradition and actors in British politics

Of fundamental importance in explaining the continued significance of the BPT is its resonance with actors. Generally it has been viewed as a superior democratic model and one that has set Britain on a peculiar, yet superior, developmental path. The BPT has, in the views of its adherents, provided for effective and efficient governance over time.

The resonance of the predominant tradition forms a crucial component in any explanation of its impact over time. Thus we must focus, albeit briefly, on the actors who have appealed to it so readily. Here we should make a crucial distinction between its appeal to the elites and its appeal to the wider population.

The role of the socio-economic and political elites in the UK is of fundamental significance to the development of the British political system over time (Gash 1979; Garrard 2002). In particular their ideas, interests and concerns to bring about the development of the predominant political tradition. However firstly we should focus on the political elite, that is to say, politicians and civil servants[13] and their attitudes. The suggestion here is that 'the British Political Tradition is inscribed not only in the institutions and processes of British politics, but also, and particularly, in the views of politicians and civil servants' (Marsh and Hall 2007: 228). A political tradition that stresses 'Westminster and Whitehall know best' fits easily with the interests and self-image of political elites because 'it reinforces the idea that the elite are knowledgeable and effective and everyone prefers such an image of themselves' (Marsh and Hall 2007: 28). Simultaneously, it reduces both scrutiny through emphasising secrecy and widespread participation to voting in periodic elections. This ensures that politicians and civil servants can operate with a degree of freedom and certainly do not have to worry about people 'looking over their shoulder'. Executive dominance too could be seen to have a similar impact in that through their dominance of Westminster and its business, they are able to control both decision-making and crucially, the agenda. Indeed the practices and processes to be found in Westminster and Whitehall can be seen to emanate from, and be supportive of, the BPT. In the attitudes of the political elite: 'the emphasis is on the need for strong and decisive, rather than responsive government' (Marsh, Richards and Smith 2001: 247).

It can also be seen that the majority of the populace has been largely supportive of the BPT over time. The BPT contains a set of cultural tendencies or beliefs that are widely held in UK society. Beer (1965) argues that faith in the BPT was widespread. This faith can be linked in part to the deferential attitudes of the populace[14] and the belief that those making decisions had the right to do so, based upon their superior wealth, knowledge and social position. However a political system that concentrates power and access in the hands of elites is well placed to steer a path through periods of criticism and declining support, offering minimal, gradual change, as we have seen.

Furthermore over time it was believed the British political system and the ideas that shaped it delivered strong and efficient government. This was encapsulated in the discourse concerning national distinctiveness which describes the British political system as superior and quintessentially British. This sense of Britishness was widely supported by members of the working class as evidenced by the widespread approval of nationalism and imperialism (Breuilly 1993). Even in the post-war period the British political system enjoyed widespread popularity and the ideas that underpinned it were left relatively unquestioned in popular discourse. As Norton argues, the British constitution 'used to be the subject of praise but little discussion' (1989: 10). This faith in its efficacy and superiority was crucial in maintaining popular support over time for the BPT.

Moreover the working class and their attitudes were important in inculcating support for the predominant tradition. The existence of a 'labour aristocracy' in the 19th century (Hobsbawm 1967) facilitated this. They argued against militancy and were hostile to the concept of class struggle. Politically, they tended to be supporters of the Liberal party and collaborationist in industrial relations. Moreover they tended to 'look down' on the rest of the working population and socially, this best-paid stratum of the working class merged with the lower middle class. It was they and their attitudes that were associated with the development of 'political fitness' or respectability c.1867. These attitudes were often characterised by loyalty to their employers, individualism and deference (McKibbon 1990). Crucially, they accepted the status quo and endorsed existing institutions such as the monarchy, Parliament and the idea that a parliament of elected representatives was the best way of securing the national interest. McKibbon argues that 'Crown and Parliament enjoyed an ideological hegemony which, if anything, increased throughout the century. The acceptability of both to the working class underwrote the existing status order and preserved the country's institutions and calls system more or less intact' (1990: 17).

This acceptance was based upon the fact that the Crown had, by the late 19th century, adopted the role of ensuring that the rules of the political game were followed, whilst Parliament performed the functional role of governance. Thus the monarchy appeared as a 'class-neutral' representation of the nation and one that signified Britain's distinctiveness from other Western nations. Indeed the monarchy was too deeply embedded in constitutional doctrine and popular consciousness ever to be seriously threatened[15] and this acted to stabilise, and on occasion, unify disparate political positions. Furthermore the British working class differed from that found in Europe. This was in part because 'a libertarian pattern of industrial relations obstructed that sense of fear and resentment which was characteristic of workers' attitudes on the continent' (McKibbon 1984: 324). Consequently an atmosphere of political conservatism pervaded much of the working class and they accepted the efficacy of existing institutions and approaches. Such attitudes were helpful to the inculcation of faith in the predominant political tradition and its discourses. Indeed the centrality of Parliament in the public's consciousness was ensured through the ritual of elections, both national and local. In this process 'the franchise was a political asset objectively worth possessing, elections themselves were crucial to the official ideology of Britain; they enhanced social stability and were a ritualized confirmation of a received form of political life' (McKibbon 1990: 21). Moreover this restricted the development of a working-class political consciousness in the UK which fundamentally critiqued existing political arrangements post Chartism.

Of course, there have been periods where faith in the BPT has dwindled and been challenged as alternative ideas have been promulgated through competing traditions and by different interests. Ideational conflict has been a hallmark feature of British history. Contingent events have been instrumental in promoting periods where the BPT has been challenged more fully than others. However challenges have to be made within an ideational and institutional environment that has been shaped by the predominant tradition. Even though faith in the BPT has been undermined since the 1970s (Marsh and Hall 2007) it still influences outcomes.

The socio-economic dimension

The idea of a predominant political tradition is based upon viewing the relationship between the ideational and the material as dialectical. As such we should briefly consider the relationship between the BPT and the socio-economic interests and relationships found in UK society over time.[16]

The BPT is not only a product of structured inequality found in British society historically, but also reinforces such inequality. This argument has two facets:

- Over time the predominant ideas of British political life were informed by the structured inequality of UK society. In this society a power bloc existed comprising socio-economic elites (Scott

1991). The political elite were largely recruited from this power bloc through various networks, processes and institutions. The BPT was both a reflection of and a narration of the alleged 'rightful position' of these elites, and it served to reinforce that position over time.
- This structural inequality remains a hallmark feature of contemporary British society to date and continues to be replicated in the membership of the political elite. Thus the predominant political tradition is linked to the ideas and interests of dominant economic groups. Furthermore the institutions and processes of British government privilege these groups and their interests.

Discussing the relationship between the political system and the socio-economic elite raises two central debates within socio-political analysis. Firstly we encounter debates concerning the relationship between socio-economic position and political power (Dunleavy and O'Leary 1987: Scott 2001).[17] Secondly we encounter discussions concerning 'the death of class' (Paluski and Waters 1996; Meiskins Wood 2000; Cannadine 2000).

Socio-economic elites and the British Political Tradition

The extent to which the capitalist state is run by and for dominant economic groups is one that has concerned 'left-leaning' political analysts of all persuasions throughout the post-war period. In particular the famous Miliband-Poulanztas debate in the 1970s[18] focused on this.

Miliband (1973) argued that the British political elite were largely drawn from the socio-economic elite, that is to say, the capitalist class. His contention was that there was direct control and interference by members of the ruling elite in the running of the capitalist state. They further entrenched their dominance through socialising those non-elite members of the state into the dominant values and ideas of the elite and manipulating the views of the populace so that they would support pro-capitalist policies. This view of the state in capitalist society was criticised by Poulantzas (1978) for being instrumentalist, agency-centric and for lacking empirical proof.[19] Poulantzas then developed the idea of 'relative autonomy' whereby the capitalist state seeks to regulate class conflict and perpetuate the capitalist system over time. To do this it requires a degree of 'relative autonomy' from the instrumental control of the capitalist class. Consequently rather than focusing on the personnel of the state we should consider the state as a structurally selective environment predisposed to forwarding the interests of capital in general. This view has itself not been free from criticism.[20]

However the notion that the state in capitalist society requires a degree of autonomy from the interests of capital can be a helpful one.[21] Later Miliband (2004) sought to accommodate consideration of the personnel of the state alongside the idea of 'relative autonomy'.[22] Similarly Scott (1991) argues that in certain circumstances, for instance an economic crisis, a government may develop policies that allow for the long-term continuation of capitalism, contra the immediate interests of the capitalist class.

Over time, there is a clear linkage between the political elite and the socio-economic elite based upon similarity of background and a series of networks that bind these groups together (Scott 1991; Bond 2007).[23] The existence of a power bloc in UK society unites the socio-economic and political elites over time. The process by which power blocs are constituted is a dynamic one and one whose membership has developed over a long period (Scott 1991; 1997). In contemporary UK society Scott suggests that it includes the major landowners and industrialists, commercial capital and merchants who are centred around a power elite, often referred to as the establishment (Scott 1991) in which the interests of the socio-economic elite are of paramount concern. Whilst we should be wary of understaning the political divisions and conflicts within classes, the idea of power blocs or: 'alignments of social groups, generally under the dominance of one of them, which is able to monopolize the levers of political powering society over a sustained period' (Scott 1991: 33) is a particularly telling one when applied to UK society historically.

Although power blocs change somewhat in their social composition over time, they remain 'exclusive' in their membership. This occurs through various strategies of class reproduction or social closure which allow for the reproduction of class dominance over time (Scott 1991). These include intermarriage and kinship connections, interconnected economic interests such as interconnected company directorships where individuals are directors of more than one company, exclusive educational background via attendance of certain public schools and universities, and cross-sphere contacts and linkages where individuals occupy various elite positions. Examples of such connections include MPs who are also company directors, former government ministers and civil servants who join the boards of private sector companies after they leave Whitehall, and business personnel who get appointed to quangos.

In the early 19th century the landed and commercial classes were the key elements in the power bloc that wielded political power. In the latter part of the 19th century powerful industrialists were incorporated into a new power bloc that comprised urban manufacturing capital alongside landed and commercial capital (Anderson 1987; Garrard 2002). In the latter part of the 20th century the UK witnessed the relative decline of manufacturing and the rise in power of 'the finance fraction' of the capitalist class (Coates 1984: 117). We should also acknowledge the interwoven nature of the City of London, the Bank of England and the Treasury (Coates 1984; Ingham 1984) and the existence of 'the Treasury view' (Kerr 2001). Through this focus on the mechanisms that allow for the reproduction of patterns of dominance, in particular through the education system, we can draw out the relationship between socio-economic inequality and political power in the UK.

Power blocs will always face demands and challenges. This conflict and contestation could and does take the form of ideational dispute. In order to maintain their dominance, these groups will have to offer concessions and create agreement from subordinate groups. This again points towards issues concerning conflict and change and continuity, suggesting that the process by which dominance is maintained is indeed a dynamic one and one that involves attempts to win support from subordinate groups (Gramsci 1971). Numerous social and political institutions and strategies might be employed by those within the power bloc to maintain their overall dominance and the centrality of their interests. For example the gradual extension of the franchise during the 19th and early 20th centuries was the accommodation of concessions albeit on the terms and at timings dominated by the socio-economic and political elites. Furthermore the development of a discourse on national distinctiveness can also be seen in this regard. Consequently the BPT was intrinsically linked to the desire of the socio-economic and political elites to maintain their dominance.

Historically the British political system was dominated by those from a socially exclusive background (Garrard 2002). In this sense the personnel of the British political system were drawn from a socio-economic elite comprised initially of the aristocracy and the commercial middle class and subsequently, in the 19th and 20th centuries, from a power bloc that included these groups and the industrial middle class. The political elite was then drawn from these groups through various networks including common social circles, attendance of certain educational establishments and membership of certain organisations and clubs. As we have seen, the ideas that shaped that political system, the

BPT, were ideas that derived from these groups and that were supportive to them. As such they were a reflection of the structural inequality in British society in terms of wealth, knowledge and power. In particular the emerging BPT reflected the concerns of the socio-economic and political elites in the face of the major social upheavals of the late 18th and 19th centuries and their desire to retain, as best as was possible, their dominant position in UK society. In turn the BPT came to narrate and reinforce the structured inequality of UK society, portraying it and elitism as both natural and desirable. Political institutions and processes that were developed reflected these ideas and they came to be the context through which dominant and competing ideas were experienced and viewed.

Structured inequality and the BPT

A second facet to this argument is that this structural inequality remains a hallmark feature of contemporary British society to date and continues to be replicated in the membership of the political elite. Patterns of recruitment to the political elite remain dominated by those who have attended certain educational establishments or undertaken certain occupations. These are also the province of the socio-economic elite (Scott 1991: Marsh 2008a). Thus the significance of socio-economic position within contemporary capitalist society remains. As Marsh, Richards and Smith argue: 'this structured inequality is reflected in the privileged access which some interests have to government, and thus it shapes, although by no means determines, political outcomes' (2001: 9). Or to put it another way 'white men with money, knowledge and power do have a privileged position within the British polity' (Marsh 2002a: 34). In this notion of structural inequality, an individual's class, gender, ethnicity and knowledge are all relevant in providing: 'actors with various structural possibilities, but any explanation of the outcomes must be in terms of both those structural possibilities and the strategic calculations of actors' (Marsh 2002a: 29).

Despite debates concerning the 'death of class' thesis (Paluski and Waters 1996; Meiskins Wood 1998; Cannadine 2000), class still remains a key factor in shaping the lifestyles, opportunities and attitudes of people in the UK (Roberts 2001), even with evident changes in the class structure in the UK. Alongside other key social divisions, primarily gender and ethnicity, UK society is characterised by structured inequality[24] in terms of class. Thus structured inequality continues to lead to inequalities of political resources that contribute to the privileging of the ideas and interests of dominant socio-economic groups. It can also be suggested that through various media the socio-economic and political elites are linked, not the least of which, by their faith in the BPT itself.

Structured inequality remained a hallmark feature of British society at the end of the 20th century, in that there was 'a persistent structural inequality that is reflected in access to money, knowledge and power; and these are the key resources used in the struggle for political influence' (Marsh 2002a: 29). On this the persistent and, in fact, growing gap between the wealthiest and poorest sections of UK society in recent years (Westergaard 1995; Marsh 2002a 27–8) should be noted. Furthermore: 'occupants of all capitalist locations are able to secure advantaged opportunities and life chances for themselves and for their families and they are able to live a life of privilege' (Scott 1991: 10).

Through a series of networks those with wealth, knowledge and power are able to advantage themselves and their life chances. Discussing the socio-economic elites, Crompton argues that similarities of background, club membership and political affiliation sustain a situation where 'the upper class in capitalist societies does manifest all the signs of being conscious of its material interests and capable of protecting them' (2000: 198). UK political elites are overwhelmingly white males who are middle class or above, if not by birth then by education. Thus membership of the political elite is itself a reflection of the structural inequalities found in capitalist society in the UK. For example Marsh and Hall (2007) point to the civil service and the extent to which its composition highlights an elitist social background. A similar point is in fact accepted by Bevir and Rhodes.[25]

This view can be extended to other members of the political elite in the UK, most notably politicians at Westminster (see Marsh 2002a: Table 2.3, ibid 30). For example British cabinets between 1970 and 1997 were dominated by those from a middle-class background or above, and by those who received a university education. In particular we should note the disproportionate influence of the middle classes and, when the Conservatives are in power, the aristocracy. Two observations can be made here. Firstly Pattie et al. (2004) clearly demonstrate how those of higher socio-economic status are more politically knowledgeable (2004: Table 3.7), more interested in and likely to discuss politics (2004: Tables 3.1 and 3.9) and crucially, more satisfied with British democracy generally (2004: Table 2.17). Thus they are more likely to be politically active (2004: Table 3.4) and to enter politics. Secondly the disproportional representation amongst UK politicians of those who have an elitist educational background through attending Oxbridge should be recognised.

Following the 2010 general election the composition of the Westminster Parliament highlighted a similar trend. Of the 650 MPs there were 143 females and 507 males. Women are significantly under-represented in the Lords, Holyrood, Stormont, and amongst the UK members of the European Parliament (Marsh 2008a: 262). In the Lords the figure was only 4 per cent, with the appointments procedure based upon 'the great and the good' criteria clearly acting as an impediment in a society where structured inequality creates both a glass ceiling for women and those from minority ethnic communities. There were only 27 MPs from a minority ethnic background. Similar trends for the under-representation of women and those from a minority ethnic background can be detected if we look at membership of quangos and local councils. One notable figure for the present discussion is that in 2005 women made up just 28 per cent of the senior civil service.

On the educational background of MPs a disproportionate representation of those who come from an environment of wealth, knowledge and power can be identified. The Sutton Trust reported in December 2005 that almost 32 per cent of MPs had attended an independent school, whilst only 7 per cent of the population was educated in this way, and a further 25 per cent had attended state grammar schools which were academically selective. This research is supported by House of Commons research (House of Commons SN 1528: 2005). Only 42 per cent of MPs had attended a comprehensive school even though such schools account for the education of the majority of the UK's youngsters. Seventy-two per cent of MPs had attended university compared to 34 per cent for the population as whole, with 43 per cent of those having attended one of the leading 13 universities[26] and 27 per cent having attended Oxbridge.[27] Eight of those in Cabinet in 2011 and six of the Shadow Cabinet studied Philosophy, Politics and Economics at Oxford. In total a third of the Labour Shadow Cabinet in 2011 also attended Oxbridge.

In terms of previous occupation the main groups represented amongst the current crop of MPs are from professional occupations and business (House of Commons SN 1528: 2005). This research also notes the increase in the number of MPs coming from the politician/political organiser category.[28] On the basis of the evidence it can be concluded that the majority of politicians are drawn from a socially exclusive background in which wealth, knowledge and power are the key resources and these are more likely to be available to those who have attended certain educational institutions and/or entered certain occupations. This trend is accentuated when senior government positions are assessed.

Focusing on the socio-economic elites we find a largely similar educational background. Only 7 per cent of UK children attend independent schools. Of the 'top' public schools the average live-in fee is c. £25,000 per annum.[29] It hardly needs saying that with schooling fees often higher than the national average income, independent schooling is open primarily to those with wealth and other key resources such as knowledge.[30] A perception of the superiority of these establishments and a recognition of the impact they have on life chances leads to a pattern of self-recruitment and closure amongst socio-economic elites. Turning to elite universities, research shows that whilst the percentage of those attending 'elite universities'[31] from state schools has increased since 1997, there remains a large degree of disproportionality of representation between fee-paying and state schools. For example 45 per cent of those attending Oxford in 2002-3 had attended a fee-paying school. At Cambridge the figure was 42 per cent.[32] The Sutton Trust (2005b) notes the extent to which UK judges and barristers have also attended independent schools and/or Oxbridge: in 2004 84 per cent of barristers and 81 per cent of judges attended Oxbridge. Recent research has also highlighted the extent to which leading journalists can also be seen to have a similar educational background (Sutton Trust 2006): over half of the UK's leading journalists attended a fee-paying school, with 37 per cent having attended the University of Oxford. Therefore a persistent pattern of structured inequality in relation to class, gender and ethnicity in UK society can be detected. These socio-economic elites, due to the advantages they have in terms of wealth, knowledge and power, are able to access educational institutions in far greater proportions. This in turn leads them to have greater life chances and for a greater number to occupy key positions in UK society.

These socio-economic elites are bound together, and to the political elite, through networks:

> which stem from family and education. Such contacts are maintained largely in an informal manner by membership of London clubs, by the social round of dinners and parties as well as more formally, in business meetings and at official events. The contacts which constitute this informal network of social relationships are important in the determination of the life chances of those who go through the public school and Oxbridge system. Their contacts both facilitate their careers and enable them to have more influence in the posts where they eventually land. (Scott 1982: 159-60)

These networks and relationships (Abercrombie and Warde 2001) which, in the past, bound the socio-economic and political elite to each other through kinship relations, marriage, financial and business relationships and common background, particularly education continue to operate today (Bond 2007). The extent to which the socio-economic elite remains a socially exclusive group that has privileged access to key resources in capitalist society and greater opportunities generally, can be demonstrated. We can undoubtedly find examples of current members of the socio-economic elite who have not been socialised via these networks, but as Abercrombie and Warde (2002) suggest, commonality of outlook and frequent contact as well as a similar material position will help to inculcate those initially outside of networks into them.

As we have noted, the political elite is largely drawn from and connected to the socio-economic elites through educational and social networks (Bond 2007) rooted in the structured inequality of UK society. Therefore we can conclude that 'Britain is ruled by a capitalist class whose economic dominance is sustained by the operations of the state and whose members are disproportionately represented in the power elite which rules the state apparatus' (Scott 1991: 151). However one point warrants repetition here. Focusing on the networks that give rise to a high degree of self-recruitment and social closure does not deny the notion of 'relative autonomy'. Both the state and government retain a degree of relative autonomy (Poulantzas 1978), facilitated by a political tradition which emphasises 'Westminster and Whitehall know best'. Jessop (1988) argue that at times political elites may impose policies or programmes 'for the good of the nation', even when these may damage the short-term interests of capital. A political tradition that stresses elitism and the notion of 'Westminster and Whitehall know best' facilitates this, particularly if inscribed into its institutions and processes. Belief in the BPT amongst the socio-economic elite assists in this process. Despite short-term losses, the acceptance that the political elite is acting in the broader interests of the nation and thus the long-term interests of capital, facilitates relative autonomy for political actors. Moreover as we have seen already elite groups accept the logic of the BPT and its four discourses.

Therefore the BPT has dovetailed neatly over time with the interests of the socio-economic elites. Through this they have been able to dominate the political process and have an influence over outcomes. That is not to say that their interests are always served in policy outcomes at the expense of other groups.[33] Rather it is to suggest that in the strategically selective environment of the British state, those actors will be better equipped, in terms of key resources, to develop strategies that allow for the maintenance of their dominance. At times this may involve concessions to the subordinate groups arising from contestation and conflict of predominant ideas and policies. Again the incremental expansion of the franchise in the 19th and early 20th centuries could be cited here. At other times this may involve not responding to the demands of subordinate groups and opposing those who offer a wholesale alternative, such as the Chartists in the 1840s, as it is important to recognise that contestation and conflict do not always result in change. Throughout these contestations the significance of a belief in the BPT cannot be understated or ignored.

In this we should also recognise that rather than having a strong state tradition, the UK has a strong government tradition. The UK has never developed a state that intervenes extensively in UK society and, in particular, in economic relations (Marquand 1988). This could clearly be explained through reference to the relationship between dominant socio-economic interests and the BPT, which emphasises the virtue of strong, decisive government. The BPT facilitates the needs of dominant socio-economic interests because it has seen the development of institutions and processes that allow for the management of the capitalist economy. Without recourse to intervention these interests would deem excessive and damaging to capital accumulation over time. As such, dominant economic interests would favour a political tradition that stresses that the political elite should be largely free to act as they will. That is not to say that the British state has not been interventionist at times, for example, during the post-war period. However the predominance of 'the Treasury View' in economic policy should be recognised. This emphasises a fundamentally negative view of the state and its role in the economy and involves 'a more or less permanent state posture of menace and rejection' (Kerr 2001: 143) towards state intervention. Nor is it to deny the 'relative autonomy' of the capitalist state. Rather it is to suggest that the interests of socio-economic elites can be served and fostered over time more effectively by a strong government tradition, such as the BPT.

It should also be noted here that this is even more the case given the need for governments to please business (Scott 1997; Philips 1999). As such the notion of a strong government tradition dovetails neatly with the interests of dominant economic groups and would certainly be preferable to an interventionist state that may regulate capitalism and/or undermine their dominance. The privileging of certain interests linked to dominant positions in the socio-economic system is relevant here. Philips (1999: 17–18) argues that:

> the conditions of corporate capitalism constrain the exercise of popular control, making the supposed freedom and equality of citizens a desperately unbalanced affair...The point here is not just that the wealthy find it easier to disseminate their views, to finance newspapers, launch pressure groups, lunch Prime Ministers. More troubling (because it is more systematic) is the fact that all governments depend upon the process of capital accumulation as the sources of incomes, growth and jobs, and must therefore ensure that the economic policies they pursue do not undermine the prosperity of the private sector. This structured privileging of corporate power means that the democratic playing field is never level.

In such an environment a political tradition that emphasises elitism and strong, decisive government fits neatly with this as it allows the political elite to offer policies that privilege the interests of dominant socio-economic groups, whilst simultaneously narrating these as in the national interest. The institutions and processes of government shaped by the BPT also facilitate the privileging of these interests (Marsh, Richards and Smith 2001) as do the asymmetries of power evident in the UK. That is not to say that the ideas and interests of socio-economic and political elites will always triumph. Rather it is to suggest that the BPT and its institutions and processes impose a selective bias towards strategies that fit neatly with established notions. In this process socio-economic elites are in a comparatively better position to develop such strategies given their superior political resources and access. The perception that the British political system and its institutions and processes have delivered economic prosperity and advantage for elite groups over time would also help to further their continued faith in the BPT.

Conclusion

In this chapter we have focused on how the predominant political tradition has been inscribed into the institutions and process of British government, thus becoming the context through which the tradition is experienced, updated and challenged. The BPT has enjoyed widespread support amongst both the socio-economic and political elites and the wider population over time. In particular the relationship between dominant socio-economic interests and the BPT should be recognised. The argument here is simple. The BPT is both a product of and supportive to the structured inequality and asymmetries of power in UK society. In particular this inequality has led to a close relationship between dominant socio-economic interests and the political elite in the form of a power bloc. This power bloc has been supportive of the BPT because it allowed their dominance and narrated it as effective, allowing the pursuit of policies largely favourable to them.

Having outlined the predominant political tradition operating in the UK we will now turn our attention to two competing political traditions which have, over time, contested aspects of or the entirety of the BPT.[34]

6
The Participatory Tradition

Introduction

In Chapters 4 and 5 we focused on the predominant political tradition in UK politics, the BPT. The BPT has had a decisive impact upon British political life over time, helping to shape the institutions, process and practices of British politics. However it has not gone uncontested or unchallenged.[1] Rather it has been critiqued and contested throughout British history by competing political traditions.

Competing political traditions offer alternative views of how politics should be conducted and are often advocated by those seeking to challenge and change the nature of politics and even social organisation within a nation. They may also be advocated by those seeking power and influence from within the political system. These traditions critique both the discourses of the predominant tradition and the institutions, processes and practices informed by it. Indeed continual ideational contestation is the backdrop for British politics (Bevir and Rhodes 2003; 2006b; Marsh and Hall 2007; Marquand 2008). There exists a long lineage of such challenges in the UK and that it is from these that change can and does, emanate. The next two chapters explain two competing traditions: the first focuses on what can be referred to as the participatory tradition.[2] This primarily contests the discourses concerning representation and responsibility at the heart of the BPT. The second considers the nationalist tradition. This contests the territorial relations and concept of national identity established by the BPT. These traditions have on occasion coalesced in the views of those demanding constitutional change in the UK.

Before focusing on the participatory tradition two key ideas warrant repetition. Firstly the resonance of the BPT and the challenges to it have not been equivalent over time. Rather an asymmetrical resonance of these traditions can be detected. Moreover competing traditions have resonated to differing degrees of intensity at differing times in British political history.[3] To explain this phenomenon we should consider the impact of contingent events, be they major points of crisis (Hay 1996) or the result of cumulative ideational contestation (Kerr 2002). Both of these can be tied to the perceived failings of the political system over time. Moreover predominant and competing traditions resonate asymmetrically in relation to the prevailing institutional, contextual and discursive environment. Consequently the BPT has and does resonate more fully. However it should be noted here that 'if the efficacy of the British political system and the view of democracy that underpins it become increasingly questioned... then this may lead to change' (Marsh and Hall 2007: 227).

Secondly whilst ideational conflict has and remains a hallmark feature of British politics we should also recognise that competing traditions contest the predominant tradition at either a macro or a micro level. More often than not, this means challenging aspects of the political system. We have examples of this from the various groups that demanded the extension of the franchise in the 19th and early 20th centuries. However on occasions they challenged numerous facets, as in the case of Chartism, or its entirety, as in the case of Charter 88. Similarly these contestations can account for change at both a macro and micro level. Two points are worth repeating here. Firstly the relationship between the predominant and competing traditions is interactive and iterative over time, in that conflict can and does produce both continuity and change. Secondly such contestations occur within an institutional and ideational context that privileges certain ideas and solutions over others.

Having outlined the idea of competing political traditions, we will now turn to an explanation of the participatory tradition.

The participatory tradition

Examining British political history we can readily identify the existence of a competing political tradition that appeals to a more participatory concept of democracy. This contestation has a long lineage amongst the work of numerous individuals and groups. Furthermore its development and resonance has occurred in relation to contingent events both nationally and globally. This competing tradition primarily challenges the discourses concerning representation and responsibility detailed in

Chapter 4. In this it draws its lineage back to Athenian Democracy[4] and the original meaning of democracy with 'the people governing themselves, without mediation through chosen representatives, directly or, if necessary, by the rotation of governing offices among the citizens' (Arblaster 1994: 60). It seeks to maximise the participation of all members of the adult population in decision-making and to widen the opportunities for those able to do so. A faith in political (and often social) equality and thus the competence of all citizens manifests itself via a stressing of popular sovereignty, frequent political participation, active involvement in public affairs and accountability to the populace. Indeed in the eyes of its advocates it is viewed as 'real' democracy as it offers more direct participation in decision-making. Furthermore the participatory tradition draws from civic republicanism and, in recent times, radical democracy.[5] From the former it draws the ideas of widespread discussion and debate amongst the citizenry and 'a commitment to the common good that is the essence of civic virtue, rather than partial interest, still less material self-interest' (Dryzek and Dunleavy 2009: 214). In its contemporary form the participatory tradition seeks to maximise popular sovereignty and to widen and deepen[6] political participation because the 'closer a community comes to realizing the democratic ideal of self-government, the more the conventional the distinction between government and governed is dissolved' (Arblaster 1994: 60). Furthermore contemporary advocates of this tradition such as Unlock Democracy or Power 2010 often appeal to some of the institutions and processes associated with a consensus model of democracy (Lijphart 1999).[7]

Turning to the development of the participatory tradition, challenges to the elitist system of rule have a long history in the UK. They can be traced back through English/British history to well before the debates between Whigs and Tories in the 18th and early 19th centuries. From well documented examples such as the 1381 Peasants Revolt,[8] through Jack Cade's Rebellion of 1450, to Kett's rebellion in 1549, the contestation of aspects of the system of rule in England and its social and political norms can readily be identified. Crucially, these disparate movements advocated greater involvement for the population and a measure of both political and legal equality. Furthermore prior to and during the British Civil Wars of the 1640s various groups sought to challenge the political and social status quo. The radical groups that emerged during this period did so 'from a society that was already religiously divided and in which social relations were severely strained' (Vallance 2009: 141). Indeed religious radicalism was hugely significant in promoting challenges to the political and social order (McGregor and Reay 1984). However it was the events of the 1640s[9] that promoted the emergence of radical political and religious groups 1646–47, the most celebrated of which are the Levellers[10] and the Diggers. The former, through their petitions[11] and finally through *The Agreement of the People* (1647), sought to further the rights of 'freeborn Englishmen'[12] on the basis of political equality. They demanded political rights, religious toleration, legal equality and justice for all. For example *The Agreement* (lines 20–5) states: 'That the people do choose themselves a Parliament once in two years... That the power of this and all future Representatives of this Nation is inferior only to those who choose them'. This can be seen as an early statement in favour of popular sovereignty and accountability. Thomas Rainsborough's avocation of government by consent during The Putney Debates July 1647[13] is further evidence of this.

The Diggers[14] advocated views of politics and society that constituted a challenge to the established order and the predominant ideas of the time[15] (Hill 1984; Meiksins Wood and Wood 1997). On notions concerning governance Winstanley (1652) argued for a society with 'no Kings, lords, lawyers or priests, and the commonwealth will be governed by older (male) citizens... (and) a national parliament of members over forty, elected by all male citizens'[16] (Meiksins Wood and Wood 1997: 88). Like the Levellers before them, the Diggers argued from a premise of political equality[17] in favour of government by consent and, more radically than Levellers such as Lilburne and Overton, the abolition of private ownership.

By the 1650s civil war radicalism had been largely defeated and during the Restoration (1660) radical ideas had been driven back (Thompson 1980). With them, notions about popular sovereignty and the widening and deepening of participation were also reduced in their resonance. The Glorious Revolution (1688) occurred on parameters narrated by Locke (1690).[18] In the context of his time Locke's ideas were radical. However despite his use of Leveller rhetoric, his radicalism had more in common, politically, with that of Cromwell or Ireton (Meiksins Wood and Wood 1997). Whilst he opposed absolutism, he sought to limit the democratic implications of his own argument. Indeed Locke's argument for government by consent was not based upon universal suffrage, popular sovereignty or participation but rather on what amounts to 'virtual representation'. As we saw in Chapter 4, it was this view and the associated interpretation of history that Whigs such as Burke forcefully proffered in the late 18th century. Parliament could represent the various interests of the people without direct election or frequent participation by the population. Indeed representation was seen as 'a means of limiting popular participation and control, and retaining the day to day powers of government in the hands of a (preferably enlightened) elite' (Arblaster 1994: 60).

Despite the activities of John Wilkes in the mid 18th century and the Society for Constitutional Information (1780), contestation of the ideas and institutions of the British polity only truly re-emerged in the wake of the upheavals of 1789. At this point, it was largely manifested as demands for wider participation and popular sovereignty in the form of the extension of the franchise and the ending of corruption. British Jacobins such as Coleridge and Wordsworth enthusiastically supported the revolution in its early stages, whilst the formation of the Sheffield Society for Constitutional Information (SSCI) in 1791 and the London Corresponding Society (LCS) in 1792 saw the revival of popular radicalism (Wright 1988). Furthermore individuals such as John Cartwright, John Horne Tooke and Thomas Hardy were instrumental in raising the cause of parliamentary reform. In Scotland in 1792–93 a number of societies were established that advocated French egalitarian symbolism.[19] Most notably for the development of the participatory tradition were writers such as Paine (1791) and Wollstonecraft (1795). Their ideas would decisively influence this tradition and later advocates of constitutional reform as we will see shortly.

It should be noted that the late 18th century 'British Radical Tradition'[20] (Derry 1967; Vallance 2009) was in no way a homogenous or uniform movement. Rather the socio-economic composition of groups differed and there were regional variances.[21] As a consequence, demands for parliamentary reform were geographically and socially uneven (Dickinson 1985). Furthermore divisions existed over the extent of reform that was desirable and the manner in which it could/should be brought about (Wright 1988). Indeed many Jacobin societies were unwilling to fully adopt Paineite republicanism, vigorous rationalism or the package of social and economic reforms outlined in the second volume of *The Rights of Man* (1792). Most artisan societies were genuinely democratic; however those with significant propertied influence hoped to restrict the vote to the propertied and the educated, thus excluding the labouring masses whom they viewed with suspicion and no small measure of disdain. Indeed whilst many societies boasted an alliance of middle-class radicals and skilled artisans, unskilled workers and casual labourers seem to have been largely unaffected by democratic and republican ideals c.1790. Thus whilst the social composition of these radical societies was new, it fell short of mass support or a genuinely working-class movement. In fact it was patriotism that resonated most widely once war with France began in 1793. Mass support for parliamentary reform tended to occur during times of economic downturn, unemployment and agricultural depression.

That said, whilst recognising differences of both content and context, we should not ignore the ideational, material and cultural continuities in these demands for political reform. These groups, however disparate, were united in their desire to see the political system based upon something other than elite rule. Thus they favoured thorough political and, on occasion social, change. Politically, this meant adopting a system of rule based upon popular sovereignty and wider and, in time, deeper political participation. The demands of groups such as the LCS and the SCCI are indicative of this desire to move in a more democratic direction. The impetus for such demands was to be found in the socio-economic and political upheavals of the late 18th century and responses to them. Although popular radicalism c.1790 often fell short of advocating universal suffrage, it did challenge key aspects of the elitist system of rule in the UK. As such at this point we can see the participatory tradition in its embryonic form. In this emergent competing tradition, writers such as Paine (1791; 1792) and Wollstonecraft (1795) were hugely influential.

Paine and Wollstonecraft

The significance of Paine's ideas to the upheavals of the late 18th century cannot be underestimated. His works *Common Sense* (1776) and *The American Crisis* (2008) were instrumental in the American struggle for independence (Nelson 2007). However it was *The Rights of Man*, (1791; 1792) which truly established his position within the participatory tradition. In it Paine:

> rejected the legacy of the past, including the Glorious Revolution of 1688 which he dismissed as sanctifying oligarchy and property, rather than liberty. All men were created equal and possessed natural rights of life, liberty, property and the pursuit of happiness. Governments should be subject to the sovereign will of the people and a written constitution. Hereditary titles, honours and privileges were iniquitous. (Wright 1988: 42)

Paine (1791; 1792) gave uncompromising voice to a burgeoning anti-elitist democratic tradition and was an inspirational figure for radical thinking and agitation both in the late 18th and 19th centuries (Derry

1967). He savaged the Whig narrative of 'an ancient constitution' as an illusion, arguing instead that government in England, based upon power, conquest and 'the usurpation of popular sovereignty...merely set new bounds to the exercise of royal tyranny' (Vallance 2009: 234). Paine also vigorously defended the French Revolution and critiqued the elitism that pervaded UK society in the form of monarchical and aristocratic rule. For example he famously stated that 'the idea of hereditary legislators is as inconsistent as that of hereditary judges, or hereditary juries; and as absurd as a hereditary mathematician, or a hereditary wise man' (Paine 1791: 63).

Clearly such attacks on the idea of hereditary principle suggest a competing view of political fitness to that advocated by Burke (1790) and highlight his belief in the equality of men and republicanism. Such sentiments also point towards the need to reform the second Chamber.[22] Indeed Paine favoured the full-scale abolition of the House of Lords. Political rights for Paine came from the laws of nature and reason. All men, whatever their status, were entitled to equal citizenship because at birth they were both free and equal. Paine's avocation of representation as 'a means of adapting the democratic principle to societies, such as the United States, which were too large to allow for personal participation by all their citizens' (Arblaster 1994: 8) stood in contrast to the elitism of Burkeian 'trusteeship'. He challenged the corruption, oppression and lack of responsibility in elite rule (Paine 1791: 130–32). Indeed Paine (1792: 173) stressed his admiration for Athenian democracy and argued that 'representation' should be seen as a means by which the impracticalities of direct democracy could be overcome, rather than the manner by which elite rule could be preserved. Finally he was deeply hostile to attempts to portray politics as something that ordinary people could not understand. He stated that 'the people's enemies take care to represent government as a thing made up of mysteries, which only they understand' (1792: 163), again demonstrating hostility towards the elitism that would later crystallise as the mantra 'Westminster and Whitehall knows best'.

Paine's arguments were not original. However he inspired both fear and loathing, and praise in almost equal measure. His power came not only from the ideas themselves, but also from his ability to express them in accessible language. Indeed he 'unshackled radicalism from its subaltern role in the unofficial opposition' (Belchem 1981 cited in Wright 1988: 42) and raised it to the status of an ideational challenge to the predominant political ideas of the late 18th and early 19th centuries. Paine stressed the need for popular (albeit male) participation and representative democracy. This and his rejection of the Whig interpretation of history set his ideas in direct opposition to those ideas and discourses that, by the 20th century, formed the BPT.

Mary Wollstonecraft's *A Vindication of the Rights of Woman* (1795) was as important to the development of the participatory tradition in the UK in that it espoused the idea of political equality and participation in a wider sense by suggesting that gender should be no impediment to political involvement.[23] Most radical discourse up to this point was 'grounded in values and faculties that were deemed to be almost exclusively masculine' (Vallance 2009: 242). In particular reason or a lack thereof, was often cited to explain women's position in society and it was on this that Wollstonecraft focused her attention. Reacting against the prevalent patriarchy of much of the Enlightenment thinking associated with 'the rights of man' (Kennedy and Mendus 1987), she sought to repudiate the ideas of Talleyrand and Rousseau. By doing this she challenged the prevalent stereotype of women as incapable of reason, education and simply made for man's pleasure. This stereotype was widely believed and inscribed into the institutions and processes of British government and its outcomes.[24] Wollstonecraft insisted that 'women had an independent right to education, employment, property and the protection of the civil law' (Bryson 1992: 24). Whilst her work focused mostly on nature and education, she did briefly touch on female suffrage, stating: 'I really think that women ought to have representatives, instead of being arbitrarily governed without having any direct share allowed them in the deliberations of government' (1795: 151). Furthermore she offered a critique of elite rule stating that 'the more equality there is established among men, the more virtue and happiness will reign in society' (1795: 15). Through this work, Wollstonecraft offered a competing view to the male-dominated elitism of the emerging BPT in her suggestion that women should be representatives in government (Wollstonecraft 1795: 25).

The significance of Paine and Wollstonecraft to the participatory tradition's development is that they both proffered a view of British politics rooted in political equality, the rights of the individual and the capabilities of all based upon reason. This ran contra the elitism of Burke and the Whig discourse of representation. Paine in particular was quite visceral in his criticism of the elites. Both authors were also wholeheartedly rejected by those elites as dangerous and subversive (Thompson 1980). Their belief in popular consent and participation was directly at odds with the view that governance should be conducted by those already in power, that is to say, the socio-economic elite. In both cases the emergence of an important contestation of the prevalent elitism of the BPT can be seen. It was through the work of these two seminal socio-political theorists that, over time, the participatory tradition became more firmly established.

The 19th century and the emergence of the participatory tradition

In the aftermath of the Napoleonic Wars, demands for parliamentary reform in the UK fluctuated in relation to contingent events, particularly those relating to the economy. This period saw further steps towards the development of the participatory tradition. However we should recognise that these challenges took both the form of macro and micro challenges to the emerging predominant tradition. Indeed many of these contestations targeted the most obvious excesses and failings of British political life and its system of elite rule. As the postwar depression took hold agitation for reform grew, culminating in the infamous Peterloo Massacre (1819). For example in 1817, 700 petitions demanding political reform were submitted to Parliament, with 60 per cent coming from the heartlands of the Industrial Revolution, such as the Midlands and the North of England (Eastwood 1972: 76). By the 1820s, although reform had not been achieved the foundations of the reform movement that powerfully emerged c.1830 had been firmly laid. Once the Tory hegemony disintegrated c.1827–29, the way was open for the revival of reform and the emergence of political unions, inspired by Attwood's Birmingham Political Union and its campaign for improved representation at Westminster.[25] Between 1830 and 1832 numerous societies were established as the reform crisis gripped the country (Cannon 1973; Thompson 1980). However the resultant 1832 Reform Act did little to address the demands for popular sovereignty and wider and deeper participation. Indeed as O'Gorman notes: 'the men, the institutions, the values and the practices were remarkably similar either side of 1832' (1989: 392).

It was dissatisfaction with 1832, alongside other factors, that inspired one of the iconic movements of the participatory tradition, Chartism. The six points of the People's Charter published in 1838 highlight a challenge to the elitist concept of democracy that was coming to dominate the British political system. Chartism was the culmination of the radical technique adopted since the end of the Napoleonic Wars of a constitutional campaign married to a mass movement, agitation and petitioning. Ideationally the influence of Paine (1791; 1792) and

Cobbett can readily be seen.[26] The socio-economic roots of Chartism have been a source of debate (Belchem 1981; Thompson 1984) as has the role played by language and culture in Chartism (Stedman-Jones 1983; Vernon 1993). However the political demands that arose out of these are beyond doubt. In seeking the establishment of a political system based upon universal male suffrage over 21,[27] the secret ballot and the removal of wealth and property as a determinant of participation, Chartism was significantly at odds with the predominant views of the socio-economic and political elites. Furthermore the Chartists advocated annual parliaments, equally sized constituencies and payments for MPs. Underpinning these demands was a belief in political equality contra the predominant notion of political 'fitness', popular sovereignty contra elite rule, and wider and more frequent participation contra the limited franchise and participation found in mid 19th century British politics. Taken together, these can be seen as contesting the predominant ideas of British political life c.1840 and became central tenets of the participatory tradition over time.

To explain the emergence and resonance of Chartism we should undoubtedly recognise the impact of contingent events such as the 1834 Poor Law Amendment Act and its consequences, the economic depressions of the late 1830s and 1840s, and the general disappointment felt by many towards the 1832 Reform Act. Chartism was driven forward by the socio-economic hardships of the day and the belief that political change offered a solution to these. Following the failure of the third Chartist petition in 1848, the emerging participatory tradition receded.[28] However two points should be recognised. Firstly whilst the Chartists failed to achieve their political aims,[29] they mobilised ordinary men and women in asserting their rights as citizens of the UK.[30] This enabled people to learn a great deal about political ideas and about how to organise themselves and it allowed a sense of class identity to develop further. They and their activities have been an iconic source of inspiration for numerous later movements including the Trade Unions, the Labour Party and, more recently, Charter 88. For this reason, the Chartists should be viewed as one of the key groups within the participatory tradition.

Demands for parliamentary reform did continue following the demise of Chartism.[31] However it was not until the early 1860s that political reform fully returned to the agenda. Here, the activities of the National Reform Union (1864)[32] and the Reform League (1865)[33] are worthy of note, as well as the impact of international events such as the Risorgimento. The latter had whittled the wide-ranging demands of

Chartism down to the sole issue of universal male suffrage, whilst the former focused on four parliamentary reforms: triennial Parliaments, the introduction of the secret ballot, equal distribution of seats and the extension of the franchise to male ratepayers. Despite their differences, it was their agitation that again helped raise demands for parliamentary reform and, in particular the extension of the franchise. Both groups advocated an increase in popular sovereignty and a widening of democracy and were, in their own way, adherents to the emerging participatory tradition. That their demands coalesced primarily on issues around the franchise highlights how adherents to the emergent participatory tradition often sought to redress the most obviously undemocratic facets of British political life rather than its entirety.

Despite the activities of the Reform groups, it was factors such as a typology of political fitness/unfitness[34] and party political intrigues that were crucially important in influencing the eventual outcome of reform in 1867 (Cowling 2005). However in the context of this discussion, one noteworthy moment in the debates of 1866–67 occurred when, having received a petition from the Kensington Society[35] in favour of female suffrage, J. S. Mill sought to amend the Reform Bill and enfranchise women on the same criteria as men. The vote on 20 May 1867 saw some 73 MPs supporting the enfranchisement of women, with 196 against. Mill's proposal was a modest one, pushing essentially for the enfranchisement of spinsters and widows rather than all women by substituting the word man with person in the section of the bill dealing with property qualifications. Like the Bill itself, this amendment fell some way short of democracy.[36] However Mill's amendment suggested that gender should not be an impediment to participation.[37] Furthermore as the first attempt to undermine the patriarchal facet of elitism in British political life it is noteworthy, as is the impetus given to Mill's actions by those advocating a more participatory concept of democracy and the inspiration it reciprocated.

Further political reforms occurred in 1872, 1883 and 1884/85. The first of these sought to tackle corruption and the influence of wealth and was something that radicals such as Paine and later John Bright had campaigned for.[38] The 1872 Ballot Act introduced the secret ballot to British politics. Its opponents maintained that an open declaration of support was 'honourable', 'manly' and 'English', whereas the secret ballot was 'cowardly' and 'continental'. Furthermore they argued that it supported paternalism and deference and was, above all, traditional. Contra this, proponents of the secret ballot such as the Philosophical Radicals, and Bright argued that secrecy and independence would allow for the freer exercise of popular sovereignty, they believed to be essential with the post-1867 growth of the electorate.[39] The 1883 Corrupts and Illegal Practices introduced limitations on electioneering and election spending. This sought to improve the process by which elections were conducted. However as with the 1872 Ballot Act it did not radically alter the discourse concerning representation, or later responsibility, despite their anti-elitist, democratic progeny. Finally in 1884/85 parliamentary reform returned to the agenda with the further extension of the franchise and redistribution of seats. Despite some campaigning from the radicals and Joseph Chamberlain's 'The Peers vs. The People' campaign in October 1884,[40] this change was not the result of popular struggles for democratisation but rather the political machinations of the ageing leaders, Gladstone and Salisbury (Hayes 1982). Indeed the resistance of Gladstone to Chamberlain's attempts to force reform of the Lords onto the agenda and the Unauthorised Programme published in July 1885[41] is notable (Rhodes-James 1978), as is the failure of 19th and early 20th century radicals to decisively push for democratisation of the Lords.[42]

Two further movements are relevant to the participatory tradition's emergence in the 19th century. Firstly the Electoral Reform Society (ERS) formed in January 1884 and then more notably, the Women's Suffrage Movement in the late 19th century. In both it is possible to detect a questioning of the ideas and processes established by the predominant tradition. Proportional Representation had been advocated by Hare (1861) and Mill (1861). However it was the arguments of ERS, under the name the Proportional Representation Society, that first fully challenged the use of SPS. To use their favoured Single Transferable Vote (STV) electoral system would undoubtedly challenge notions such as strong, single-party governance. It would also offer voters more sophisticated choices and largely proportional outcomes. An examination of ERS's history highlights the argument that the participatory tradition has resonated at varying intensities. Following their initial formation, as discussions of changes to the British political system were occurring in 1884/85, their critique of the British political electoral system has resonated intermittently. They actively campaigned in 1884/85 and were then inactive from 1888 to 1904. Since then they have continued to campaign for STV, for example, during the Speaker's Conference on Electoral Reform in 1917. Between the 1930s and 1970s electoral reform in the UK lost a 'live' issue and ERS struggled. However since then the issue has undoubtedly resonated more widely in response to contingent events. In particular following the election victories of Thatcher, Blair and most recently the Conservative-Liberal Democrat coalition concerns regarding the democratic credentials of the governments that have been formed[43] have assisted the resonance of ERS's critique.

For their part, the Women's Suffrage Movement also challenged the established ideas and practices of the British political system. Both the Suffragists and Suffragettes built upon the work of earlier feminist writers, in particular but not only, Wollstonecraft (1795). They also based their views on Mill and Taylor (1869). Both Suffragists like Fawcett and militants like Sylvia Pankhurst, in their own way, saw themselves as part of a tradition of radicalism that dated back through the 18th and 19th centuries and beyond. Holton argues that the Women's Suffrage movement was built around 'the common human attributes of men and women and the consequent social injustice involved in their unequal treatment' (2002: 9). Undoubtedly the desire for female suffrage challenged the widely believed stereotypes of women and their alleged inferiority. As we have seen, a political tradition steeped in elitism could easily accommodate ideas concerning male superiority and female inferiority. Contra this, the Women's Suffrage Movement sought to proclaim and secure the political equality of women, alongside demands for intellectual freedom and social reform (Holton 2002). Whilst much attention has rightly focused on divisions between 'constitutionalists and militants', and the social composition of both the Suffragists and the Suffragettes, the desire for the vote contra the elitism of the BPT formed part of a broader attempt to challenge the unequal treatment of women (Holton 2002). Once again the role of contingent factors such as the election of a radical Liberal government in 1905 and their failure to address the demands of the Women's Suffrage Movement was instrumental in promoting the resonance and militancy of this ideational challenge.

Summary

By the end of the 19th century the participatory tradition had developed. As we have seen, its lineage can be traced back to the British Civil War and beyond, and exists in challenging the elitist system of rule in the UK. However it was throughout the late 18th and 19th century that it came to fruition, as the predominant tradition itself developed. Paine (1791; 1792) and Wollstonecraft (1795) most famously gave powerful voice to these anti-elitist demands for political equality, popular sovereignty and wider and deeper political participation. However it was also those that they influenced who helped develop this tradition, through their actions and crucially, their demands. By challenging the predominant ideas and values of British political life, they played their part in the process of change and continuity in Britain's political development. This process proved to be a slow one and in many cases, the predominant tradition and its adherents amongst the socio-economic and political elite successfully thwarted this challenge. Not all aspects of the participatory tradition were fulfilled. For example demands for annual or even triennial parliaments would undoubtedly have widened and deepened democracy in the UK, but were never close to being accepted. Nor were all of the undemocratic, elitist features of British political life thoroughly campaigned against, as in the case of the reform of the Lords. However we can see not only the development of a competing political tradition with a rich and diverse history, but also changes that derive, in part, from that tradition and the activities of its adherents.

On occasion, during the development of participatory traditions, these challenges focused on aspects of the political system by demanding specific reforms, in particular the extension of the franchise. On other occasions these challenges focused on wider political reform as in the case of the Chartist movement. Furthermore we should recognise that the initial challenges to elitism targeted the most obvious vestiges of undemocratic behaviour and elite rule such as the vote and how the seats were distributed. Indeed in line with the prevailing patriarchal attitudes of the day, much of the focus was on extending the vote to men. Post 1867, attention switched to demands for further democratisation in the form of the votes for women and changes to the electoral system. That there were differences between them and often, limitations to the extent of democracy advocated by these numerous groups, does not detract from their desire to see political, and on occasion, social change instituted in the UK. By the 20th century the participatory tradition incorporated the demands for more democratic governance on a number of levels including the contestation of the patriarchal attitudes of the predominant tradition associated with Wollstonecraft (1795) and later, the campaign for Women's Suffrage. We can also see its influence on a significant section of the newly formed Labour party (Tant 1993).

As with the development of any political tradition, the process by which the participatory tradition developed was a dynamic one and involved responses to the prevailing ideational, institutional and discursive context. By the early 20th century the participatory tradition contested the BPT by suggesting that representatives should be more representative socially, accountable and elected by all of the adult population. It also stated the idea that the government should be directly responsible to the populace more frequently than ever before. For those who drew from the participatory tradition 'Westminster and Whitehall' did not know best. Rather they were merely there to facilitate democratic governance by overcoming the logistical problems identified by writers such as Paine. In the process of its emergence this tradition had engaged numerous individuals in the process of democratic politics for the first time, in this way developing the foundations for a rich tradition of protest and dissent that exist to this day. Finally the participatory tradition also implicitly and explicitly contested the BPT's discourse concerning change by rejecting the Whig interpretation of history. Contra this, it appealed to the idea of an ancient set of inalienable rights and freedoms that had been lost and needed rediscovery.

Having outlined the development of the participatory tradition in the 19th century, we should now turn to its more recent renaissance.

The participatory tradition in the late 20th century

Since the beginning of the 20th century the participatory tradition has continued to contest the dominance of the BPT, albeit at differing intensities at different times. For a substantial part of the 20th century there was a broad consensus over the political structures and the 'rules of the political game' in the British polity (Forman 2002). Indeed the institutions and processes of the British political system were treated with respect and no small amount of reverence (Norton 1989). It was only from the 1960s onwards that the ideas, institutions and processes of British political life came to be increasingly questioned and critiqued. This occurred as a consequence of various contingent events including: the post-war decline of the British economy, membership of the EU since 1973, concerns regarding overly mighty government,[44] the questioning of the efficacy of 'the union' and growing interest in devolution in the 1970s,[45] Thatcherism and Conservative hegemony at Westminster, and party polarisation in the 1980s. These events promoted the resurgence of the participatory tradition and its emphasis on popular sovereignty and wider and deeper political participation. In turn, this promoted the demands for constitutional reform and influenced the eventual reforms enacted by Labour post 1997.[46]

This resurgence can be seen most readily in the formation of both the Campaign for Freedom of Information (CFOI) in 1984 (Tant 1993) and Charter 88 in 1988 (Evans 1995). Both of these pressure groups were formed in the 1980s at the height of Thatcherism. CFOI sought to challenge the secrecy of the British political system which was rooted in, and complimentary to, the BPT. Since the 1970s both major political parties had offered to tackle secrecy in British government when in opposition, but failed to take action when in power.[47] CFOI emerged initially in response to the failure of Clement Freud's FOI Bill in 1979. However it was re-launched in 1984 in response to the approach of the Thatcher governments, their opposition to a statutory right to know, and crucially, their actions in cases such as the Tisdall Case (1983) and the Ponting Case (1985). The campaign acted as an umbrella group for those campaigning for more openness in British government and sought to 'win the war of ideas in 'High' politics' (Evans 2003: 1999) by convincing members of the elite of the need for FOI legislation. Throughout the Thatcher and Major years CFOI sought to influence outcomes at Westminster and was, to a degree, successful.[48] However it was their success in working with Labour and Liberal politicians in the mid to late 1980s and early 1990s that helped sustain interest on the opposition benches for FOI. Whilst the resulting Freedom of Information Act (2000) failed to satisfy their demands and had been substantially de-radicalised from the 1997 *Your Right To Know* White Paper (Marsh and Hall 2007), CFOI's challenge to the BPT should be recognised. In arguing for more openness in government they sought to promote one of the most basic facets of a more participatory approach to democracy. The ability to participate in public affairs requires knowledge/information in order to hold decision-makers to account and/or make decisions. Such a view runs contra the established processes and practices of the BPT.

Charter 88 offered a wholesale critique of the institutions and processes of the British political system from a participatory perspective (Evans 1995). Their critique of the British political system and the political tradition that underpins it was evident from the outset.[49] They demanded sweeping reform of the British political system[50] and were undoubtedly driven in part by the excesses of the Thatcher governments during the 1980s[51] (Erdos 2009). In particular the failure of the British political system to constrain an overly mighty executive, which on the basis of a minority of the popular vote in three successive elections, was increasingly authoritarian.[52] However they themselves also (correctly) regarded themselves as the heir to a long running tradition 'of demands for constitutional rights in Britain, which stretches from the barons who forced the Magna Carta on King John, to the working men who drew up the People's Charter in 1838, to the women at the beginning of this century who demanded universal suffrage' (The Original Charter 88).

Furthermore Charter 88's origins were influenced 'by the affluence and mobility of the post-World War II era [which] had prompted a 'radical dislocation of social attitudes' in Britain, resulting in the death of 'old social and political deference' and new demands for 'public participation and greater openness' (Erdos 2009: 540) and the emergence of post-material attitudes. Charter 88 architects on the political left sought to appeal beyond narrow working-class issues and onto broader ideas such as power and democracy in UK society. This saw 'a new focus on the need to remove traditionalist monarchical and aristocratic aspects of Britain's governance structure and, more positively, to encourage the empowerment of civil society and democracy (Erdos 2009: 540). Here both civic republican – and now radical democratic – ideas were evident, the latter highlighting the process of continuity and development in the participatory tradition.

The significance of Charter 88 and their challenge to the BPT can be seen in a number of ways. Firstly they offered what amounts to the most complete expression of the participatory tradition in recent years, contesting numerous aspects of the institutions, processes and practices of the BPT. Key players such as Stuart Weir and Anthony Barnett believed in 'a humanistic critique of both the prevailing system and the dominant elite tradition; and a belief in its transformative potential' (Evans 2003: 35). Furthermore in identifying the historical antecedents to their challenge they appealed to and developed a long-running tradition of critiquing elite rule in the UK. Secondly they successfully influenced certain actors in both Westminster and Whitehall. In particular they worked well with Labour politicians such as John Smith, Robin Cook and Alistair Darling, as well as members of the media, academia and think tanks such as the IPPR. Indeed their attempts to influence the thinking of the Labour party in the late 1980s and early 1990s (Evans 1995) were crucial to their attempt to turn critique into policy. They undoubtedly influenced the constitutional reform agenda of the 1990s (Dunleavy 2009) by producing detailed evidence, expertise and argument for debates and discussions on constitutional issues.

Furthermore their participation in the development of devolution through engagement with the Scottish Constitutional Convention played a role in influencing the eventual 1998 settlement (Hall 2009). Finally they raised the level of debate and discussion of Britain's constitutional arrangements by highlighting Labour's historic acceptance of the BPT as well as challenging some of the most deeply embedded myths concerning British political development. However we should recognise that once in government, the Labour party did not enact constitutional reform as Charter 88 would have wanted, instead 'cherry picking' to a degree those reforms they would enact (Flinders 2009). Moreover those reforms that were pursued, were either: adopted in line with the ideas and institutions of the predominant political tradition as in the case of the Human Rights Act, de-radicalised as in the case of FOI, or not instituted as in the case of electoral reform (Marsh and Hall 2007; Marsh 2008a). Only Scottish devolution was introduced in its original guise and this was done primarily due to political expediency (Marsh and Hall 2007).

Post 1997, Charter 88 encountered various problems,[53] not the least of which was Labour's continued reverence for the BPT. Indeed Labour's 'failure to honour its commitment to hold a referendum on electoral reform for the House of Commons' (Erdos 2009: 543) symbolised Labour's attitude and resulted in the Charter 88's 2001 election campaign highlighting Labour's broken promises on constitutional reform. Furthermore Charter 88's insider strategy had also led them to lose momentum and when that did not bear fruit as they had hoped, they reached an impasse. They also had financial problems and in 2003/4, they formed strategic alliances with the left-leaning New Politics Network (NPN) and Active Citizens Transform. In recent years, however, this challenge to the BPT has been reinvigorated with the merger of Charter 88 and NPN as Unlock Democracy. This movement continues to campaign for constitutional reform in the UK. In particular alongside ERS, Make Votes Count and Power 2010,[54] Unlock Democracy have campaigned on issues regarding democratisation such as Lords reforms and electoral reform.

Thus the participatory tradition and its adherents continues to contest the BPT through such contemporary debates. Indeed it has had an impact upon various constitutional reforms, including Scottish devolution via the work of the Consultative Steering Group and the establishment of the Standing Orders for the Scottish Parliament.[55] With issues over MPs' expenses and then the election result of 2010 bringing electoral reform and 'recall' more squarely onto the political agenda than at any time in recent years, there are undoubtedly opportunities for adherents to the participatory tradition. The latter proposal fits neatly with the participatory tradition, allowing the electorate to hold their representatives to account for their conduct far more effectively than under current arrangements. The referendum on introducing the Alternative Vote promised by the Coalition has been welcomed by Unlock Democracy as a step towards a more democratic political system, although it does not deliver proportionality.

Extensions and qualifications on the participatory tradition

When discussing the BPT we considered the linkage between that particular tradition and actors in British politics. We also considered the existence of a socio-economic dimension to the BPT. As such some brief comment on similar issues pertaining to the participatory tradition is required.

On the relationship between these competing traditions and actors in British politics, the participatory tradition has, over time, found greater resonance with those of a liberal or socialist persuasion. For example the architects of Charter 88, and many of its prominent signatories, came from the left (Rustin 2009) and the movement found supporters amongst the Labour and Liberal grass roots. This is hardly surprising given that its critique of the elitism of the BPT arises from notions concerning equality and rights. Nor is it surprising that those of the Conservative party have proven resistant to and even derisory of the participatory tradition. In the 19th century the views of Paine (1791) and Wollstonecraft (1795) and those they inspired were viewed with suspicion and fear by the overwhelming majority of the socio-economic and political elite. Neither the Whigs nor the Tories favoured popular sovereignty and democracy. Many of their successors in the Liberals and the Conservatives retained much of the suspicion towards popular sovereignty and wider and deeper participation. Although the Liberal party has become the mainstream party of constitutional reform since its revival in the 1970s, it has not at an elite level fully supported the participatory tradition. For example the Liberal Democrat leadership failed to fully endorse Charter 88, despite its popularity amongst the grass roots (Erdos 2009: 543). Even the Labour party which initially drew from the participatory tradition quickly became 'constitutionalized' (Tant 1993) and for most of its history, was largely supportive of the BPT. The most recent example of this trend can be seen in the experience of Charter 88. Despite working closely with Labour politicians, they:

> did not succeed in persuading the Labour Party of the need to adopt a holistic or systematic approach to democratic renewal. With the benefit of hindsight it is possible to go further and suggest that although Charter 88 sat at the centre of a powerful epistemic community it did not achieve a deeper ideological shift within the Labour Party away from its traditional acquiescence with majoritarianism. (Flinders 2009: 654–5)

In its post-1997 constitutional reform programme, the Labour party has remained largely committed to the BPT.[56] Therefore across the party system the participatory tradition has had few consistent adherents.

Amongst the population there has also been a lack of consistent and widespread resonance for the participatory tradition. Since the heady days of 50,000 members and the millions of signatures on the Chartist petitions of 1842 and 1848[57] and the c.100,000 members in the NUWSS, notions concerning popular and participatory democracy have not secured widespread acceptance in recent years. Although this brief overview is not the place to develop a detailed analysis of the failure of the participatory view of democracy to permeate into popular consciousness we can undoubtedly see the 85,000 signatories to Charter 88 or the limited membership of modern groups such as the ERS[58] as evidence for this. This is not to suggest that these groups have not secured influence, rather they have not secured widespread support for their critique amongst the population at large. It should be noted, however, that the resonance of these critiques is linked to contingent events.

Finally we should make brief reference to the relationship between socio-economic interests and the participatory tradition. Much attention has been focused onto the socio-economic background of movements such as the Levellers, Chartism and Women's Suffrage.[59] The social composition of the Levellers represented 'small and 'middling' proprietors, craftsmen, traders and yeomen farmers' (Meiksins Wood and Wood 1997: 82), whilst the Diggers drew from farm labourers (Hill 1984). Derry (1967: xi) argues that radicalism was often linked to nonconformity and the Celtic fringe, and in the late 18th century sprang from the Enlightenment. Research has highlighted the extent to which Chartism was overwhelmingly a working-class movement, led by men but with a significant female membership (Thompson 1984; Wright 1988). The Women's Suffrage Movement was initially dominated by middle-class women. However over time working-class women became far more prominent amongst its rank and file (Holton 1986). Charter 88 drew upon post-material interests (Erdos 2009) and was supported by famous left-wing academics such as Eric Hobsbawm and Stuart Hall. We should clearly be wary of homogenising those who advocate the participatory tradition as there may be different emphases in different movements or in different parts of the UK (Kenny 1999). However those arguing from the participatory tradition are united by opposition to elitism in UK politics and its manifestation in the predominant political tradition, the BPT.

Conclusion

A competing political tradition rooted in a participatory view of democracy has over time contested the predominant tradition and its institutions and processes. Contra the BPT, the participatory tradition advances a concept of democracy based upon popular sovereignty and wider and deeper political participation. In particular notions concerning the commonality and equality of human attributes and the right of everyone to have an equal say in how their lives are governed have figured prominently. That these arguments have developed over time highlights again the dynamic nature of political traditions. They are not static nor time-bound. In their campaigns the adherents to this competing tradition have targeted the institutions, processes and practices of British political life, seeking various reforms that would democratise British politics and society.

This conflict and contestation occurs at both a micro or macro level in the sense of challenging either aspects of the political system or its entirety. Similarly it can account for change at both a macro and micro level. However two points are worth repeating here. Firstly political traditions resonate asymmetrically in relation to the prevailing institutional, contextual and discursive context. Thus the participatory tradition has operated in a context that privileges the predominant tradition and we should recognise the continuities that emanate from this. Furthermore as we have seen, the participatory tradition has resonated at differing intensities at differing times and this can best be explained in relation to contingent events. Events such as the formation of the Conservative-Liberal Democrat coalition in 2010 and its proposals to reinvigorate UK democracy via 'recall' and a referendum on electoral reform suggest that adherents to the participatory tradition will continue to contest the predominant tradition for the foreseeable future.

Having identified our first competing tradition, the participatory tradition, we will now turn our attention to a second: the nationalist tradition.

7
The Nationalist Tradition

Introduction

The BPT has, as we have seen, been the predominant political tradition in the UK. However it has not gone uncontested. In Chapter 6 we focused on the challenge over time from the participatory tradition. In this chapter we will turn our attention to the nationalist tradition.[1] This tradition, in various guises, contests the territorial relations and concepts of national identity encapsulated within and promulgated by, the BPT.[2] Before turning to the nationalist tradition, a brief summary of the territorial relations established by the BPT is required.

Historically the UK has been, and remains, a composite state with a complex pattern of territorial relations and politics. The formal creation of the UK occurred across the 17th and 18th centuries. Prior to this Wales had been gradually brought under English Rule from the 12th century onwards. Royal authority over Wales was defined in two Acts of Parliament in 1536 and 1543. The Union of the Crowns occurred in 1603, whilst Scotland was formally unified with England in the 1707 Act of Union. Indeed: 'the incorporation of Scotland in 1707 created a unified state and market within the island archipelago' (Preston 2004: 53). The creation of the UK formally culminated in the 1800 Act of Union with Ireland. Once underway, the process of 'making' the UK flourished 'on the back of military (and imperial) success, economic innovation and political repression' (Preston 2004: 53) throughout the 18th and 19th centuries. In summary, the fundamentals of UK territorial politics historically have been viewed as a legally sovereign Parliament counterbalanced chiefly by territorial representation, local government and a degree of administrative decentralisation (Holliday 1999).

The UK has traditionally been seen as a unitary state. This narration was linked to the Westminster Model (WM) and its key doctrine, parliamentary sovereignty. Despite the crudeness and inaccuracy of the simple unitary state paradigm (and the WM), actors across the political spectrum believed in this description and the efficacy of what it described. In reality, ideas such as parliamentary sovereignty and the unitary state are narrations of the discourses of the BPT and in particular its key mantra that 'Westminster and Whitehall know best'. Furthermore they are linked to the discourse concerning national distinctiveness. This stresses a sense of Britishness and exceptionalism contra the political systems found in Europe and the USA. It emphasises unionism and, in the past, empire. This discourse intersects with the BPT's discourse concerning change which suggests that Britain's mode of development had been proven to be superior contra that of other states. The British political system was seen as something altogether different politically (and culturally) to that found in Europe and the USA, as it provided for representative and responsible government as well as for a gradual development over time contra the upheavals evident elsewhere. These four discourses assisted in homogenising a socio-economic and political system that contained both vast inequalities and diversity across and within the regions of the UK. They also allowed for the perpetuation of patterns of dominance and inequalities of wealth, knowledge and power. Thus they served the interests of the socio-economic and political elites, allowing for the latter's continued dominance of UK society and capital accumulation, acting as an integratory force, particularly during times of social and political upheaval.

Challenging Britain: the nationalist tradition

Despite widespread acceptance of BPT across the UK,[3] contestation of the BPT occurs on the national-territorial level by the nationalist tradition. We can identify the existence of different identities and political traditions in the different parts of the UK (Kenny 1999; Preston 2004)[4] which challenge aspects of the BPT or its entirety. The most well-documented example of this can be seen in Northern Ireland through Irish Nationalism of various complexions. However there exists a long history of challenges to the constitutional position of Scotland and, in the 20th century, Wales. Each of these examples takes core nationalist assumptions and adds some regional flavour in the form of a concept of national identity and the nature or extent of their demands.

For the nationalist tradition the target has been the notions of centralisation of power and unionism. It critiques both the notions of the unitary state and Britain itself. Over time independence, self-determination and decentralisation have been advocated contra the dominance of Westminster and Whitehall.[5] To do this the nationalist tradition has stressed the inalienable right of peoples to self-determination. This idea traces it intellectual heritage to the Rousseauian notion of the 'general will' and popular sovereignty (Rousseau 1762) and J. S. Mill's suggestion that 'the boundaries of government should coincide, in the main, with those of nationality' (1861: 298). The nationalist tradition stresses notions such as 'internal colonialism' (Hechter 1998),[6] where the centre has been in a historically advantaged position economically, socially and politically, seeing self-determination as the remedy to this. Furthermore it appeals to competing senses of national identity in the form of Irishness,[7] Scottishness,[8] and Welshness[9] contra the discourse concerning national distinctiveness which emphasises Britishness.[10] Although Britain is a modern construct (Colley 2003) these separate senses of national identity appeal to longer-standing notions of identity emanating from pre-modern communities and their language, culture, myths and history.

The challenges mounted towards unionism and the territorial integrity of the UK by nationalists in Ireland, Scotland and Wales all emanate from this competing political tradition. Moreover the nationalist tradition challenges the discourse concerning change by proposing a radical rupture with existing territorial relations. To adopt the ideas of independence and self-government advocated by Sinn Fein, the Scottish National Party (SNP) and Plaid Cymru would end the territorial politics developed on these isles since the 16th century onwards. Contemporary nationalists in Ireland, Scotland and Wales advocate separatism and thus the break-up of the UK. Indeed in an effort to thwart this potential, as well as challenges to their electoral hegemony, New Labour introduced devolution to Scotland and Wales.

A number of important points should be recognised before we turn to the specific examples of the nationalist tradition. Firstly there has been a long history of contesting these central aspects of the BPT in the constituent parts of the UK. In these we should recognise points of commonality in each challenge which comprises the nationalist tradition. However we should also recognise variances between the expressions of this tradition. This is linked to the different political complexions and histories of Ireland, Scotland and Wales and views concerning the efficacy of the union. For example the nationalism in both Ireland and

Scotland has historically been primarily political in nature, contesting ideas about governance. Until recently, Welsh nationalism was primarily cultural in flavour, focusing primarily on language via the activities of Plaid Cymru (1925) and The Welsh Language Society (1962). However in recent years Welsh Nationalism has increasingly demanded greater independence and even self-determination for Wales.

Secondly we should recognise competing concepts of national identity within the nationalist tradition. The BPT offers a concept of national distinctiveness and Britishness. However despite support from both mainstream parties and elements of the population, assimilation to this sense of national identity was by no means total. Many people across Ireland, Scotland and Wales retained a distinct sense of their national identity (Boyce 1996; Brown, McCrone and Paterson 1996; Elwyn Jones 1994)[11] as well as a belief in both ancient rights lost and an identity under threat.

Thirdly we should again recognise the importance of contingent events in promoting the resonance of this tradition. This can be linked to the idea of historical grievances(s) felt by members of each nation over time. Numerous examples can be cited here including: the impact of the Great Famine between 1845 and 1852 in Ireland or the 1870 Ballot Act that assisted the rise of Irish Nationalism at Westminster, through to the failure of Britain's economy in the 1960s and 1970s and the discovery of North Sea Oil. In the 1980s the experience of Thatcherism performed a similar role through the treatment of 'hunger strikers' in Northern Ireland, the Miners Strike 1984–85 in Wales, or the early introduction of the Poll Tax in Scotland. Indeed it was this prolonged period of Conservative hegemony that prompted the most recent resurgence of Scottish and Welsh nationalism.[12] Disquiet at how the Tory government's programme, in particular how their economic policy with its emphasis on low public spending and the virtues of the free market impacted upon Scotland and Wales,[13] prompted such a resurgence. We can also point to the impact of devolution on each country since 1997 as the possible impetus for further change and contestations[14] of the BPT.

Fourthly the nationalist tradition intersects with the participatory tradition. This can be seen in its contestation of centralisation and executive dominance over 'the Celtic Fringe' historically and, since the 1980s, in the idea of the democratic deficit. The elitism of the BPT produces a democratic deficit as a matter of course and nationalists have historically been concerned about how those at Westminster and Whitehall governed the UK, even before the advent of universal suffrage. For example in Ireland during the Great Famine from 1845 to 1852, we can readily find criticism of the British government's handling of the crisis[15] and their motivations. In the 1980s, as dissatisfaction with how the BPT delivered governance for Scotland and Wales grew, so did reference to the idea of a democratic deficit. Despite repeatedly electing MPs from parties other than the Conservatives, both areas were governed by that party from Westminster and Whitehall, and not in a manner that was popular. As such, the demands of nationalists (and others),[16] have often focused on critiquing the democratic aspects of territorial politics, seeing the remedy in decentralisation and self-determination. In this respect they often appeal to the participatory tradition when framing their arguments.

Having outlined the core of the nationalist tradition, we should now briefly turn to its various expressions across the UK. Given both the duration and intensity of the contestation, we will start with the nationalist tradition in Ireland.

Ireland

Of the nationalist challenges to the BPT, the most prominent historically has been in Ireland.[17] The main features of nationalism in Ireland 'have been race, religion and a strong sense of territorial unity and integrity; and in all its modes it has been profoundly influenced by the power and proximity of Britain' (Boyce 1995: 19). England's involvement in Ireland can be traced back to the 12th century. However by the 15th century English authority in Ireland had dissipated. This was followed by the Tudor reconquest of Ireland which established asymmetrical relations as Ireland was constitutionally denoted as a dependent from 1494. The 17th century witnessed the strengthening of English rule via the Wars of the Three Kingdoms[18] and the Williamite Wars.[19] By the end of 18th century Ireland was formally united with England via the Act of Union (1800) and the Irish Parliament in Dublin that had existed since 1297 was removed. However unlike their Welsh and Scottish counterparts, the majority of the Irish did not embrace either Englishness or later, Britishness. Rather they retained a clearer sense of distinctiveness from Britain, both in terms of national identity and political aspiration. As such the history of Ireland has been marked by challenges to English, and then British rule. Prior to 1800 notable examples include Henry Grattan's Irish Patriot Party and the Society of United Irishmen in the 1790s. Following the Act of Union, these challenges intensified via the activities of Young Irelanders in the 1840s and the Irish Republican

Brotherhood (IRB). Since then, Irish Nationalism has been a prominent feature of British politics.[20]

The Nationalist challenge in Ireland

The demands of Irish Nationalism have varied over time, as have its methods; however some common themes can be detected. Nationalism in Ireland arose as 'a political response to internal colonization; and the ethnic identity of the periphery provides a basis for the movement of resistance. Regional inequality and ethnic identity in Ireland created nationalism' (Boyce 1995: 377). The nationalist challenge in Ireland has often appealed back to the 'Gaelic tradition',[21] suggesting that the Gaels 'in some sense represent the Irish in the infancy of their race' (Boyce 1995: 25).[22] In invoking the idea of an historic ancestry and identity, as with the discourse of 'the Freeborn Englishmen', the suggestion is that at some point in the past the Irish were encroached upon by conquerors, namely the English. From this, a strong cultural nationalist tradition developed, which stressed the Gaelic tradition and a sense of Irish cultural and national identity. This emphasised the Gaelic language, mythology and symbolism as well as Gaelic culture.

This discourse has coalesced with reference to historical grievances over time, be it alleged atrocities by, or neglect from, England. Numerous examples of either could be cited by Irish nationalists to rally people to the cause, including the alleged atrocities at Drogheda in 1649, the failure to carry out Catholic emancipation in 1800 and the Great Famine itself. The Irish felt from England 'a deeply rooted and frequently nurtured English conviction of inferiority' (Jenkins 2006: 4), which underpinned attitudes from the centre towards Ireland into the 19th century and beyond. Indeed Boyce (1995: 20) argues that abstract notions such as the inalienable rights of the Irish or the arguments of thinkers such as Paine[23] were rarely appealed to by pre-20th century Irish nationalists. Rather they tended to appeal to notions about alleged injustice and 'historical wrongs' emanating from England and the English.

Irish nationalism was and remains, a complex phenomenon.[24] The mainstream of Irish nationalism mounted 'an attack not only on England, the alleged originator of Ireland's ills, but on the Protestant minority in Ireland, who sheltered behind the British Protestants' skirts' (Boyce 1995: 382). This highlights a belief that injustice and inequity was imbued into the very fabric of the Union. In the 19th century this took the form of attacking Protestant power and privilege. However it also developed into the desire for self-government within the union, and even independence. In this, Britain was seen as both a threat to their distinctiveness and an obstacle to progress for the Irish majority who remained culturally, politically and economically marginalised. Thus it was on a competing sense of Irish identity that the political nationalism in Ireland was built. Despite this complexity, the nationalist tradition has found expression in Ireland via demands for constitutional change. Indeed:

> it's demands have ranged across the whole spectrum of constitutional relations, from the kingdom of Ireland, subordinate to the British crown but not to the British parliament, to outright separation; but it has consistently emphasised the importance of parliamentary independence and parliamentary government, with cultural themes, playing a significant, but essentially subordinate role. (Boyce 1995: 19)

The nationalist challenge in Ireland has, since the late 18th century, therefore focused upon contesting governance by Westminster and Whitehall. In the 19th century this took the form of both demands for independence, and the well-documented issue of Home Rule.[25]

The most radical manifestation of the nationalist tradition in Ireland, the call for Irish independence, can be found in the Irish Rebellion of 1798, the Irish Republican Brotherhood (1858) and the Fenian rising of the 1860s. The latter believed that Ireland should realise its inalienable right to independence and self-government and that this could only be achieved via armed insurrection. Fenians such as John O'Mahony stated their belief in both republicanism and democracy, saying that the 'common people are the rightful rulers of their own destiny' (cited in McGee 2007: 16). The heirs to these views were the architects of famous events such as the 1916 Easter Rising (Townsend 2006) and the partition of Ireland in 1922. Since the late 1960s, the demand for an independent Ireland has found expression in paramilitary organisations such as the Provisional IRA and the Irish National Liberation Army. As part of this demand for independence we should recognise that a strong physical tradition,[26] which harks back to Fenianism, remained via the Republican Paramilitaries.

The most notable example of the Nationalist tradition in Ireland is Sinn Fein. Established by Arthur Griffiths in 1905, Sinn Fein began as pro-monarchist organisation before committing to the creation of an Irish republic in 1917. After the First World War the party, having won 73 out of 105 Irish seats at Westminster, became more prominent. Its MPs met in Dublin and declared themselves Dail Eireann (the Parliament of Ireland). They also played a prominent role in the Irish War of Independence 1919–21, and the eventual partition in the Anglo-Irish Treaty (1922). Sinn Fein's nationalist challenge starts from the premise that Ireland is naturally a single political unit. They argue that 'prior to the Norman invasion from England in 1169, the Irish had their own system of law, culture and language and their own political and social structures. Following the invasion, the island continued to be governed as a single political unit, as a colony of Britain, until 1921: (Sinn Fein website).

Britain, in this discourse, is viewed a colonial aggressor and occupying power. For example they state 'throughout the 19th Century and until partition in the 20th Century the British Government provided its colonial rule in Ireland with a cover of 'democracy'. In the changed conditions of a partitioned Ireland it now used the wishes of Irish Unionists in North East Ireland as justification for its continued occupation' (Sinn Fein website).

Thus Sinn Fein's expression of the nationalist tradition has an anti-colonial flavour, viewing a united, independent Ireland as an inalienable right. As such Sinn Fein contest the territorial relations established by the BPT and the discourses concerning both national distinctiveness and change. More broadly, Sinn Fein is seen as a democratic socialist party (Garner and Kelly 1998).

More moderate expressions of the nationalist tradition came from Isaac Butt, the Irish Parliamentary Party, and demands for Home Rule. The issue of Home Rule became the predominant issue in British politics during the late 19th century as a consequence of Butt's creation of the Home Government Association and the introduction of the Ballot Act in 1872. Moreover Gladstone's failure to pacify Ireland during his first ministry and the impact of the agricultural depression assisted in the rise of both the Davitt's Land League (1879) and more famously, the charismatic Parnell. Contra previous demands such as O'Connell's Repeal Movement, Home Rule meant the creation of an All Ireland Parliament or Assembly with a degree of legislative power alongside continued Irish participation in the Union. Gladstone's Home Rule Bill (1886) offered the latter with various powers reserved to Westminster and Whitehall such as the right to declare war, make treaties and mint coinage. Such a transfer of power clearly involves some change to the executive dominance and the notion that 'Westminster and Whitehall know best'. Furthermore it challenges the sense of Britishness promulgated by the predominant tradition. However whilst Home Rule was viewed by its 19th century opponents such as Chamberlain and Salisbury as a radical rupture with existing territorial relations and therefore a challenge to BPT's discourse about change, such devolutionary approaches can now be viewed as offering much consistency with the BPT (Hall 2009). Indeed Home Rule, like the devolution settlements of the 1990s, should be viewed as an attempt to preserve the union and thus maintain rather than undermine the union.[27] In the last 40 years this more moderate expression of Irish Nationalism is associated with the SDLP. From its beginnings in 1970 the SDLP favoured the establishment of a devolved administration with power-sharing structures. However the failure of attempts at power-sharing such as the Sunningdale Agreement (1974) saw the party advocate the construction of all-Ireland institutions with a prominent role for the Irish republic (Murray and Tonge 2005).

Scotland

In Scotland, the nationalist tradition has an equally long, if less turbulent, history. Scotland's position within the union has received less contestation than that of Ireland, until recently. The inclusion of Scotland into the UK formally occurred in 1707 and this established the territorial relations for the next 300 years. Despite the concerns of many Scots at the time: 'the 1707 Acts of Union constituted not so much 'an unequal treaty' as measures of expediency by the English and Scottish political elites who each had their own different reasons at the time for reaching agreement upon a deal' (Forman 2002: 79). The development of a political system, whose territorial relations were centred at Westminster and Whitehall, facilitated the pursuit of these. However differences between aspects of the governance of Scotland and the rest of the UK remained. It is from these that contestation of the BPT and its territorial relations emanated.

In framing and maintaining the union with Scotland economic considerations were crucial (Mitchell 2001). The Union was forged during a period of economic expansion and growing prosperity for the socioeconomic elites. In Scotland there were concerns regarding the subsuming of the Scottish identity under an English one (Whatley 2008). However unlike in Ireland these were put aside or accommodated, as two patrician classes for economic and political gains forged the union (Brown, McCrone and Paterson 1996: 3-7). Much public opinion was initially unpersuaded as to the virtue of 'the Union' (Harvie 1998). However its architects believed they were doing the best for Scotland (Whatley 2008: 35).[28] Any concerns however were quickly offset by a number of factors.[29]

Once established, a broad consensus existed over the constitutional position of Scotland (Mitchell 2002) which was underpinned by belief in the emerging discourses of the BPT. However ideational contestation did remain. There were those who appealed to competing ideas such as Scottish independence. The basis for such demands was found primarily in the sense of Scottishness that remained. Thus Scottish integration was partial. The major institutions of civic life in Scotland retained a separate Scottish identity precisely because Scotland's elites negotiated to retain control over law, education, religion and local government (Paterson 2000). This steady but constant stressing of 'difference' between aspects of Scotland and Britain would, over time, become increasingly important. It provided the basis for the sense of distinctiveness which underscored later demands for a degree of self-government or independence. Furthermore the beginnings of contestation of core tenets of the predominant tradition such as centralisation, unionism and Britishness can be seen here. As such, even in the 19th century the notion of Britain as a unified entity and its predominant political tradition, were not universally accepted in Scotland.

The formation of the *National Association for the Vindication of Scottish Rights* (1853) highlights the complexity of views of territorial relations. Their manifesto 'contained no explicit criticism of the union but it did deplore what it regarded as English neglect of Scottish political interests' (Forman 2003: 79).[30] On one level, this demonstrates the degree to which the ideas of the BPT had become accepted even amongst critics. However these critics did see an intrinsic asymmetry, or English bias, in the Union and thus were, to a degree, contesting the constitutional status quo.[31] There was limited resonance for demands for reform amongst the Scottish electorate at this point given the perceived success of 'the Union'. However it should also be recognised that the Scottish Office was reinstated in 1885 suggesting the idea of concessions, albeit minor ones,[32] being given by Westminster.

Thus a sense of Scottish political-cultural identity did persist in the 19th century.[33] This was rooted in the existence of some distinctive political and cultural institutions and practices. The political aspect of this identity has been described as 'unionist nationalism' (Brown, McCrone and Paterson 1996: 11).[34] Through the existence of separate legal and educational systems and a sense of religious distinctiveness, the Scots were able to preserve a degree of separate identity within the UK. As long as the union delivered tangible benefits for Scotland, demands for constitutional change would be somewhat muted in their resonance, but, that said, they did exist. Therefore faith in the union, and therefore 'unionism', was centrally significant to maintaining acceptance of the institutions and processes of the BPT.

The nationalist challenge in Scotland

Debate on Scotland's constitutional status was a feature of Scottish politics during the 19th and 20th centuries (Mitchell 1996: 4) and various attempts were made to articulate the demand for a degree of self-government. Lindsay (1991) argues that Scottish Nationalism involves four strands: first, a romanticised, semi-mystic form which focuses on shared history and community; second, a minimal state nationalism that emphasises decentralisation and green politics; third, a left-wing strand that views nationalism as the route towards more socialist policies; and fourth, a view that sees nationalism as a vehicle for modernisation which can be both left and right wing. Scottish Nationalists have appealed over time to such notions or combinations thereof.

The early manifestations of the nationalist tradition in Scotland can be found in the late 19th and early 20th centuries. The Scottish Home Rule Association (SHRA) was established in 1886 and defined its aims in 1887 via *The Union of 1707 viewed financially* (Morton 2000). These aims made the SHRA 'the first parliamentary political Scottish national movement' (Morton 2000: 116) and included a desire to 'promote the establishment of a legislature sitting in Scotland, with full control over all purely Scottish questions, and with an Executive Government responsible to it and the Crown' (Morton 2000). Had these demands been actualised, they would have represented some departure from the BPT. As such, the SHRA offered a challenge to key aspects of existing territorial relations. It also provides evidence of continual contestation of both, as does the fact that the House of Commons carried a Scottish Home Rule motion on 3 April 1894. The first meeting of the Scottish National Convention was on 15 November 1924, with a further one was convened after the Second World War. Although these challenges stalled due to lack of resonance with a public largely convinced of the virtues of the Union, their existence clearly demonstrates that there have always been contestations of Scotland's traditional constitutional position. Moreover these were followed by the establishment of the National Party of Scotland in 1928 (NPS) and the Scottish Party (SP) in 1930.

Since the mid 20th century, the primary expression of the nationalist tradition in Scotland can be found in the Scottish National Party (SNP). Given their ascendance to governance in Scotland in 2007, both their rise and relationship to the nationalist tradition should be explained.

The SNP was formed in 1934 through a merger of the NPS and the SP[35] and initially led by John MacCormick.[36] At this point they were 'a resilient little sect rather than a political movement' (Evans 2003: 226) as they lacked a coherent ideology or policy programme beyond the issue of independence. Over time, they married this to what they described in the 1970s as a social democratic programme.[37] Since 1987, however, social democracy has sat a little more comfortably with the SNP, albeit a social democracy that has increasingly come to be 'Neo-liberalism with a Heart' (Cuthbert and Cuthbert 2009). However the heart and soul of the SNP lies not in concepts of left or right, but rather in a commitment to Scottish nationhood and independence (Hassan 2009).[38]

The SNP's first success came in 1945 when they won the Motherwell by-election.[39] The motivation for this was dissatisfaction with Scotland's position in the union as many Scots believed that they 'were suffering disproportionately from the neglect of Westminster'.[40] The SNP doubled its share of the Scottish vote between 1964 and 1966 from 2.4 per cent to 5 per cent. However the victory of Winnie Ewing in the 1967 Hamilton by-election marked the first phase of modern Scottish politics.[41] This demonstration of the growth of the SNP prompted Wilson to institute *The Royal Commission on the Constitution*, which began the process that culminated in the offering of devolution to the Scots in the late 1970s.

Throughout the 1970s the SNP increased its prominence and increasingly came to replace the Conservatives as Labour's direct opponent in Scotland (Devine 2008), at least in the minds of Labour politicians. The SNP was able to find a new focal point for their cause in the discovery of North Sea Oil, which ratcheted up their appeal to an increasingly disillusioned and dissatisfied section of the Scottish electorate. Their campaign 'Its Scotland's Oil' helped speed their rise. The 'Oil' was merely the confirmation of the inequity of the Union for many Scots and offered the opportunity for economic independence at a time of a UK-wide economic downturn. Dissatisfaction with the union and North Sea Oil helped to stimulate the process of politicising Scottish identity and the SNP were the primary beneficiaries of this. Thus the challenge to the BPT and its unionism epitomised in demands for independence was given wider resonance. The effect of this could be seen almost immediately. In the two elections of 1974 the SNP secured 21.9 per cent and 30.4 per cent of the vote in Scotland respectively, a dramatic increase on their 1970 figure of 11.4 per cent. Moreover the Labour government's small and declining majority undoubtedly assisted them. Labour was increasingly reliant upon Scottish and Welsh seats for overall victory at Westminster (Devine 2008c). After the election of October 1974, the Labour party only had a majority of four,[42] whilst the SNP had gained four seats, reaching a new high of 11. This increased Labour's reliance upon other parties and led them to offer concessions, or consider policies that previously would have been viewed as 'beyond the pale', including devolution.[43] Here party politics and electoral realities at Westminster acted as one of the key contingent factors promoting the nationalist contestation of the BPT.

The failure of the devolution referenda in 1979[44] was followed by the final defeat of the Callaghan government on 28 March 1979. The ensuing general election saw the return to government of a party almost wholly convinced of the virtues of the BPT. The approach of the Thatcher government, culminating in the events surrounding the Poll Tax,[45] increased the resonance of demands for constitutional reform in Scotland. As well as promoting those who supported devolution (O'Neill 2004) it also assisted the nationalist tradition in the guise of the SNP (Hassan 2009). Indeed it was Thatcher's 'monolithic unionism, a political rather than an economic force that created the conditions for the resurgence of Welsh, and even more so, Scottish distinctiveness' (Ward 2004: 168). Moreover the length of time the Thatcher government spent in office led to the perception that rule from the centre in London could in fact be equated to Conservative rule and policy they did not want, regardless of how Scotland voted. This was the democratic deficit in action.

In 1979 the combination of the referendum defeat and election losses had a devastating effect on the SNP (Mitchell 2009). Two notable trends emerged from this. Firstly a fundamentalist opposition to accepting an assembly emerged in the SNP. Secondly the 1979 group was formed, which sought to promote a more left-wing approach and 'Scottish Resistance'. Following their demise and the SNP's return of only two seats of 72 contested in 1983, the party sought to rebuild. However it was the increasing dissatisfaction with Scotland's position within the UK, and by definition the BPT, that reinvigorated the rise of the SNP and this challenge from the nationalist tradition. In 1987 the SNP won 14 per cent of the votes and three seats in the general election. In local elections in Scotland the SNP faired well, achieving, for example, 21.3 per cent of the vote and 113 seats in 1988. However they were not the only beneficiaries of Thatcher's approach to territorial politics – all the main opposition parties sought to capitalise as the belief grew that old territorial consensus and all that underpinned it no longer delivered (Mitchell 2002). This polarisation between a government, whose faith in the BPT was unshakeable, and its various opponents in Scotland, reached its height during the controversy surrounding the Poll Tax.[46] Again, this benefitted the SNP, who, along with numerous Labour members, argued for non-registration and non-payment.[47] Labour's defeat in the Glasgow Govan by-election of November 1988 by the SNP showed the extent to which the SNP was increasingly in touch with public frustrations. The SNP then worked alongside the Anti-Poll Tax Federation at the forefront of the 'Can't Pay, Won't Pay Campaign'.

Whilst Labour and the Liberal Democrats participated in the Scottish Constitutional Convention[48] (SCC) post 1989, it is unsurprising that the independence-seeking SNP chose not to join. The SCC did contain challenges to the predominant tradition.[49] However the nationalist position of the SNP represents the most radical challenge to the territorial aspects of the BPT and one not supported by many other members of the convention. Despite this, the SNP had further electoral success in 1992, winning 21.5 per cent of the votes. The fact that the SNP had won nearly a quarter of the vote in Scotland in 1992 suggested to many in the Labour party that independence was becoming more attractive to Scots (Bennie, Brand and Mitchell 1997) and that dissatisfaction with both Labour and the constitutional status quo was growing. Labour responded by increasing its neo-nationalist rhetoric and, under the leadership of John Smith, pushing for devolution. They saw this as a way of preserving the union in the face of a growing support for independence and as a way of staving of the threat to their electoral hegemony posed by the SNP.

Post 1997 the SNP campaigned in favour of creating a Scottish Parliament with tax-varying powers alongside Labour and the Liberal Democrats. The SNP had dropped their fundamentalist view on independence, instead supporting devolution from a gradualist perspective, believing that it would be the first step towards achieving Scottish independence. Once the Scotland Act (1998) had been passed and the first Scottish parliamentary elections had taken place in 1999, the SNP became the main opposition party in Scotland. Compared to their position at Westminster where they had only six seats post 1997 they won a total of 35 seats at Holyrood. Eighty per cent of these seats were delivered under the regional list portion of AMS.[50] In 2003, the SNP lost both seats and votes. However with 27 seats they retained their position as both the second largest and official opposition party.

The key moment for the nationalist tradition in Scotland came with the SNP's victory in the 2007 Scottish Parliamentary Election. They obtained 47 seats to Labour's 46. Not only was this a shift in Scottish politics, but it also heralded the potential beginnings of a major challenge to the BPT and the Union itself, as the SNP now had the opportunity to form a government. Two points should be noted here. Firstly the SNP has increased its number of constituency seats from nine to 21 at the expense of Labour. Secondly their success was not confined to the Holyrood Elections.[51] Once victorious the SNP sought to form a coalition. However only the Green party would join,[52] leaving Alex Salmond to lead the first minority administration since Scottish devolution began.

Since then the SNP has sought to assert itself[53] and its views. On 3 September 2007 Salmond announced the re-branding of the Scottish Executive, as the Scottish government.[54] The stated reason for this was that research had suggested that the term 'executive' was meaningless to many people, whereas government would be understood far more widely. The significance of this move should not be underestimated though.[55] Since its election the SNP has repeatedly referred to its intention to hold a referendum on independence. In August 2007 Salmond announced a consultative exercise on Scotland's future constitutional position entitled *Choosing Scotland's Future: The National Conversation* which culminated in the publication of a draft referendum bill in February 2010. This included three possible future directions for Scotland: a continuation of the current settlement with at best only minimal change, extensions to the powers of the Scotland Parliament, and an independent Scotland. Undoubtedly the latter two options would raise major questions regarding the consequences of the devolution process. As ever, independence would constitute the most profound challenge to the BPT to date.[56] Despite the withdrawal of the bill in September 2010, the SNP victory has posed fundamental questions for the devolution settlement and the constitutional position of Scotland, opening up the possibility of further contestation of the Union and therefore aspects of BPT. Indeed their growing support may well highlight the failure of Labour's devolution strategy.[57]

Wales

The history of Wales within the Union is somewhat different to that of Ireland and Scotland. Wales was finally linked with England via the Laws of Wales Acts 1536–43. This created a single legal jurisdiction and a single state, governed from the centre. Furthermore the anglicising tendencies operating in Wales from the 16th century onwards can be seen in the removal of the Welsh language from the administrative and judicial systems of Wales. Indeed it was only the use of Welsh in religious practice in Wales that had prevented a greater decline (Elwyn Jones 1994). All this formalised a process of conquest by the English that had been occurring since the end of the 13th century with the defeat of Llywelyn ap Gruffydd. The brief resurgence of Welsh political independence at the beginning of the 15th century under Owain Glyndwr did little to ultimately disrupt the hegemony of England over Wales. This had seen the development of shared political and governmental institutions under the English king and the Marcher lords.[58] By the 16th century 'the practice of politics in Wales was the prerogative of the aristocracy and the gentry. The aristocracy exercised the greatest political power across England and Wales and maintained it by complicated political manoeuvrings and intrigues in court and across the country' (Elwyn Jones 1994: 83). This pattern of relations continued largely unchanged into the 18th century, with Wales being, in governmental terms, dominated by England.

The nationalist challenge in Wales

That said, persistent differences remained between England and Wales, which over time gave rise to a sense of distinctiveness and a variant of the nationalist tradition. These differences were to be found in the Welsh language, culture and identity. Despite the anglicising tendencies of the Union and the promulgation of Britishness, the idea of Wales experienced a 'renaissance' (Elwyn Jones 1994) in the 18th century. At the same time we find resurgence in scholarly interest in Welsh history, language, culture and traditions.[59] By the 19th century a greater sense of 'Welshness' existed amongst the populace. However this coexisted 'with few strains...with loyalty to the monarch, British state and empire' (Elwyn Jones 1994: 209). Thus in the 18th and 19th centuries Welshness remained somewhat ill-defined (Morgan 1998). That which did exist could sit easily for most alongside key signifiers of Britishness and the Union. Moreover the economic dominance of Britain globally underpinned this faith in the Union, its key discourses and its efficacy. The romantic view of Welshness that existed was linked to literary activity which promulgated a sense of Welsh history and tradition. In this historical figures such as Owain Glyndwr became semi-mythic national heroes. Also during the 19th century Welshness was increasingly linked to religious non-conformity, in particular Methodism. Moreover the publication of the 'Blue Books'[60] in 1847 caused deep resentment in Wales and fostered a sense of injustice. Indeed the myth of a distinctive, long-running Welsh gwerin or 'folk' sat well alongside 19th century popular radicalism and non-conformity and these coalesced into an increasingly clear sense of Welshness. The emergence of politicians from relatively humble backgrounds such as T. E. Ellis and Lloyd George added to this belief. However 'the overriding impression left, even to sympathizers ... was of a land whose concerns were still largely of interest to folklorists and antiquarians' (Morgan 1998: 4).

At the same time, the use of the Welsh language was in decline. For example 54.4 per cent of the population spoke Welsh in 1891. By the 1960s the number had fallen to 26 per cent. This decline was promoted by an education system which prioritised fluency in English, the demands of the economy, and the proliferation of English via newspapers, periodicals, books and later, radio and television. Bilingualism also grew due to economic migration into Wales over time and because key community figures such as religious ministers came to associate 'English' with respectability. It was a combination of this sense of Welsh cultural identity and its potential loss that sparked the resurgence of Welsh Nationalism in the 20th century. Initially, this involved challenging the dominance of Britishness.

The lack of distinctive Welsh political identity meant that Welsh nationalism lacked a political dimension until recently. Rather it sought 'parity with England and the recognition of Welsh rights (Elwyn Jones 1994: 246). A sense of injustice did follow the publication of 'The Blue Books' but this fell way short of the injustice felt in Ireland. Nor were there separate institutions such as those in Scotland to foster a sense of administrative distinctiveness.[61] However the idea of distinctive Welsh needs could be more clearly seen than before. For example The Welsh Sunday Closing Act (1881) was the first legislation designed exclusively for Wales and in 1893 the University of Wales was founded.

The emergence of the Young Wales movement[62] (1894–96) saw the first major attempt to add political notions to cultural nationalism in Wales. This movement was influenced by the Young Ireland Movement in the mid 19th century and drew support from the major Liberals in Wales such as Ellis, Lloyd George and D. A. Thomas. Young Wales argued for Welsh Home Rule and the issue came onto the political agenda again just prior to the First World War when E. T. John proposed a bill for Welsh Home Rule. Indeed Welshness could and did find supporters in both the Liberals and emergent Labour parties. However the idea of Welsh Home Rule could not generate either public interest or support, and thus Welsh nationalism remained largely a cultural phenomenon. The dominant issues in Wales post First World War were largely economic ones,[63] yet the issue of Home Rule for Wales was not seen to provide the answer for the majority of the population. Lloyd George offered tokenistic support to the idea and in 1922 a Government of Wales Bill was presented to Parliament. However it did not get past the first reading. Faith in the Union and Britishness remained intact. With the increasing dominance of Labour in Welsh politics, demands for independence and separatism remained marginal at best. This was due in no small part to Labour's by now well-established faith in the BPT. As Morgan notes: 'In 1945, and for several years afterwards, Welsh Nationalism seemed as dead as the druids ... there was in short no Welsh De Valera and no Welsh Sinn Fein. Nor did Welsh Nationalism show the vitality of the SNP North of the border' (1998: 376).

The formation of Plaid Cymru (1925) saw the birth of Wales's first nationalist party. The party contained a wide range of views, some of which veered towards the anti-democratic and authoritarian (Elwyn Jones 1994: 260). Despite these divisions members of this new party all agreed on the primary importance of preserving the Welsh language. However before the Second World War, they had little influence. They had agreed on a policy for self-government in 1932, seeing this as the best means to preserve Welsh cultural identity. However this did not necessarily equate to independence at this point. In 1945, they fought eight seats but lost seven deposits. Having come to prominence during the Llyn incident (1936)[64] Plaid suffered a loss of support during the war due to its support for conscientious objection. After the war it made little headway. By 1959 they had managed to secure 10 per cent of the vote in Wales. However 17 of their 20 candidates still lost their deposits. They remained a largely rurally orientated, small party lacking organisation and support in urbanised, English-speaking areas.

During the late 1950s and early 1960s the nationalist tradition in Wales received a boost. The 'Parliament for Wales' Campaign had been founded in 1949 and a Plaid Cymru chose to support it. Between 1950 and 1956 this campaign garnered a modicum of support across Wales. However it was too ill-focused to provide a permanent basis for the nationalist challenge (Morgan 1998). The Tryweryn Affair[65] in the late 1950s and demands for a separate Welsh television channel were important. Most significantly in 1962, leading Plaid member Saunders Lewis gave a BBC lecture on the decline of the Welsh Language.[66] In it he argued that the preservation of the Welsh language was of greater significance than political independence. Moreover he argued that direct action might be required.

The formation of the Welsh Language Society (1962) came from this. Members engaged in sit-ins and mass demonstrations to promote the cause. The results were apparent as government offices and universities started to adopt bilingualism. In 1967 the Welsh Language Act gave Welsh parity with English. However direct action such as damaging road signs and sabotage resulted in frequent court appearances and caused some damage to Plaid's reputation. The paramilitary activities of the Free Wales Army[67] did not help. Furthermore despite the breakthrough victory of Gwynfor Evans in the Carmarthenshire by-election of 1966 and major swings in by elections in Rhondda West (1967) and Caerphilly (1968), Plaid still struggled to turn its popular support into electoral strength at Westminster. The core of their campaigns focused on local and economic issues and increasingly Labour came to view Plaid Cymru with increasing suspicion. As with the SNP in Scotland, this perceived threat to their electoral hegemony promoted Wilson to establish the Royal Commission in 1968. However with both Labour and the Conservatives committed to a unionism and the BPT, the nationalist challenge remained largely peripheral.

The 1970 election saw Plaid Cymru unable to build upon their by-election successes, returning no seats, despite getting 175,016 votes. Pressure for recognition of the Welsh language in the education system kept Welsh Nationalism alive as did the Kilbrandon Report recommendations for an elected Assembly for Wales. The election of February 1974 saw Plaid Cymru take two seats from Labour in rural areas with high unemployment. By the election of October 1974 it added a further seat to this. With nationalist feeling evident in Wales, both via Plaid and beyond, Labour politicians were increasingly concerned about the possibility for their continued electoral dominance in Wales. Plaid Cymru's MPs supported devolution in the late 1970s, believing it would provide opportunities for the furthering of Welsh interests and Welshness. However the failure to secure a successful referendum result in March 1979[68] highlighted that 'however powerful their sense of cultural and historical identity the Welsh were, in political and economic terms, strictly unionist' (Morgan 1998: 405).

Though their constitution of 1976 Plaid stated that their aim was to secure self-government for Wales, but they downplayed political nationalism in the 1979 election,[69] concentrating again on socio-economic problems. Indeed during the 1980s their tendency towards left-wing and green politics became increasingly apparent. Throughout the Thatcher years notions such as the democratic deficit and the inequity of the union gained further support in Wales as a consequence of election results and the impact of Thatcherite polices. In particular the Miners' Strike 1984–85 had a devastating impact on Wales and seemed to confirm to many that governance from Westminster did not serve Welsh needs. In a country traditionally hostile to the Conservative party the experience of Thatcherism magnified concerns regarding the Union. However such concerns did not translate into widespread support for the political nationalism of Plaid Cymru. Nor did it increase support for Welsh Devolution.[70]

Since the establishment of the Welsh Assembly in 1999 Plaid Cymru has become the main opposition party, winning 15 seats in 2007 and entering a coalition government with the Labour party. They now favour independence, viewing devolution as a stepping stone towards achieving full independent status for Wales within the EU and the UN. Alongside this they retain their concern for Welsh cultural identity, as does the Welsh Language Society. Welsh Nationalism can be seen as an example of the nationalist tradition and thus a challenge to the BPT and its four discourses. By proposing decentralisation, self-government and Welshness it challenges the predominant concepts of political life and identity within the UK.

Conclusion

In this chapter, we have considered the nationalist tradition in the UK and its various expressions in Ireland, Scotland and Wales. This tradition has continually contested the four discourses of the BPT by stressing independence, self-determination and competing national identities. It rejects the centralisation of power and executive dominance emphasised by the BPT, as well as its emphasis on unionism and Britishness. Furthermore in proposing dramatic changes to the territorial relations established by the BPT, it challenges the discourse about change. Indeed the nationalist tradition in one manifestation or another can be seen contesting the predominant political tradition across modern British history. This can be found in both demands for Home Rule, separatism and the preservation of national identity.

However the resonance of the nationalist tradition vis-à-vis the BPT has not been constant or consistent. Rather an asymmetrical resonance of traditions can be detected in two ways. Firstly contingent events have led to the nationalist tradition resonating at differing intensities in different time periods. This has proven to be particularly true in the case of the recent Scottish and Welsh Devolution where declining faith in efficacy of the Union as a result of contingent events prompted the rise of the nationalist parties and demands for constitutional change. Promoted by this and concerns about their electoral hegemony in

Scotland and Wales, Labour then devolved power in 1998.[71] Secondly we can see the nationalist tradition resonating at differing intensities in the constituent parts of the UK at differing times. Whilst the nationalist tradition in Ireland has burned most intensely, the Scottish and Welsh manifestations of this competing tradition have been intermittent. Finally as we have seen, predominant and competing traditions resonate asymmetrically in relation to the prevailing institutional, contextual and discursive environment. Thus whilst the nationalist tradition contests the BPT, this occurs in a context that privileges certain solutions over others. As such the BPT has and does resonate more fully. Hence a degree of path dependency in recent developments such as devolution can be detected (Hall 2009).

However the questioning and contestation of the BPT can and does lead to changes in UK territorial relations over time, be it in the creation of the Irish Free State or the emergence of the recent devolution settlements. Over time, the challenges of nationalists in Ireland, Scotland and Wales have resulted in changes to the territorial relations of the UK. For example the creation of the Northern Ireland Assembly, the Scottish Parliament and the Welsh Assembly was the most recent phase of a long-term process of contestation of the territorial relations established by the 19th century. Despite the resonance of, and faith in, the traditional territorial relations, there were always those who favoured constitutional change. Their views were rooted in competing concepts of democracy and territorial relations. These competing views built upon and were facilitated by a sense of national distinctiveness that was retained over time. Historically Celtic distinctiveness culturally and politically within the Union had a ratchet-like effect on territorial relations, driving small, incremental concessions over time. This process is likely to continue and may be amplified by the post-1997 devolution settlement. Undoubtedly there have already been changes and the first ten years of devolution have witnessed the emergence of policy divergence, coalition governance and an embryonic multi-party system, much of which can be explained by the unintended consequences of the use of AMS.

However the BPT remains a powerful integratory force and will continue to be so. It continues to influence territorial politics in the UK. Crucially it continues to inform the attitudes and responses of key actors. Faced with increasing contestation of traditional territorial relations, actors devised a solution within a discursive framework that dovetailed as neatly as possible with prevailing norms. In this way the asymmetrical power relations between the centre and periphery emanating from the BPT continued to inform, albeit in slightly revised fashion, territorial relations post 1998. For example Executive-Legislative relations at Holyrood have been conducted in a manner similar to those found at Westminster historically (Arter 2004). Thus in many ways devolution does not demonstrate a break with the past and the development of 'new politics' and MLG. Rather it highlights the continued importance of the predominant ideas that have shaped British political life and long-established patterns of dominance and asymmetry in an updated form. Central government still wields a unique set of resources in a political system whose hallmark features remain structured inequality and asymmetrical power relations. As such the BPT remains centrally significant in territorial relations post 1998.

Whilst the possibility for further change in the devolution settlement through the extension of the powers of the Scottish Parliament and Welsh Assembly may occur in the near future, the idea of an independent Scotland or Wales, or a united Ireland, the most fundamental breaks with the prevailing territorial relations and the BPT remains, at this point, highly unlikely. That said devolution undoubtedly involves a dynamic that is likely to lead to further contestation and conflict of the dominant ideas of British politics. Furthermore we have yet to witness the true test of the solidity and efficacy of the 1998 settlement. This is likely to occur since the Conservative party has returned to power in 2010, albeit as part of a coalition. Their faith in the core tenets of the BPT remains unshaken, and how they respond to demands for further change if and when this occurs, remains to be seen. Moreover the coalition's programme of public sector cuts is unlikely to be welcomed in the devolved areas, whose political leanings are often viewed as more social democratic in tone.[72] Recent events such as the victory of the SNP in Scotland in 2007, the establishment of the Calman Commission (2008), the Scotland Bill 2010[73] and the 2011 Referendum on extending the powers of the Welsh Assembly serve only to highlight the fact that the possibility for further conflict and change exists within UK territorial relations remains.

Conclusion

In considering the relationship between political traditions and UK politics this book has dealt with two major concerns. Firstly it has considered a range of usages of political tradition in relation to British politics. Secondly it has offered a detailed exposition of the political traditions that have decisively shaped the institutions, processes and practices of British political life.

In the context of this work, four broad criticisms of traditional narratives of British political life have been identified:

- As a consequence of the dominance of the WM and the positivism of Anglophone political science there has been a lack of detailed focus on the role played by ideas in shaping the institutions, processes and practices of British political life. Indeed there has been a tendency to either ignore the ideational underpinnings of the British political system or take them as given.
- The link between dominant ideas and dominant socio-economic interests is left unexplored in conventional accounts of British political life. This has led to an undervaluing of the impact of structured inequality and asymmetrical power relations to British politics historically.
- When combined, these tendencies help perpetuate a benign and uncritical self-image of the British political system that masks the reality of British political life.
- Traditional narratives offer insufficient conceptualisations of key meta-theoretical issues. In particular on change and continuity, conventional accounts of Britain's political development offer a perspective that unpersuasively alleges the gradual, peaceful evolution of the British political system.

As we have seen, a focus on political traditions necessitates an explicit focus on ideas. However the classical approach to the BPT suffers from many of the criticisms above as well as many more dealt with in Chapter 1. The critical approach to the BPT, whilst not free from criticism, has been underdeveloped and largely ignored in accounts of British politics.

More recent approaches which focus on the importance of ideas fare no better when seeking to explain British political life. Bevir and Rhodes's 'new interpretivism' has attracted much attention, but ultimately lacks heuristic value. It ignores notions such as dominance, hierarchy and asymmetry and offers flawed conceptualisations of both meta-theoretical issues and notions such as tradition and dilemma. Significantly, Bevir and Rhodes's concept of change and continuity is unconvincing and fails to account for the demonstrable continuities in British politics. For his part, Marquand fails to adequately address the key relationships between ideas and institutions and the material and the ideational.

In response to the above, a concept of the political traditions operating in the UK has been offered that develops and extends the critical view of the BPT. Examining modern UK history we can clearly identify the existence of a predominant political tradition, referred to as the British Political Tradition (BPT). This is based upon four key discourses. The first of these are:

- A discourse which stresses a limited liberal notion of representation and the elitist view that politicians are best suited to make decisions on behalf of the populace. Politicians have come to view themselves as the guardians and executors of the national interest and are willing to act against the expressed will of the public or in the face of substantial public opposition.
- A discourse which stresses a conservative notion of responsibility and the view that strong, decisive government is the most effective, efficient and desirable form of government. This can be seen in the belief in the virtue of centralisation of power through the notions of parliamentary sovereignty, the unitary state and unionism.

Taken together these two discourses coalesce into an elitist view of democracy and the predominant mantra of governance in the UK: that 'Westminster and Whitehall knows best'.

These sit alongside two further discourses:

- A discourse concerning change which emphasises the virtues of continuity, gradualism, flexibility and stability. The British developmental

path is seen as setting Britain apart from other Western democracies and is emblematic of a superior approach.
- A discourse concerning national distinctiveness which stresses British superiority politically (and culturally). This emphasis on British exceptionalism is associated with the view above.

When combined these four discourses form the BPT. Over time this predominant political traditions has come to function as a 'common understanding' of the political system which is widely appealed to by both politicians and scholars alike.

The BPT underpins and informs the institutions and practices of British government, usually associated with the WM narrative. The WM narrative portrays parliamentary sovereignty and strong, centralised government benignly in that they are seen as democratic, desirable and effective. They have allegedly served the UK well and are a superior form of government. However this has always been a self-image rather than an accurate description of British political life. Instead such notions are expressions of the BPT, underpinning and ensuring the predominance of the political elite at the centre historically. Processes such as the use of SPS and government secrecy are also linked to the BPT as is faith in them. Actors within and beyond the British state have believed in and continue to believe in the efficacy of this approach.

Furthermore the BPT establishes and maintains institutional hierarchies and embodies power relations. This explains how patterns of behaviour at Westminster and Whitehall became replicated both over time and elsewhere.[1] The BPT informed the set of institutions and practices that governed Britain. These in turn helped to further inculcate and perpetuate patterns of elite dominance within the political system and outcomes that generally favoured their continued dominance. Moreover these institutions and processes became the context for future debates and discussions, leading to a strategically selective environment that privileges certain ideas over others. Through this perspective we can persuasively explain both the development of the British political system and the fate of the various constitutional reforms enacted since 1997.

Finally we have considered how the predominant political tradition is reflective of the ideas and interests of dominant socio-economic groups and how it reinforces those ideas and interests. The suggestion here is simple. The BPT both reflects and reinforces the structured inequality and asymmetries of power in UK society. In particular this inequality has led to a close relationship between dominant socio-economic interests and the political elite in the form of a power bloc. This power bloc has been supportive of the BPT because it allowed their dominance and narrated it as effective, efficient and in the national interest. Above all, the BPT has allowed the pursuit of policies largely favourable to these elites. However support for the BPT has not only been found amongst the elites; rather the predominant political tradition has found support over time amongst large sections of the populace as well.

Despite its predominance, the BPT has not gone uncontested. Indeed there is a long lineage of challenges to it and it is from these that change can and does emanate. We have identified the existence of a competing political tradition based upon a more participatory concept of democracy. This tradition has challenged the elitist nature of UK democracy. The importance of this tradition can be seen in recent demands for constitutional reform emanating from Charter 88, CFOI, ERS and Unlock Democracy.

We also considered the nationalist tradition and its various expressions in Ireland, Scotland and Wales. This tradition challenges the territorial integrity of the UK, stressing instead independence, self-determination and competing national identities. It rejects the centralisation of power and executive dominance emphasised by the BPT, challenging the unionism and Britishness of the predominant tradition. The impact of this tradition can be seen in the development of UK territorial politics. Indeed historical demands for constitutional change in the constituent parts of the UK as well as recent developments such as devolution can be persuasively explained by the utilisation of the notion of predominant and competing political traditions.

However the resonance of the BPT and the challenges to it have not been constant. Rather an asymmetrical resonance of traditions can be detected in two ways. Firstly contingent events lead to predominant and competing traditions resonating at differing intensities at different times. Secondly predominant and competing traditions resonate asymmetrically in relation to the prevailing institutional, contextual and discursive environment. Thus whilst this contestation is continual it occurs in a context that privileges certain solutions over others. An integral facet of the asymmetrical political landscape in the UK is the asymmetrical resonance of ideas and traditions within that landscape. As such the BPT has and does resonate more fully. However contestation of the predominant tradition can and does lead to change.

Ideational conflict forms the backdrop to the British political system. This occurs at both a micro or macro level in the sense of challenging either aspects of the political system or its entirety. Indeed the relationship between the predominant and competing traditions is interactive and iterative over time. As contestations of the predominant tradition occur within an institutional and ideational context that privileges certain ideas and solutions over others, alongside change, a degree of path dependency in the British political system can be detected. However we should also recognise the impact of unintended consequences such as those seen in devolution post 1998 as offering the possibility for further contestation of the predominant tradition and thus further change.

With demands for reform of the British political system an increasingly prominent feature of discourse and debate in recent years, considering how political traditions have shaped the British political system has clear heuristic value. Moreover with further reform promised by the Conservative-Liberal Democrat coalition,[2] the need to explain the process by which such proposals develop and how the prevailing ideational, institutional and discursive context impacts upon the nature and development, or lack thereof, of British political life will remain as pressing as ever.

Notes

Introduction

1. See for example the comment in the *Daily Express* (19 December 1997): 'This country's distinctive contribution to civilisation has been the development of stable institutions of representative government.'
2. This approach is linked to the governance thesis, which is itself becoming a new orthodoxy (Kerr and Kettell 2006).

1 'Variations on a Theme': Political Tradition in Explanations of British Politics

1. We should recognise, as Chadwick (2000: 288-9) does, that 'the distinction between real politics and ideas is artificial – politics is a linguistic practice and our understanding of any political practice is incomplete if it does not refer to the discourses that surround and construct it'.
2. Hall (1986: 19) defines 'institutions' as: 'the formal rules, compliance procedures, and the standard operating practices that structure the relationship between individual in various units of the polity and the economy'.
3. Similarly in a widely read textbook, Dearlove and Saunders (1991: 70) describe the Westminster Model as 'a cabinet system of government where close two party electoral competition produces a party duopoly in the Commons and an alternating monopoly of the executive that is mandated and able to implement the programme it put before the electorate so that representative and reasonable government is secured'.
4. Lijphart juxtaposes the Westminster Model of Democracy with a Consensus Model of Democracy. The latter will be raised in Chapter 6.
5. The Asymmetrical Power Model (Marsh, Richards and Smith 2001: 2003; Marsh 2008a) offers a more accurate description of how the British political system functions.
6. For example in a later co-authored work, he suggested that 'the men who drafted the Treaty of Union carefully left every institution in England and every institution in Scotland untouched by the Act, provided that the existence of such an institution was consistent with the main objects of the Act...the essential unity of the people' (Dicey and Rait 1920: 362).
7. For example Bogdanor goes so far as to suggest that 'the profoundly unitary nature of the UK, as expressed in the supremacy of Parliament' (1979:7) was the defining feature of territorial relations in the UK.
8. See for example Bogdanor (1999), Mitchell (2000) and McGarvey and Cairney (2008).
9. Johnson argues that 'in retrospect, it is hardly short of astonishing that this faith in the virtues and vigour of a bundle of conventions and institutional practices shaped mainly over a century ago should have endured so long'

10. For example Midwinter, Keating and Mitchell (1991: 2) argued that 'the UK remains a unitary state, in which ultimate sovereignty resides in Parliament'.
11. As we saw earlier the lack of theory in British politics is an increasingly identified weakness of analyses of British politics (Greenleaf 1983a; McAnulla 2006a; Kerr and Kettell 2006).
12. See for example Bill Jones et al. *Politics UK* (2004)
13. It is worth noting in passing here that in the many constitutional reforms proposed since Birch originally discussed this idea little has been done to alter this. In cases where reform proposals have been advanced, the claim to make the system more representative, such as the 'People's Peers' or the Wakeham Commission Report (2000), a closer inspection highlights the extent to which the result would likely to be to preserve the specialist and unrepresentative nature of politicians due to the nature of the appointments process.
14. Marsh and Hall (2007: 222) suggest that debates about responsibility were implicit in those occurring about representation that had characterised the late 18th and 19th centuries. The same notion of responsibility was implicit in the Tory, Whig and Liberal discourses concerning representation, a point that will be dealt with in greater depth later.
15. Broadly, in the UK the Liberals stressed that responsible government would be achieved via accountability to Parliament whereas Conservatives placed their emphasis on the desirability of a strong executive that was able to govern.
16. It is highly debatable whether Bevir and Rhodes overcome this in their own work, given how they conceptualise the relationship between ideas and institutions. For a greater exploration of this see Chapter 2.
17. It should be noted here that the Asymmetrical Powel Model (APM) developed by Marsh, Richards and Smith (2001; 2003) also utilises the BPT as a central tenet of its overall organising perspective and the more recent work of Batters (2005) and Marsh and Hall (2007) has built upon this critical perspective.
18. Tant's analysis of British democracy is reminiscent of Rousseau's oft-quoted observation that 'the English people believes itself to be free; it is gravely mistaken; it is free only during election of members of parliament; as soon as the members are elected, the people are enslaved; it is nothing. In the brief moment of its freedom, the English people makes such a use of that freedom that it deserves to lose it' (cited in Cress 1987: xi) and the subject of Lord Hailsham's 1976 Dimbleby Lecture 'Elective Dictatorship'.
19. This is a trend that, it could be argued, continues unabated. See for example New Labour's failure to honour their manifesto commitments to hold referendums on both membership of the Single European Currency and, significantly, electoral reform for Westminster elections. For a convincing explanation of the latter see Marsh and Hall (2007).
20. As already noted The British Political Tradition forms a central part of the APM developed by Marsh, Richards and Smith (2001; 2003). It is also

discussed in detail by McAnulla (2006a) and developed in detail by Marsh and Hall (2007).
21. Historical Institutionalism is a branch of social science whose method involves analysing institutions in order to identify sequences or patterns of social, political and economic behaviour across time. Charles Tilly's Coercion, capital and European states (1990) defines it as a method for measuring 'big structures, large processes, and (making) huge comparisons. As such it is explicitly concerned with the notion of continuity and change over time. Critics argue that it privileges the former over the latter. For an engaging discussion of Historical Institutionalism see D. Marsh, E. Batters and H. Savigny, *Historical Institutionalism: Beyond Pierson and Skocpol* (unpublished paper: available online).
22. For discussion of this see for example Hay (2002), Marsh, Batters and Savigny (2004: available online), Schmidt (2006).
23. This view forms a key part of Bevir and Rhodes's critique of the existing usage of the BPT (Bevir and Rhodes 2003).
24. Marsh (2003) suggests there are five overall positions concerning the relationship between institutions and ideas. He identifies them as (i) Institutionalism (ii) Idealism (iii) The Additive Approach (iv) The Discourse Analytical Approach (v) The Dialectical Approach. Of these Marsh advocates a dialectical approach. For details see Marsh (2003: unpublished paper available online).
25. For discussion and explanation of the fate of Freedom of Information under New Labour see Batters (2005) and Marsh and Hall (2007).
26. The stages of the morphogenetic cycle are (i) structural conditioning (ii) social interaction (iii) structural elaboration or reproduction.
27. Hay states that 'what is required instead is a recognition of the complex interaction of material and ideational factors. Political outcomes are, in short, neither a simple reflection of actors' intentions and understandings, nor of the contexts which give rise to such intentions and understandings. Rather, they are a product of the impact of the strategies actors devise as means to realise their intentions upon a context which favours certain strategies over others and does so irrespective of the intentions of the actors themselves' (2002: 208).
28. See for example Norton (1984) and Punnett (1987) whose reverence for the British political system and its development barely conceals their conservatism.

2 Tradition or Traditions?

1. Nor is the concept of political tradition peculiar to British politics. See for example R. Hofstadter, *The American Political Tradition* (1948).
2. We should note here that McAnulla (2006b) persuasively suggests that their interpretivism has not fully overcome the problems of positivism. This will be explained more fully later in this chapter.
3. Hay (2002) offers a detailed analysis and critique of the methodology of positivist political science. In particular he highlights the parsimony of positivist approaches to political analysis and critiques their 'naturalism' (2002: 59–89).

224 Notes

4. For a detailed discussion and evaluation of the relative merits of these approaches see Marsh (2008a).
5. Firstly Bevir and Rhodes suggest that the interpretive approach identifies important empirical gaps in the WM by distinguishing the fundamental changes in British government. Essentially Bevir and Rhodes (2003; 2004) argue that the WM is an outdated and unconvincing description of British politics. Secondly the interpretive approach decentres institutions and thus avoids the idea that institutions fix the behaviour of individuals within them rather than being products of that behaviour. For Bevir and Rhodes, change is rooted in the beliefs, attitudes and preferences of individual actors. Concepts such as tradition and dilemma are available to political scientists as explanatory devices if this approach is adopted. Thirdly it is suggested that this approach opens up new research agendas and questions regarding British government and techniques, such as ethnography and history, are excellent tools for identifying beliefs and actions as well as explaining such beliefs and actions. Fourthly it raises key theoretical issues regarding the pluralising of policy-making and diversification of government structures. It therefore lends support to the idea of bottom-up forms of decision-making as an analytical view. Finally it focuses upon observation and tries to get below and behind the surface of official accounts to find the texture and depth, as well as allowing interviewees to explain meaning of their actions.
6. It should be noted that Marsh and Hall (2007) conceptualise this continual contestation somewhat differently to Bevir and Rhodes.
7. Marsh and Hall (2006: 6) suggest that Bevir and Rhodes breach their own rules concerning 'intellectual honesty' by undervaluing alternative approaches.
8. Bevir and Rhodes (2008a) refer to the Westminster tradition for the first time. Readers are left to assume that this is the narrative of the institutions and practices usually associated with the WM.
9. To suggest that actors may hold a mistaken beliefs or set of beliefs is easily accommodated within critical realist ontology and epistemology.
10. It is interesting to note again the similarity between this view and the oft-cited view of Marx (1851). See K. Marx, 'The Eighteenth Brumaire of Louis Bonaparte, 1851' in D. McLellan (1977).
11. The free floating nature of Bevir and Rhodes's political traditions can also be seen in their antipathy towards questions regarding power and dominance (2008a: 174).
12. This is one of the reasons that the APM (Marsh 2008a) offers a more persuasive view of British politics than the DPM because it accepts and develops this idea. The APM states that the British polity is characterised by structured inequality in society, an elitist political tradition, asymmetries of power, exchange relationships between actors in the system of governance, a strong, if segmented, executive and limited external constraints on executive power.
13. See for example Lord Irvine's statement that the constitutional reforms were 'tailored to the particular needs of the UK constitution'.
14. We should recognise that there have been longstanding classical approaches to change that social and political analysts have utilised. These range from evolutionary perspectives of early sociologists like Herbert Spencer, through

the systems theory of Talcott Parsons, to the historical materialism of Marxism.
15. For example Blyth (2002) argues that structures and institutions account for continuity and stability whereas agency and ideational factors account for change. Whilst such a suggestion hardly seems to grasp the complexity of the problem, it does illuminate how even those with theoretically informed views of continuity and change such as Historical Institutionalists can oversimplify complex questions (Marsh 2007).
16. Structuralism assumes that social and political change is confined to marginal modifications of behaviour within the context of a definitive set of rule or laws that structure social and political life and that crucially remain essentially static over time (Hay 2002a). Although it is undoubtedly easier to assume that institutions, practices, structures and ideas exhibit some consistency over time, this leaves political analysis as the mapping of an essentially static, if at times, uneven terrain. Thus structuralist accounts suffer most obviously from a lack of temporality, presenting a picture of structures as almost trans-temporal phenomena.
17. Intentionalist or agency-centric approaches fair no better when attempting to explain change and continuity. Focusing on the role of agency as the contingent factor promoting change implies the absence of constraints upon action. Thus we see a world postulated where many outcomes are possible because 'there are essentially no rules of the game and there is no close correspondence between observed and intended outcomes' (Hay 2002: 135). Taken to its purest form, intentionalism conceptualises time as 'merely the unfolding of preferences instantiated in action (Hay 1997: 13). However the suggestion that constraints, be they structural, material, ideational or cultural, do not exist or have an impact upon actions makes it difficult to explain outcomes when there is no close correspondence between intention and outcomes.
18. These include a tendency to interpret the past in the light of present day British constitutional settlement and a view of British parliamentary democracy as the apogee of political development. The Whig approach can be summarised thus, 'it is part and parcel of the Whig interpretation of history that it studies the past with reference to the present' (Butterfield 1965: 11).
19. Kerr (2002: 331) notes that whilst political scientists often invoke evolutionary concepts of change 'these words are often invoked in an ad hoc way, rather than being embedded within a proper explanatory framework'. In particular we might suggest that Norton (1984), Punnett (1987) and Hanson and Walles (1990) all do this.
20. For an excellent overview of this see D. Marsh, 'Marxism' in Marsh and Stoker (2002).
21. Marsh (2002) argues that this change has been prompted by three factors: (i) theoretical critiques from both inside and outside Marxism (ii) the inability of economism to persuasively explain economic, social and political developments (iii) economic, social and political developments in the world have stimulated new theoretical developments.
22. For details of each approach and a critical evaluation see Hay (2002: 143–150).

226 *Notes*

23. He highlights the theories of Comte, Spencer and Durkheim as offering the first widely read usage of evolution. The approach then experienced a brief resurgence 'between the 1950s and the early 1970s in the work of structural-functional theorists such as Talcott Parsons' (Kerr 2002: 332).
24. This can be explained because it was seen as trying to incorporate the objective reasoning of the natural sciences into explanations of historical change over time and was damaged by its association with social Darwinism and Nazism (Kerr 2002: 332).
25. We should also recognise the importance of political realities and electoral concerns as motivating factors here.
26. For some discussion of this see M. Hall (2010) *'Political Traditions and continuity in UK Politics: A Discourse concerning Representation'* (unpublished paper: available from author).

3 Exploring Tradition

1. Hobsbawm (1983a: 2–3) defines 'invented traditions' as 'a set of practices, normally governed by overtly or tacitly accepted rules and of a ritual or symbolic nature, which seek to inculcate certain values and norms of behaviour by repetition, which automatically implies continuity with the past. In fact, where possible, they normally attempt to establish continuity with a suitable historic past ... However in so far as there is such reference to a historic past, the peculiarity of 'invented traditions' is that the continuity with it is largely factitious'.
2. The obvious exception to this is Shils's *Tradition* (1981).
3. For an introduction to the diverse range of social theorists concerned with the relationship between culture and identity, see chapter 12 in Haralambos and Holborn (2004).
4. In particular the importance of the work of neo-Marxists and discourse analysts should be recognised.
5. Preston suggests that 'the notion of political-cultural identity points to the way in which individuals and groups locate themselves with reference to the ordered political-communities (polities) within which they take themselves to dwell; the way they handle questions of power and authority. The immediate local will provide the person with a series of sources of practical knowledge: family, neighbourhood, organisation, institution and media. Thereafter, agents form networks and lodge themselves in dispersed groups, and these groupings of persons order their relationships with other groups within the wider community. Finally individuals and groups order their understandings of contingent, shifting patterns of power and authority in continually reworked memory. This can take a series of forms: the material of folk traditions, common sense and local ideology (the material of little traditions); the histories of organisations and institutions; the ideas of current in the public sphere and media; the official truths affirmed in the machineries of states; and ideas of nation (the material of great traditions). In these various spheres we are looking at the production, dissemination and practical effects of sets of ideas about how the polity and its inhabitants are ordered and might develop (the range of possibilities/permissible

lines of prospective action. Over time, there will be a series of elite political projects, each way of reading and reacting to shifting circumstances, each shaping distinctive forms of life and patterns of understanding' (Preston 2004: 2–3).
6. McAnulla (2007) notes that Shils has been criticised for offering an essentialist account of tradition that suggests that traditions have essential or unchanging characteristics. Shils (1981) does not account for what might make a particular characteristic essential or open to adaptation. However, McAnulla (2007: 12) suggests that we may read his work in such a way that 'in principle any particular element of a tradition could be open to challenge'.
7. Concurring with Giddens (1994 cited in McAnulla 2007), we note that beyond these two examples, conservative theorists have themselves been surprisingly reticent in their theoretical reflections on the concept of tradition.
8. For overviews of Marxist and neo-Marxist approaches to culture, see Barker's *Cultural Studies: Theory and Practice* (2003), and Strinati's An Introduction to Theories of Popular Culture (2004).
9. This idea (the constitutive other) is widely appealed to in social theory. It refers to the construction of identity vis-à-vis that which it is not. Cahoone describes the 'other' thus: 'what appear to be cultural units – human beings, words, meanings, ideas, philosophical systems, social organisations – are maintained in their apparent unity only through an active process of exclusion, opposition and hierachization. Other phenomena or units must be represented as foreign or "other" through representing a hierarchical dualism in which the unit is privileged or favoured, and the other is devalued some way' (1996: 159).
10. As Anderson argues, 'Traditionalism and empiricism henceforward fuse as a single legitimating system: traditionalism sanctions the present by deriving it from the past, empiricism shackles the future by riveting it to the present' (1964: 32). Whilst such 'sanctions' and 'shackles' are not 'unbreakable', we should recognise that they can act as powerful constraints upon action and outcomes. This can account for the perpetuation and persistence of patterns of rule and power relations and as such, a measure of path dependency with the pre-existing will be discernible.
11. Tant uses the word 'constitutionalization' to describe the process by which the Labour party in its infancy quickly went from being a party that viewed democracy in more participatory terms, to a party largely convinced of the virtue of the British Political Tradition (Tant 1993).
12. Relatedly Hobsbawm (1983a: 9) suggests that there are three overlapping types of 'invented traditions' that perform functions in society: firstly, those that establish or symbolise social cohesion or the membership of real or artificial communities, secondly, those establishing or legitimising institutions, status or relations to authority, and Finally those whose main purpose is socialisation, the inculcation of beliefs, value systems and conventions of behaviour.
13. This point is recognised by Marx's oft-quoted but insufficiently utilised statement that 'men make their own history but they do not make it as they please nor under conditions of their own choosing...rather they make it

under the circumstances they find before them, under given and imposed conditions' (K. Marx, 'The Eighteenth Brumaire of Louis Bonaparte, 1851' in D. McLellan (1977).
14. For example, the elitist assumptions of the predominant political tradition in the UK have been left unrecognised or unexplored in mainstream analyses of the institutions and procedures they underpin.
15. These include Burke (1790); Erskine May (1844; 1862) Bagehot (1867); Dicey (1885); Jennings (1936; 1941); Birch (1964); and Beer (1965).
16. Numerous examples of movements whose views challenge or contest established notions of territorial organisation in different nation states could be identified globally. See, for example, the Basque Separatism movement in Spain or Breton Nationalism in France.
17. It is for this reason that, contra Rhodes, Wanna and Weller (2009: 45), we should consider 'dead' traditions such as Chartism.
18. This critique is one that draws explicit influence from previous constitutional challenges including Chartism.

4 The British Political Tradition Revisited

1. See for example the comparison referred to by Marsh and Hall (2007) between debates in Denmark over the notion of active citizenship and the notion of 'subjects' that has been prevalent in the UK. Such ideas are crucial in informing the nature of the political system and the extent of participation that occurs thereafter. Or to put it another way, the idea of subjects is informed by, supports and upholds an elitist concept of democracy such as that found in the UK.
2. A contemporary example of this can be seen in relation to the Iraq War (Kettell 2006).
3. Vernon identifies contestation over: 'the meaning of the constitution as the master narrative of English politics' (1993: 333). These debates concerning representation and responsibility could be seen as part of the historical debate(s) over the nature of governance and rule in the UK which can be readily identified across English, and then British History. In these debates, whilst a radical discourse can be seen on occasion, the Tory and Whig discourses were, at this point, the predominant perspectives.
4. See for example Bagehot (1867), Dicey (1885) and Jennings (1936; 1941).
5. Marsh and Tant summarise this: 'some familiar ideas thus emerge, we can see the emphasis upon: hierarchical social and political organization; the initiation of policy by the head of government and the need for 'order' if harmonious society and good government is to be ensured' (1989: 7).
6. Vernon correctly notes that: 'it is simply not sufficient to assert that any discourse used by a class reflects their consciousness as members of that class' (1993: 330). However we should also recognise that socio-economic position can and does influence (but not determine) how we come to understand the world, its structures and our place within them. Thus we should seek to uncover the dynamic process by which material and ideational factors interact in an iterative and reciprocal manner in the formation of any political identity.

7. It should be recognised that the Whigs did not speak with a unified political voice, nor was Burke's the loudest of those voices when he became MP for Bristol in 1774.
8. Although he appears to suggest that the constituents' wishes were important, at the time of his writings less than 5 per cent of the adult population could vote.
9. For example, we might recognise here the influence of Plato's thought regarding the role of Philosopher Kings and Guardians (Annas 1981), his critique of Athenian democracy and the political competence of the majority. However we should recognise that Plato was equally scathing with regard to oligarchs and their obsession with wealth, property and self interest (Annas 1981: 299).
10. Not only does it reduce the means to ensure politicians' accountability to the will of the people primarily to periodic voting; it also ensured a notable lack of popular influence or participation in policy-making. Trusteeship also lacks the capacity to generate sufficient popular interest in politics between elections. Indeed in recent years its legacy has been a dislocation between politicians and the public which has proven incapable of sustaining or re-establishing respect between them as trust in politicians is damaged by scandals such as Cash for Questions, and Parliamentary Expenses. It is interesting to note here how contemporary criticisms of the UK's political system often target these ideas. See for example the arguments of the Liberal Democrats, Unlock Democracy, Power 2010, The Electoral Reform Society and CFOI.
11. See for example his statement on the 9 February 1790 that 'the French had shown themselves the ablest architects of ruin that had hitherto existed in the world. In a very short space of time they had completely pulled down to the ground, their monarchy, their church, their nobility, their law, their revenue, their army, their navy, their commerce, their arts and their manufactures' (cited in O'Brien 2002: 213).
12. It should be noted that radicalism was a broad and imprecise view incorporating a variety of opinions (Thompson 1980).
13. For example, Thompson notes that even the Westminster Committee, did not lead: 'an independent, populist, still less working class movement' (1980: 509).
14. Recent research on the notion of deference in the 19th century suggests that it was often based upon conditionality and implicit negotiation. That is to say, 'respect was given in return for performing paternalistic duties thought appropriate to wealth and position' (Garrard 2002: 264). However at its heart deference in the 18th and 19th centuries was still rooted in inequalities of wealth and asymmetrical power relations which would influence both the conditions and the substance and conduct of implicit negotiations.
15. He stated that 'he was fully convinced that the country possessed at the present moment a legislature which answered all the good purposes of legislation...he should always feel his duty to resist such measures (reform) when proposed by others' (Canon 1973: 201).
16. For example, Hanson and Walles's suggestion that Britain is set apart: 'most sharply from most other countries...(by) the slowness and gradualness of

the evolutionary process by which she achieved her modernisation' (1990: 3 is indicative of this trend.
17. See for example the popular disturbances evident during the Reform Crisis of 1830–32 and the Hyde Park Riots of July 1866.
18. See for example the opposition of Viscount Palmerston as indicative of the attitude of many MPs towards popular sovereignty and the lasting influence of Burke.
19. Here we could reference the various failed attempts at reform in the 1850s as evidence.
20. It should also be noted that gaining the vote did not necessarily gain the middle classes equal political power and influence with the Aristocracy. Indeed Garrard (2002) notes that it was not until after the 1880s that the landed classes' dominance began to diminish but in no way disappeared.
21. We should again recognise here as O'Gorman (1989) and Vernon (1993) do, that political influence in Victorian Britain extended beyond the vote. That said, politics in this period remained vastly asymmetrical in terms of the possibility of or opportunity to influence outcomes due to the structured inequalities of UK society and their manifestations in the political process.
22. See for example, Lord John Russell's suggestion in 1853 that only those should be enfranchised who had given: 'good proof of prudence' (cited in Hoppen 2000: 239), although how this was to be ascertained was unclear.
23. See for example Gladstone's famous statement that 'every man who is not presumably incapacitated by some consideration or personal unfitness or of political danger is morally entitled to come within the pale of the constitution. Of course in giving utterance to such a proposition I do not recede from the protest I have previously made against sudden, or violent, or excessive or intoxicating change' (Hansard May 1864). The Burkeian element to his view of change, as well as his antipathy to the notion of popular sovereignty underpinning the notion that 'political danger' and 'personal unfitness' cannot be underestimated.
24. Davis and Tanner demonstrate that 'although the late Victorian borough franchise remained exclusive, in was not in any conscious way selective – certainly not in the way its founders intended, distinguishing a 'respectable' electorate from the residuum' (1996: 327). This clearly demonstrates the significance of unintended consequences.
25. This was more the case following the 1872 Ballot Act and the 1883 Corrupt and Illegal Practices Act.
26. See for example, the notion that 'the rich and wise are not to have, by explicit law, more votes than the poor and stupid' (Bagehot 1867: 162).
27. Bagehot (1867: 182), like Gladstone before him, did suggest that artisans should have members to speak for them.
28. To cite Bagehot: 'the English people possibly even above other free nations, is fair' and 'a free nation rarely can be – and the English nation is not quick of apprehension. It only comprehends what is familiar to it – what comes in its own experience, what squares with its own thoughts' (Bagehot 1867: 152).
29. The mantra 'Westminster and Whitehall knows best' does not preclude discussion, debate and disagreement within and between the institutions of governance in the UK. Indeed this is commonplace as policy is developed

and deliberated upon. Rather it suggests firstly that political wisdom is to be found primarily amongst the political elite and thus, supreme decision-making power should reside with them. Secondly it suggests that they (the political elite) are the supreme arbiters of the national interest and should be free to govern largely as they see fit. Given that the parameters established by the BPT ('the rules of the game') have found widespread support amongst that elite and beyond, those opportunities that do exist for wider involvement in policy-making and governance occur on an uneven playing field in which, politicians, and more specifically the executive wield a unique set of resources. Moreover much of the rancour we witness at Westminster masks the reality of executive dominance of Parliament, creating, more often than not, the illusion of opportunity for influence rather than the actuality.

30. Even Rhodes et al. recognise this antipathy when they refer to: 'an elite or top down view of representative democracy that will have no truck with participatory ideas' (2009: 71).
31. Such a view of the nature of UK democracy could be appealed to when attempting to explain the increasing problems concerning political participation in the UK in recent years. For such an approach see D. Marsh, T. O'Toole and S. Jones, *Young People and Politics in the UK* (2007).
32. Despite the fact that the Parliament Act of 1911 involved a removal of the House of Lords' power of veto in all circumstances barring an attempt to extend the lifetime of a parliament beyond five years, we should note that the aristocracy retained a disproportionate influence in the British political system. This can be seen not only in the fact that they retained their own chamber but also in the Lords' ability to amend and influence law-making, and thus affect outcomes.
33. Since 1911 there have been numerous reforms to the House of Lords. These include the reduction of the delaying power to a single year (1949), the introduction of the Life Peerage and women to the chamber (1958) and the more recent removal of all but 92 of the hereditary peers (1999). We should however note here that the long-term fate of the House of Lords remains to be decided as various options for reform exist, ranging from total appointment to total election.
34. Dicey suggested that ministerial responsibility had two meanings. Firstly it referred to the liability of Ministers to lose their offices if they could retain the confidence of the House of Commons (Dicey 1885: 155). Secondly it meant the legal responsibility of every Minister for every Act of Parliament in which he takes part (Dicey 1885: 155). The first aspect of ministerial responsibility was not enshrined in law but highlighted the central significance of Parliament in relation to the executive, as Dicey saw it. This suggested that accountability to Parliament occupied a central position within the British political system.
35. In his famous speech at Crystal Palace on 24 June 1872 Disraeli stated that the three great objects of the national party were; to maintain the political institutions of the UK through support for the monarchy, the House of Lords and the church; to protect the Empire of England; and to raise the condition of the 'English' people. It was this blend of traditionalism, nationalism and social reform, all conducted in the name of national order and balance that defined what became know as Tory Democracy.

36. McAnulla (2006a) identifies British nationalism as a cross-cutting idea in British politics. However my characterization of it is somewhat broader. I use the wider notion of Britishness as a key tenet of the BPT. Clearly, a sense of British nationalism would form part of this. However that alone does not fully capture the extent to which a distinctive sense of British national identity was developed. Nor does it fully demonstrate the extent to which there was both a political and cultural dimension to this identity.
37. The phrase that Westminster is 'the mother of all Parliaments' is actually a misquotation of John Bright and his phrase that 'England is the mother of all Parliaments' (18 January 1865). We should however note that this famous English Radical whilst arguing for the extension of the franchise, evoked the idea of something exceptional or distinctive about the political system of his country.
38. Even a cursory examination of works such as Bagehot (1867) and Dicey (1885) highlights the fact that the elitism of the BPT was somewhat masked behind a self-congratulatory narration of the British political system.
39. See for example the internal party battles of the 1950s and the early 1980s discussed in detail by Tant (1993) as evidence for this trend.
40. The impact of elitism and the idea that 'Westminster and Whitehall knows best' can be seen in the responses of politicians responsible for or supportive of unpopular policies such as the Poll Tax, the invasion of Iraq and, more recently, the removal of the cap on university tuition fees. The suggestion that public disapproval of government policy is not to be explained by the limitations or failures of the policy itself but rather, that the populace do not understand why the policy is necessary and/or desirable is a notable trend. Therefore rather than adjust or even scrap it, what is required is the re-narration or 'spinning' of the original policy.
41. These contestations will be dealt with in Chapters 6 and 7.

5 The British Political Tradition and Political Life in the UK

1. Contra authors such as Gamble (1994), the argument here is that the UK has a strong government tradition. Contra Gamble's argument that the UK has a strong state tradition, I appeal to the notion that the UK has a non-state tradition, which is commonplace in the literature to describe the UK as having a non-state tradition (Loughlin and Peters 1997). Marquand (1988) argues that the UK has never had state that consistently intervenes in either civil society or, crucially, the economy. This is an important observation given the manner in which the BPT neatly fits with the attitudes and needs of dominant economic interests.
2. See for example the debates over constitutional reform that have periodically arisen in the UK.
3. See for example the creation of the Scottish Parliament in 1999 (Hall 2009) of the introduction of the Freedom of Information Act (Batters 2005).
4. For example Judge (2005: 24) roundly dismisses the WM as 'over simplified', as holding 'crude assumptions about the nature of power' and of creating 'false dualities'.

Notes 233

5. As was suggested in Chapter 2, this continued belief in the WM, however misplaced raises problems for Bevir and Rhodes's view of political traditions.
6. See for example the House of Lords, *Completing the Reform* London, Cm 5921 HMSO 2001.
7. Contestation of the existing territorial relations can be detected across British history (Brown, Paterson, McCrone 1996, Paterson 2000, and Kee 2000) and will be dealt with in Chapter 7.
8. For example, The White Paper on Scottish Devolution (1997) stated unequivocally that the government's intention was to establish: 'a fair and just settlement for Scotland within the framework of the United Kingdom – a settlement which will be good for Scotland and the United Kingdom' (Scotland's Parliament 1997: Foreword). Immediately, we should note that the intention was to work within the pre-existing framework of 'the Union'. Labour believed that: 'the Union will be strengthened by recognising the claims of Scotland, Wales and the regions with strong identities of their own. The government's devolution proposals, by meeting these aspirations, will not only safeguard but also enhance the union' (Scotland's Parliament 1997: 3:1).
9. The UK now uses a range of electoral systems. The Additional Member system is used for Scottish parliamentary; Welsh Assembly and GLA elections. The Single Transferable Vote is used for Northern Ireland Assembly elections and Scottish local elections. The Regional Party List is used for European Parliamentary elections and the Supplementary Vote is used for the London Mayoral elections.
10. We should note here that they have not relaxed their opposition to electoral reform per se and will campaign against its introduction in the referendum. Indeed this issue may test the unity of the coalition as no other does.
11. In doing so it is debateable whether they will benefit in the long term. They are clearly not guaranteed of victory in any referendum and AV does not necessarily lead to coalition governance, unlike STV and other proportional or hybrid systems. Thus the situation the Liberal Democrats found themselves in May 2010 is in no way guaranteed if AV is introduced.
12. This continued influence is best captured by the Asymmetrical Power Model (Marsh, Richards and Smith 2001; 2003; Marsh 2008a), which recognises the fundamental realities of British economic, social and political life far more accurately than that described by the WM or the DPM.
13. We should recognise here that there is and has been historically a degree of 'crossover' between the political elite and the socio-economic elites in the UK. This will be considered in more depth shortly.
14. This deference was never complete or total and there have been periods in both the 19th and late 20th centuries when aspects of the political system were widely questioned as we will see in the subsequent chapters.
15. Thompson (1984) notes that anti-royal feeling was more likely to take the form of attacks on a particular monarch, rather than republicanism per se. This trend can be seen in many of the 19th century reform groups discussed in Chapter 5, which, despite appealing to Paine (1791; 1792), did not appropriate his republicanism.
16. Whilst we should be wary of simply reading off support for the predominant tradition from a socio-economic position, we should also recognise that the latter can and does influence (though not determine) the former.

17. Marsh (2002a) discusses the relationship between economics and power in the UK political system. He offers a more convincing explanation than the pluralism of mainstream analyses of British politics and suggests the idea that socio-economic factors enable and constrain agents through affording key resources unequally. They do not however determine it.
18. For discussion of this debate see P. Dunleavy and B. O'Leary, *Theories of the State* (1987) and C. Hay, *Marxism and the State* (1999c).
19. See for example the coverage in Dearlove and Saunders (2000).
20. Marsh (2002b: 161–2) identifies four criticisms of Poulanztas. Firstly there is no explanation of how the state knows what is in the best interests of capitalism. Secondly the argument is still economistic and deterministic. Thirdly Poulanztas privileges social class over other forms of structured inequality found in capitalist society such as gender and ethnicity. Finally the view fails to give an independent role to ideas and is thus essentially, materialist. We should also note that given his structuralism, Poulanztas views any policy that does not benefit the capitalist class directly as a mere concession to the workers. This does not attribute any power or influence to influence outcomes to the working class. Thus he negates agency.
21. This was recognised as such by Miliband himself in his later work. See for example Miliband (2004).
22. See for example his comment: 'the character of (the state's) leading personnel, the pressures exercised by the dominant economic class and the structural constraints imposed by the mode of production' (Miliband 2004: 77) which points to both a role for elites and a recognition that there might be structural constraints imposed by the capitalist system which mean their direct interests may not be directly served in the short term.
23. Scott argues that 'a ruling class exists where there is both political domination and political rule by a capitalist class. This requires that there be a power bloc dominated by the capitalist class, a power elite recruited from this power bloc, and in which the capitalist is disproportionately represented, and that there are mechanisms which ensure that the state operates in the interests of the capitalist class and the reproduction of capital' (1991: 124).
24. It should be noted here that the notion of structured inequality does not privilege class. Rather it seeks to identify patterns of inequality in society and how they are replicated and reinforced over time.
25. Discussing the Northcote-Trevelyan Reforms of 1854, Bevir and Rhodes concede that the reforms: 'sought not only to preserve the privileges of the gentry, but also to forge a link between the higher civil service and the humanities provided by Oxford' (2003: 163). Their examination of the background of permanent secretaries between 1970 and 1998 (2003: 171) highlights the narrow class and educational backgrounds of the occupants of these positions as well as highlighting the fact that in this period there were only five female permanent secretaries and none from minority ethnic communities. We should also note here the length of service of these individuals. The average length of service for these individuals was 25 to 30 years. Given this scenario, it is likely that permanent secretaries will develop attitudes informed by the arrangements and institutional culture they find before them, a culture that is inscribed with the BPT.

26. The Sutton Trust Report (December 2005) suggests that these universities were the top ranked institutions in a range of publications including *The Times* and the FT. These are known as the Sutton 13.
27. Of those Prime Ministers who have attended University, only Gordon Brown did not attend Oxford or Cambridge.
28. Indeed we should recognise the increasing importance of the route from being a 'political professional' such as a Special Political Advisor (SPAD) to being an MP. For example all three of the main party leaders in 2011 have progressed from being a SPAD to being an MP as did notable former Labour ministers such as Charles Clarke and David Miliband.
29. For example the fee for entry into Eton College in September 2010 was £29,862. That the current leaders of the three main parties David Cameron, George Osbourne and Nick Clegg attended schools whose fees are above the national average income should also be noted here.
30. Informal networks and connections networks are integral to the recruitment of wealthier individuals who have themselves not attended either fee-paying schools or elite universities.
31. As earlier I use the Sutton 13 criteria here.
32. We should also note that the term 'state school' employed in much of the analysis of this issue offers a broad and unsatisfactory categorisation which homogenises the array of different types of state school. A welcome addition to research of patterns of structured inequality and its replication via the education system would be a disaggregated approach to the term 'state school' as a staring point for analysis.
33. Although as Marsh (2008a) suggests, this is likely to be the case more often than not.
34. Whilst this contestation is continual we should recognise that it occurs in a context that privileges certain solutions over others and it resonates to differing intensities in relation to contingent events. As such integral to recognising the asymmetrical political landscape in the UK is recognising the asymmetrical resonance of ideas and traditions.

6 The Participatory Tradition

1. We should note here that the very notion of dominance implies a relation to subordinate or competing other(s).
2. Held argues that, in general terms, democracy: 'could reasonably be divided into two broad types: direct or participatory democracy (a system of decision making about public affairs in which citizens are directly involved and liberal or representative democracy (a system of rule embracing elected officers who undertake to 'represent' the interests and/or views of citizens within a framework of the rule of law' (2006: 4). Although we might, as Held does, disaggregate these broad classifications further, for the purposes of this discussion of political traditions they remain a useful schema.
3. Rhodes, Wanna and Weller (2009: 45) state they are only concerned with 'live traditions', which they define as: 'those key traditions that underlie the beliefs and shape the practices of elite actors of the core executives in their respective polities'. In the context of our present discussion, this approach

is problematic on a number of levels. Firstly to imply a typology of live vs. dead traditions offers a simple duality, which fails to grasp the potentially fluctuating influence of traditions over time. For example, they (2009: 45) describe Chartism as a dead tradition. However groups such as Charter 88 and more recently Unlock Democracy and Power 2010 appeal either overtly or subconsciously to that tradition. Furthermore Charter 88 has influenced New Labour politicians and the process of constitutional reform since 1997, and has thus had an impact upon the political elite to an extent (Evans 1995; Hall 2009). Therefore to characterise Chartism as a dead tradition fails to grasp the contemporary impact of that tradition in relation to contingent events. Moreover by focusing only on 'live' traditions we reduce our capacity to explain change and continuity over time and in doing so we also potentially reify live traditions.
4. It should be noted that political participation in the Athenian city-state was restricted to adult male citizens who had completed their military training as ephebes.
5. In *Hegemony and Socialist Strategy* (1985), Laclau and Mouffe define radical democracy as a state of permanent struggle and contestation: 'in which the irreducible plurality of different struggles would receive their proper recognition' (Callinicos 2007: 346). As post-Marxists they reject economic determinism and the idea that class struggle is the most important antagonism in society, in favour of recognising all struggles against domination and exploitation. Other social antagonisms include gender, ethnicity, age, sexual orientation and locality. Such antagonisms are endemic in the nature of society. Laclau and Mouffe argue for the creation of a radical democracy of 'agonistic (contest) pluralism' to resolve the problems and issues faced within society. Radical-democratic ideas join two strands of democratic thought. Firstly radical democrats believe in wider and deeper participation in public decision-making. Citizens should have a more direct role in making public choices or at the very least engage far more deeply with political issues. Furthermore radical democrats believe that institutions and processes should ensure that politicians and officials will respond to their concerns and judgments. Thus it stands in stark contrast to the BPT. Secondly radical democrats favour deliberative democracy. Rather than the politics of power and interest as in Liberal Democracy, radical democrats favour a situation where citizens consider issues and problems by reasoning together about how best to resolve them. Thus radical democracy appeals to the long-established ideas of civic republicanism.
6. Widening participation involves extending the range of those able to participate and the means by which they can do so. Deepening participation means creating more opportunities for decision-making directly by the populace and more methods for holding politicians to account.
7. Contra what he defines as the Westminster Model of Democracy, Lijphart identifies the following features of the Consensus Model: (i) executive power sharing in broad coalition cabinets (ii) Executive-Legislative balance of power (iii) A multiparty system (iv) Proportional Representation (v) Interest Group corporatism (vi) Federal and decentralised government (vii) Strong bicameralism (viii) Constitutional Rigidity (ix) Judicial Review (x) Central

Bank Independence. We should note however that Lijphart does not explore the ideational underpinnings of either model or approach to democracy.
8. See for example Froissart's description of John Ball: 'he tried to prove...that from the beginning all men were created equal by the nature and that servitude had been introduced by the unjust and evil oppression of men against the will of god ' (cited in Hilton 2003: 222).
9. Vallance (2009) identifies the following: the Long Parliament 1640–42 and the attacks on the personal rule of Charles I, the impact of the first civil war and the search for settlement 1642–47; and the establishment of a republic in 1649, following the trial and execution of the king.
10. Having become 'the most celebrated of all English Radical movements' (Vallance 2009: 128), the Levellers prominence in narrations of the Civil War has been questioned by recent historians such as Worden (2001). In particular questions concerning the political motivations of Levellers such as Lilburne and the prominence they have been afforded in contemporary narrations reflects the normative assumptions and concerns of 'leftish' historians have been raised. However: new research suggests that key Leveller writers such as Lilburne, Overton and Wildman were indeed politically connected and motivated (see for example P. Baker and E. Vernon, *Foundations of Freedom* (2011)
11. See for example the petition entitled *A Remonstrance of Many Thousand Citizens* (1645).
12. This phrase refers to a collection of liberties, franchises and privileges which are seen as a uniform set of citizenship entitlements (Foxley 2004). It is often associated with the idea of 'the Norman Yoke', referring to the repressive ideas and practices instituted by William I and his descendents. For Levellers like of Lilburne, these emanated, at least in part, from the English legal tradition. Once established this phrase has taken on a major significance in radical thinking, with the Diggers, William Godwin and Militant Suffragettes harking back to the idea of an ancient set of rights and freedoms that need to be rediscovered or re-established. We should note here the appeal to a sense of national identity in the phrase, a point we will return to briefly in Chapter 6.
13. During the debates, Rainsborough famously stated: 'For really I think that the poorest he that is in England hath a life to live, as the greatest he; and therefore truly, sir, I think it's clear, that every man that is to live under a government ought first by his own consent to put himself under that government; and I do think that the poorest man in England is not at all bound in a strict sense to that government that he hath not had a voice to put himself under' (cited in Thompson 1980: 24).
14. They were also known as the True Levellers and were few in number.
15. In *The Law of Freedom in a Platform* (1652), Winstanley suggests that government should be aimed at: 'common preservation, freedom, peace and cooperation...(with)...free enjoyment of Earth, liberated from the bondage of landlords and masters' (cited in Meiksins Wood and Wood 1997: 88).
16. Meiksins Wood and Wood note that Winstanley remained: 'in many ways bound to the patriarchialism and assumptions about the exclusion of women from the political sphere' (1997: 89).

17. Although we should recognise here that Winstanley suggests younger men will labour whilst only men over 40 years of age may govern.
18. There has been heated debate over Locke's relationship to both radicalism and democracy. For example, R. Ashcraft, *Revolutionary Politics and Locke's Two Treatises of Government* (1986) argues for a link between Locke and popular radicalism. Contra this, N. Wood, *John Locke and Agrarian Capitalism* (1984) and E. Meiksins Wood, *'Locke against democracy: Representation, Consent and Suffrage in the Two Treatises'* (1992), argues that Locke should be seen as a theorist of 'rising capitalism' and the advocate of the interests of the progressive land-owning class.
19. The closure of the meetings of Scottish reformers in Edinburgh in December 1793 led to the trial and deportation to Australia of the 'Scottish Martyrs'. These actions were soon followed by legal proceedings against English Radicals. Thirteen members of the LCS were tried for treason, albeit unsuccessfully.
20. Numerous writers have noted the problems of arguing for the existence of a 'British radical tradition'. These concerns centre around, firstly, the use of 'British' as opposed to 'English' radicalism. This problem reflects the complex territorial relations in UK history and concerns about 'cultural nationalist' assumptions impinging upon historical interpretation. Secondly the use of the word 'radical' has also been seen as problematic, due to its changing meaning over time and the importance of the context vis-à-vis that meaning. Thirdly it has been suggested that discussions of a 'radical tradition' are inherently normative and impose modern terms and ideas on the past in a search for continuity and political ancestry. For a discussion of these problems see Vallance (2009).
21. For example, the LCS contained members from both the middling and artisan classes, and sought to advance parliamentary reforms such as male suffrage, annual parliaments and the removal of rotten boroughs. It did this by public meetings and found support amongst London artisans as well as influencing radicals in Birmingham, Manchester, Leeds and Edinburgh. However its view of reform was gradualist and thus, somewhat Whiggish. Moreover it was largely bereft of the language of class (Vallance 2009). Beyond London, other cities such as Bristol, Hull and Liverpool were incapable of sustaining radical societies.
22. For example Paine argued that: 'no reason can be given why a house of legislation should be composed entirely of whose occupation consists entirely in letting landed property, than why it should be composed of those who hire, or of brewers, or bakers, or any other separate class of men' (1792: 228).
23. We should note that feminist theory did not begin with Wollstonecraft, nor was she the first person to suggest that women had an inalienable right to participate fully in political and social institutions and the economy (Bryson 1992). Wollstonecraft is however the most widely known and widely read of this broader trend.
24. Numerous laws could be cited to demonstrate the extent to which outcomes in British politics reflected the stereotypes of women.
25. Attwood's primary concerns' were for the removal of credit restrictions and the printing of more paper money. However he saw the need for political reform to achieve this and the BPU claimed to speak for the common

interest contra the interests of the ruling aristocracy. That said, in his speeches Attwood fell short of advocating universal suffrage (Vallance 2009).
26. We should recognise that it was not the entirety of Paineite thinking that influenced the Chartists as both the Declaration of Rights (1839) and the National Charter Association (1840) constitution recognised that 'legislative power as essentially and rightfully vested in the monarch, the peers and the duly elected commons of the realm, in Parliament assembled' (cited in Vallance 2009: 392).
27. Lovett claimed that the initial draft of the Charter included female suffrage too, but that this was dropped so as not to damage the cause of getting men the vote.
28. The Chartist Movement continued into the late 1850s with their final national convention occurring in 1858.
29. Five of the six points of the People's Charter had been enacted by 1918.
30. As Wright notes: 'Chartist branches at the local level, like those of the Owenites, provided a substantial menu of recreational, educational and religious activities which amounted to an alternative culture...It was more than a political campaign; it was a living experience, based upon a democratic radical culture, where the emphasis was placed on mutuality, self-respect and a profound sense of independence.' (1988: 139).
31. Throughout the 1840s and 1850s there were between 40 and 50 'Reform' MPs at Westminster. Mainly from aristocratic backgrounds, these radical parliamentarians did much to keep the notion of parliamentary reform alive following the demise of Chartism. However as Taylor (1995: 163) notes, they were much more concerned with the redistribution of parliamentary seats than with the extension of the franchise.
32. The National Reform Union was established in 1864 and was made up of many members of the Liberal party. It was primarily middle class in terms of its social composition.
33. The Reform League (1865) was formed by members of the Universal League for the Material Elevation of the Industrious Classes and included many former Chartists. It is most famously associated with the demonstrations in Trafalgar Square and Hyde Park in 1866 and reform agitation throughout the winter of the same year.
34. See Chapter 4 for a discussion of this.
35. The Kensington Society was formed as a discussion group in 1865 by 11 women. They presented their petition for the enfranchisement of women to two MPs known to be sympathetic to their demands, Henry Fawcett and John Stuart Mill. Mill presented the petition of 1500 signatures on 7 June 1866. Post 1867 they formed the London Society for Women's Suffrage to push for political equality between men and women. Over time, similar societies were formed in large cities such as Manchester, eventually merging as the National Union of Women's Suffrage Societies in 1897.
36. See Chapter 4 on this.
37. Mill and his wife Harriet Taylor published a number of pieces advocating the enfranchisement of women, the most famous of which is *The Subjection of Women* (1869), published some years after Taylor's death.

38. Notable radicals, however, such as Lord John Russell opposed the introduction of the secret ballot, believing it would eventually lead to universal suffrage.
39. Bright also believed that it might lessen the grip of the Conservative party over the counties (Kinzer 1982).
40. In a speech at Denbigh, Chamberlain asked: 'Are the Lords to dictate to us, the people of England? ... Are you going to be governed by yourselves? Or will you submit to an oligarchy which is a mere accident of birth?' (cited in Judd 1977: 118).
41. Amongst its proposals were demands for the introduction of universal male suffrage, Lords Reform and payment of MPs. However Chamberlain's motives were as much tactical as ideological, as he sought to appeal to newly enfranchised voters in the counties and also outmanoeuvre the Whiggish elements in the Liberal party.
42. As was suggested in Chapter 4, the ongoing saga of Lords Reform should be seen in the light of the impact of the BPT over time.
43. In the case of Thatcher and Blair, the concern is regarding the lack of democratic mandate and popular support won. For example, in 1997 the Labour government won 44 per cent of the vote and 64 per cent of the seats. Thatcher for her part never won more than 43.9 per cent of the vote she received in 1979, despite receiving larger parliamentary majorities in 1983 and 1987. The election of 2010 continued the trend towards disproportional outcomes with the largest single party, the Conservatives, receiving 36 per cent of the vote and 47 per cent of the seats.
44. This can be seen most obviously in leading Conservative Lord Hailsham's 1976 Dimbleby Lecture where he coined the phrase 'elective dictatorship' to describe the British political system. It should be noted here that he made this analysis whilst in opposition, and was then remarkably quiet when an even more powerful government emerged in the 1980s lead by Mrs Thatcher.
45. This will be dealt with in Chapter 7.
46. We should recognise here that although demands for constitutional reform were important, the actual reforms themselves were often introduced in a manner that dissatisfied campaigners due to their lack of radicalism. For example Freedom of Information stalled before they were completed, as in the case of Lords' Reform or were abandoned entirely as in the case of electoral reform (Marsh and Hall 2007).
47. For details on this see Evans (2003: 194–7).
48. Evans (2003: 199–208).
49. The opening words of the Charter stated tellingly: 'We have been brought up in Britain to believe that we are free: that our Parliament is the mother of democracy; that our liberty is the envy of the world; that our system of justice is always fair; that the guardians of our safety, the police and security services, are subject to democratic, legal control; that our civil service is impartial; that our cities and communities maintain a proud identity; that our press is brave and honest. Today such beliefs are increasingly implausible. The gap between reality and the received ideas of Britain's 'unwritten constitution' has widened to a degree that many find hard to endure. Yet this year we are invited to celebrate the third centenary of the Glorious Revolution of

1688, which established what was to become the United Kingdom's sovereign formula. In the name of freedom, our political, human and social rights are being curtailed while the powers of the executive have increased, are increasing and ought to be diminished' (The Original Charter 88.
50. They demanded a new constitutional settlement to: (i) Enshrine, by means of a Bill of Rights, such civil liberties as the right to peaceful assembly, to freedom of association, to freedom from discrimination, to freedom from detention without trial, to trial by jury, to privacy and to freedom of expression. (ii) Subject executive powers and prerogatives, by whomsoever exercised, to the rule of law. (iii) Establish freedom of information and open government. (iv) Create a fair electoral system of proportional representation. (v) Reform the upper house to establish a democratic, non-hereditary second chamber. (vi) Place the executive under the power of a democratically renewed parliament and all agencies of the state under the rule of law. (vii) Ensure the independence of a reformed judiciary. (viii) Provide legal remedies for all abuses of power by the state and the officials of central and local government. (ix) Guarantee an equitable distribution of power between local, regional and national government. (x) Draw up a written constitution, anchored in the idea of universal citizenship that incorporates these reforms. (The Original Charter 88)
51. Indeed the antipathy of the Conservative party towards the demands of Charter 88 were immediately highlighted by Conservative MP John Patten's response in December 1988 that 'Charter 88 is a loser's Charter...with no big ideas' and the response of Margaret Thatcher, both discussed at length in Evans (1995).
52. Examples of this behaviour could be seen in the abolition of the GLC; the banning of trade union rights at GCHQ and attacks on free speech in relation to the broadcasting ban on Sinn Fein.
53. For consideration of the success and legacy of Charter 88, see the special issue of Parliamentary Affairs Vol. 62, No. 4 (October 2009).
54. Power 2010 developed as an attempt to promote the findings of the Power Inquiry established in 2004, which investigated the condition of UK democracy. Its report *Power to the People* (2006) made 30 recommendations including a rebalancing of power away from the executive and unaccountable bodies towards Parliament and local government, great responsiveness and choice in both the electoral and party system, and more direct and focused involvement for citizens in decision- and policy-making. Given its critique of executive dominance and promotion of more directly democratic notions Power 2010 should be seen as one of the most recent additions to the participatory tradition.
55. The Standing Orders of the Scottish Parliament were established by the Consultative Steering Group's (CSG) document, *Shaping Scotland's Parliament* (December 1998). The CSG did not see the traditional institutions and processes of Westminster politics as something to replicate. Rather, they were deeply critical of the elitist concept of democracy found there and operated from a more participatory view. The CSG brought forward proposals that challenged established notions such as executive dominance and that 'Westminster and Whitehall knows best'. Therefore, it is possible to identify the process of

continual ideational contestation and the influence of competing traditions in the recommendations of the CSG (Marsh and Hall 2007).
56. See for example the arguments of Batters (2005), Marsh and Hall (2007) and Hall (2009) regarding the impact of the BPT on aspects of New Labour's constitutional reforms since 1997.
57. The petition of 1842 had 3 million signatures on it, whilst official estimates place the figure for the 1848 petition at 1,957, 496, with many false signatories. There has been much debate concerning the authenticity of the signatures on the Charter and the accuracy of parliamentary estimates. For a discussion of this, see Vallance (2009: 419–20).
58. The ERS currently has 1500 paying members.
59. See for example Manning (1991) on the Levellers, Thompson (1984) on the Chartists, and Holton (2002) on the Women's Suffrage Movement.

7 The Nationalist Tradition

1. Due to the discourse concerning national distinctiveness we should recognise that the BPT contains nationalist elements. These can be seen, for example, in the unionist attitudes and responses of its adherents.
2. Neither Bevir and Rhodes (2003; 2006) nor Marquand (2008) recognise the importance of national identity and the contestations arising from this as centrally significant to the political traditions of the UK.
3. See Chapters 4 and 5 for discussion of this.
4. Preston (2004: 82–91) suggests that whilst Britishness may be viewed as the 'grand tradition' of these isles, various few traditions have existed that have been centred around sub-national or regional identities.
5. We should recognise here that whilst there have always been 'dissenters from the union', there was also enthusiasm for the union found in Ireland, Scotland and Wales historically (Gardiner 2004).
6. At its most extreme this idea has informed the anti-colonial arguments of Irish Nationalists such as those from Sinn Fein to the Irish National Liberation Army.
7. See Foster et al. (2001) for an introduction to this.
8. See Brown, McCrone and Paterson (1996) for an introduction to this.
9. See Elywn Jones (1994) for an introduction to this.
10. For discussion of the varieties of national identities within the UK and their relationship to each other see R. Cohen *Fuzzy Boundaries* (1994). We should note here that: 'multiple identities are a natural feature of the human condition' (Davies 2000: 10–11) and that people often adopt more than one such identity. Evidence from the Scottish Social Attitudes Survey on National Identity (2005), demonstrates that this is certainly the case in relation to the UK.
11. For example, in the case of Scotland this was assisted through a sense of apartness in religion, education and law (Paterson 2000; Gardiner 2004) and the retention of separate institutions for these. Thus a degree of conflict or contestation existed historically between a sense of Britishness and Scottishness, which for a long time manifested itself as 'cultural sub-nationalism' (Nairn 1981: 173). This was not the political nationalism of the SNP, rather it was:

'an assertion of Scottish-ness on the part of an amorphous group of interests and individuals whose identity is caught up with that of Scotland' (Kellas 1973). As such territorial relations have involved both a degree of assimilation alongside a degree of social and cultural autonomy. No matter how peripheral it may have seemed historically, this sense of social, cultural and political distinctiveness contained elements that over time came to coalesce into demands for greater autonomy. For example on an institutional level, the Scottish Office was established in 1885 as were special parliamentary procedures for Scottish affairs in the Commons, although the former was used to impose Westminster rule (Brown, McCrone and Paterson 1996). The significance of these concessions and this sense of distinctiveness had a ratchet-like effect over time: 'constantly forcing small but cumulative concessions' (Mitchell 2002: 238). The preservation of this sense of Scottish distinctiveness would however prove to be an important foundation for contestation of the BPT via demands for both devolution and independence (Hall 2009).

12. The Thatcher government has been seen as the 'apogee' of the BPT (Marsh and Tant 1989). Mrs Thatcher viewed English dominance of the Union as both natural and desirable and was certainly perceived by many Scots and Welsh as anti-Celtic. She was to comment in her memoirs that 'the union is inevitably dominated by England by reason of its greater population. The Scots being a historic nation with a proud past will inevitably resent some expressions of it from time to time' (Thatcher 1993: 624). Moreover Thatcherism and Mrs Thatcher herself appealed to 'a synthesis of recrudescent British nationalism and a neo-liberal political economy' (O'Neill 2004: 72) in which a sense of Britishness was fundamental. However it was a specific concept of that term that was used. For Thatcher: 'Britishness meant Englishness or at the very least English dominance; unionism in constitutional terms meant the constitutional status quo' (Finlay 2008) and, thus, England dominating in the UK. She was at pains to point this out in her memoirs when stating that 'The Tory party is not of course, an English party but a Unionist one' (Thatcher 1993: 624).

13. Many of her policies, particularly those such as privatisation and opting out of local government control in areas such as education, found little resonance in Scotland or Wales. In particular the Thatcherite belief in the virtue of neo-liberal individualism ran contrary to both the more traditional values of community and belief in the virtues of social democratic institutions, such as the welfare state and the NHS. Indeed socio-economic factors were central to Celtic dissatisfaction in the 1980s (Finlay 2008). Thatcher's free market policies seemed to add to the economic woes of the regions of the UK as 'the deregulation of economic and fiscal policy during the Thatcher years accelerated the long-term structural shift in the regional focus of the British economy' (O' Neill 2004: 73). While the South East of England seemed to benefit from her policies, other regions of the UK experienced economic decline. For example, in Scotland, by 1985/86 £2.4 billion out of a total £4.7 billion of capital invested in Scottish manufacturing industry had moved southwards and unemployment had almost doubled from 5.7 per cent in 1979 to 11.1 per cent in 1986. In contrast, England, or at least one part of England, seemed to experience 'good times' as a consequence of Thatcherite

economics. It is hardly surprising that in Scotland the economic benefits of the union, which were fundamental to its establishment in 1707 and had become increasingly questioned in the 1970s, were more widely critiqued during the Thatcher era. Indeed 'the perceived failure of the British two party system to deliver concrete economic gains for Scotland' (Evans 2003: 234) was fundamental in driving further questioning of the Union and its efficacy for the Scottish. At the same time the revenue from North Sea Oil was still coming in, adding £62 million a year to the Treasury. However the regional subsidies that had previously been used to overcome economic and social disparities between the regions of the UK dwindled because of the government's belief that such subsidies reflected a dependency culture and, thus, flew in the face of the enterprise culture that Thatcherism so forcefully sought to engender. Such actions further confirmed to many that the union, the government and the prime minister did not have Celtic interests at heart. She 'saw Scotland (and Wales) as an outpost of the dependency culture she was determined to extirpate' (Bogdanor 2001: 195). As a consequence of her neo-liberalism, she wished to reduce the role of government and devolution would add an extra layer of government. Mrs Thatcher even saw both the Scottish and Welsh Offices as part of the problem, believing that their 'very structure added a layer of bureaucracy standing in the way of reforms that were paying such dividends in England' (1993: 619) and that devolution would further exacerbate what she perceived as this problem. In her view, Scottish Office Ministers: 'saw themselves as standing up of Scotland against me and the parsimony of Whitehall' (1993: 619).
14. This could be seen in the unintended consequences of devolution (Hall 2009). For example we could focus on the further rise of the SNP post 1998, initially as the opposition party and since 2007, as the party in power at Holyrood. It could also be seen in the Richards Commission (2005); the Government of Wales Act (2006); and demands for parity with the Scottish Parliament.
15. For example, the renowned nationalist John Mitchel wrote in 1860: 'I have called it an artificial famine...The English, indeed, call the famine a 'dispensation of Providence;' and ascribe it entirely to the blight on potatoes. But potatoes failed in like manner all over Europe; yet there was no famine, save in Ireland. The British account of the matter, then, is first, a fraud; second, a blasphemy. The Almighty indeed, sent the potato blight but the English created the famine' (1860: 219).
16. See for example 'The Claim of Right' (1989: 50) and the arguments of the Scottish Constitutional Convention.
17. It should be recognised in passing that Ulster Unionism appeals to a support of the predominant political tradition in the UK. Ulster Unionism became prominent at the turn of the 20th century as Irish Home Rule became increasingly a possibility. This saw the creation of the Ulster Unionist Council in 1905. Prominent unionists from Sir Edward Carson to the Reverend Ian Paisley have appealed to the discourses of the BPT in their defence of Ulster and desire for the preservation of the constitutional status quo.
18. These were an interwoven series of conflicts that gripped England, Scotland and Ireland after these three countries came under the rule of Charles 1st. Most notable amongst these were the Civil Wars 1642–49 and 1650–51

and the Irish Confederate Wars 1641–53. The latter included the infamous Cromwellian conquest of Ireland in 1649, which would feature prominently in Irish Nationalist memory and rhetoric over time.
19. The Williamite War 1688–91 was fought between the Catholic King James II and the Protestant William of Orange. It resulted in the defeat of James and the Protestant Ascendancy in Ireland during the 18th and 19th century, whereby Ireland was dominated economically, socially and politically by a Protestant land-owning elite.
20. For an introduction to the history of the Irish question see Kennedy-Pipe (1997) or Hoppen (1998).
21. For a discussion of the features of this see J. T. Kuhn, *Celtic Culture: An Historical Encyclopaedia* (2006).
22. It should be noted here that the Gaels themselves were invaders, conquering Ireland between 500 BCE and 300 BCE. For many Irish Nationalists this reality has either overlooked, or seen as 'the last good invasion'.
23. Paine's ideas and those of the French Revolution (1789) influenced the Society of United Irishmen.
24. The nationalist challenge in Ireland has intersected with and been influenced by both religion and economics. On the former, however, simplistic dualisms that equate nationalism with Catholicism and unionism with Protestantism, do not grasp the colourful and complex nature of the relationship between religion and nationalism in Ireland. Famous nationalist leaders such as the Catholic O'Connell and the Protestant Parnell differed in their religious faith but are rightly viewed as important in the history of Irish Nationalism. Indeed before the 20th century many of the prominent nationalist leaders were Protestants. However despite religious differences, until the late 19th century: 'Irish nationalist leaders were remarkably successful in promoting the idea of unity and fraternity within the nation' (Boyce 1995: 22). It was only by the early 20th century that divisions over religion were to manifest themselves in line with clearer distinctions politically with the rise of Ulster Unionism.
25. For details on Home Rule and its significance as an issue in late 19th and early 20th century politics see O'Day (1998) and Jackson (2003).
26. This refers to the willingness to engage in and utilise violence to further political ends.
27. We should recognise that through the impact of unintended consequences and the continual contestation between predominant and competing traditions, the recent devolutions may lead to further challenges to both the Union and the predominant tradition. This trend may be seen in the rise to power of the SNP in 2007 and their attempts to further promote the idea of Scottish independence. It can also be seen in the recommendations of the Calman Commission and the Scotland Bill 2010. Moreover this trend can also be seen in the development of Welsh devolution since 1998 via the Government of Wales Act 2006 as well as the proposed referendum on further extensions to the powers of the Welsh Assembly.
28. Nor were they, as members of the political and socio-economic elite, likely to respond or give weight to opinion from outside their class given the ideational norms of the time.

29. Firstly guarantees for established civic and religious institutions in Scotland were given. In particular the maintenance of the Protestant religion was crucial, even if the Church of Scotland became less significant over time (Brown, McCrone and Paterson 1996). Nods were also made towards Scottish distinctiveness as we saw earlier. Special procedures and institutions recognising Scottish distinctiveness kept alive the idea that Scotland should be treated differently, whilst Scots were able to take advantage of the economic opportunities that the Union presented, both within the territory of the UK and beyond its borders, through the Empire. Secondly the political stability that followed, in contrast to earlier upheavals, helped and a degree of patronage for key individuals in Scottish society assuaged concerns. Thirdly by the mid to late 18th century, due to the apparent economic benefits from the Empire, Scots became convinced that 'the Union' worked as if it offered trading and colonial opportunities. That the union involved no small measure of asymmetrical relations between centre and periphery did not fundamentally undermine faith in the Union or the ideas that underpinned it. Indeed, by the mid 19th century the degree of acceptance was such that it became commonplace to refer to Scotland as North Britain (Devine 2008). Had it not been for her separate legal and administrative systems Scotland may well have become 'a mere province of England' (Bogdanor 2001: 111). Finally deliberate attempts were made to play down Scottish identity and replace it with a sense of Britishness. This new sense of national identity stressed the efficacy of the Union, its institutions, its culture, and the empire. The economic success of the 19th century helped facilitate this process, which in turn helped bind the Scots and in particular the Scottish elites, into the UK (Evans 2003; Ward 2004). Moreover the union and its apparent success confirmed to the socio-economic and political elites across the UK the virtue of the BPT and the approach taken.
30. This was written by their founder W. E. Aytoun.
31. Aytoun demanded the restoration of the office of the Secretary of State for Scotland which had been abolished in 1746 following the Jacobite rebellion and an increase in the levels of Scottish representation at Westminster in proportion to that of Wales and Ireland.
32. Here we could point again to the idea that the Scottish Office was used over time to impose Westminster's control over Scotland (Brown, Paterson and McCrone 1996).
33. Devine (2008b) notes how this sense of Scottishness harked back to an older notion of Scotland.
34. Essentially, this meant that many Scots came to believe that Scotland's interests were best served by being in 'the Union'. Thus, to be a nationalist meant being a unionist and faith in the BPT was maintained. Indeed we can suggest that unionism was predominant. The nationalist element it was believed, allowed Scotland to retain a degree of its distinctiveness and prevented the subsuming of Scotland into England as a mere province.
35. For details of this merger see Finlay (2009).
36. MacCormick had left the Labour party to campaign for Scottish devolution and fought local and parliamentary seats throughout the 1930s, albeit with little success.

37. It should be recognised that their initial claims in this regard were somewhat debatable (Hassan 2009).
38. For detailed coverage of the history of the SNP see P. Lynch, *SNP: The History of the Scottish National Party*, (2002) and G. Hassan (ed) *The Modern SNP: From Protest to Power* (2009).
39. An opinion poll concerning the desirability of a Scottish Parliament held in 1947 saw 76 per cent of respondents say they favoured the creation of one (Evans 2003: 226), which further suggests a measure of support for the nationalist position.
40. In 1949 two million Scots signed 'a Scottish Covenant' calling for a home rule Scottish Parliament within the UK. This covenant found little resonance amongst the political elite, as demonstrated by Attlee's refusal to meet MacCormick to discuss it. The Labour party was preoccupied with its post-war social democratic programme and, having just won its first landslide victory, was convinced of the virtues of the central tenets of the BPT. In particular they believed that 'centralization in economic and social planning and a strong union...(were)...a recipe for industrial growth and regional development (Evans 2003: 225). Nor did it undermine the view amongst Scottish socio-economic and political elites that the union continued to work in their favour.
41. Hassan (2009) notes that modern Scottish politics is normally divided into three periods: Beginning with Hamilton 1967 through to 1979 and the failure to meet the Cunningham threshold in the devolution referendum; then from the election of the Conservatives in 1979 through to New Labour in 1997; and finally the post-1997 period.
42. This was the second election of 1974. The first, in February, had seen Labour only win enough seats to form a minority government.
43. For details of the initial attempt at Scottish devolution see for example Bogdanor (2001) and O'Neill (2004). For a discussion of these events in relation to the BPT see Hall (2009) available online.
44. George Cunningham, a Labour backbencher and staunch opponent of devolution, successfully tabled an amendment to the Referendum Act that stated that, if less than 40 per cent of those entitled to vote were to vote 'Yes', then orders for the repeal of the legislation would have to go before Parliament. The result of the poll held on 1 March 1979 saw a majority of those who voted favouring devolution, with 32.9 per cent of the total electorate voting 'Yes' and only 30.8 per cent voting 'No'. However 36.3 per cent of the electorate did not vote and the 'Cunningham threshold' was not met.
45. For details of this see Butler, Adonis and Travers (1994).
46. For detailed discussion of the significance of the Poll Tax in promoting contestation of the BPT in Scotland see Hall (2009).
47. Within the leadership of the Labour party however the view that dominated was best expressed by Donald Dewar at the 1988 Labour Party Conference. He argued that to adopt a strategy that involved supporting law breaking would damage Labour's electoral credibility. Labour's governmental aspirations and its faith that sooner or later it would be returned to government showed a faith in the traditional approach to British politics. In essence, they wanted to work within the system and within the ideas and structures prescribed by the BPT.

48. In 1988, the Campaign for the Scottish Assembly established a Constitutional Steering Committee (Bogdanor 2001). This committee, whose membership was drawn from a cross-section of groups and institutions (Edwards 1989: 2) issued 'the Claim of Right' on 6th July 1988 and also called for a SCC to be established. The Convention had a wide, cross-party, membership including 57 Scottish MPs (49 Labour and 8 Liberal democrats) and 7 MEPS; however it is hardly surprising that, as staunch advocates of the constitutional status quo, the union and the BPT, the Conservatives should decline to join. The convention drew up two documents. Firstly, in 1990 it produced *'Towards Scotland's Parliament'* and, secondly, in 1995 it published *'Scotland's Parliament, Scotland's Right'* both of which were hugely influential in the devolution settlement of 1998 (Bogdanor 2001; Mitchell 2002; Pilkington 2002).
49. This can be seen primarily through the influence of the participatory tradition via the Liberal Democrats on the SCC and Charter 88, who had convinced the Labour party to support the introduction of the Additional Member System (AMS). This has had important and perhaps, unforeseen consequences since 1998 and can be seen as a significant deviation from the norm at Westminster –single-party government.
50. This should be viewed as an unintended consequence of the use of a more proportional system and one that decisively changed the political landscape in Scotland.
51. In the 2007 local elections, they doubled their number of seats, winning 363 council seats out of 1,224. This made them the largest group in Scottish local government and helped them feature in coalitions in 12 out of 32 local administrations.
52. The Liberal Democrats, their most likely coalition partners, found themselves unable to get over the stumbling block of the SNP's pro-independence stance. Despite being committed to devolution, the Liberal Democrats were not separatists, believing instead in both the notion of Britain and the union. This faith in key aspects of the BPT, including the sanctity of the Union and the virtue of Britishness, meant that a coalition with openly separatist SNP was simply untenable. Once again ideational factors influenced outcomes in the devolution process.
53. One of their first actions was to streamline the number of departments to five, appointing all five 'cabinet secretaries' from the ranks of the SNP.
54. Salmond was not the first Scottish leader to use this phrase since 1998. Henry Mcleish received criticism from Westminster MPs for using the term 'Scottish Government' during Question Time in January 2001 and the Procedures Committee had already suggested the change.
55. The fact that the first document to bear this name change was the SNP's legislative programme and that the change was roundly condemned in Westminster and Whitehall, is worthy of note.
56. It should be remembered that the ability to cede from the union is not held by the Scottish Parliament or the Scottish Executive. This remains one of the powers reserved for Westminster under the terms of the 1998 Scotland Act.
57. It should be noted again that notions of the Union and of Britishness remain popular with the majority of the Scots post devolution. This was

demonstrated in the elections of 2007 where over 60 per cent of the seats at Holyrood went to pro-union parties.
58. These were powerful and trusted lords appointed by the English king and empowered to protect and defend the border between England and Wales. To facilitate this they were able to wage war, administer laws, collect feudal dues and establish market towns.
59. The publication of Thomas Pennant's *A Tour of Wales* (1778) and the formation of London Welsh societies such as The Cymmrodorion Society (1751) and The Gwyneddigion Society (1770). The latter society encouraged cultural debate and discussion in Welsh and took over the Eisteddfod in 1789. It also considered radical ideas such as those proposed by Thomas Paine, leading to its repression in 1794.
60. 'The Blue Books' were the report of Commissioners into the state of education in Wales published in 1847. The report suggested that Welsh was an impediment to progress, seeing English as the language of promotion. Moreover they suggested that the Welsh were ignorant and immoral as a consequence. Such attitudes reflected English middle-class attitudes towards Wales. However despite offering many balanced judgements on the quality of education in Wales, they enraged many in Wales and were widely denounced by Welsh leaders. The 'Blue Book' controversy 'helped foster a sense of nationality through outrage in the face of insult' (Elwyn Jones 1994: 289).
61. The Welsh Office was not created until 1965 by the Wilson government. Indeed previous Labour leaders such as Attlee had dismissed the idea as 'an unnecessary duplication of administration' (Morgan 1998: 377). The Conservatives had created a Ministry for Welsh Affairs as part of the role of Home Secretary in 1951. However this was viewed as an attempt to simply undermine what remained of the Liberals support by a nation hostile to the Conservatives. Both main parties' attitudes to Welsh governance demonstrated their faith in institutions and processes of the BPT.
62. This movement was short-lived and deeply divided along economic and regional lines (Elwyn Jones 1994).
63. Specific examples include the Miners Strike of 1921 and the General Strike 1926. More general problems such as unemployment and industrial relations were part of Welsh politics.
64. Three of Plaid's main members had committed a symbolic act of arson, burning down part of an RAF Training school. The government's alleged biased handling, in which they moved the case to the Old Bailey assisted Plaid.
65. The village of Tryweryn was flooded to provide a reservoir for Liverpool caused great resentment across Wales.
66. For details see Morgan (1982: 382–3).
67. The Free Wales Army conducted parades and manoeuvres and engaged in acts of intimidation including bombing campaigns, one of which cost a young child his hands. They faded after two of their leading activists were imprisoned in (1969).
68. Only 11.8 per cent of the total electorate of Wales voted for devolution, whilst 46.5 per cent voted against.

69. Their 1979 manifesto contained only two lines concerned with Welsh self government.
70. In the Welsh Devolution referendum of 1997 50.1 per cent of those that voted were in favour of the creation of the Welsh Assembly. However only 50 per cent of the electorate voted, suggesting a degree of antipathy towards the issue. It should, however, be noted that since its creation, support for the Assembly and the extension of its powers has risen. Indeed the fact that a referendum on extending the powers for the Welsh Assembly is due to be held in on 5 May 2011 suggests that support levels have risen for the existence of the Assembly per se.
71. By the 1990s Labour also saw devolution as a way of protecting Scotland and Wales from the Conservatives and asserting the 'settled will' of the Scots and the Welsh.
72. The notion that Scottish (and Welsh) politics has a different, more left-leaning complexion is an interesting one. Regarding Scotland, it is also a point that has been identified by authors in the past (Brown, McCrone, Paterson and Surridge 1999). The suggestion is that the Scots are more collectivist in their leanings and more disposed towards state-intervention as a solution. For example the ESRC Devolution Briefing No. 21 states that 'public opinion in Scotland is in line with that in England on most issues, but with a small but consistent bias towards more collectivist and egalitarian solutions' (2005: 3). It goes on to suggest that 'most of the policy divergences so far show Scotland cleaving to liberal social values and social democratic welfare-state attitudes abandoned in England, rather than pioneering new ones' (ESRC 2005: 6).
73. The Scotland Bill 2010 arises partly, though not entirely, from the recommendations of the Calman Commission report. The Bill seeks to amend the 1998 Scotland Act in a number of ways including the ability for the Scottish Parliament to legislate for a 'Scottish income tax' and also set 'devolved taxes'. It also proposes increased powers for Holyrood to run Scottish elections as well as power regarding the control of air weapons, drink driving and speed limits.

Conclusion

1. For example, the development of both centre–periphery and Executive–Legislative relations in the Scottish devolution settlement has clearly been influenced by pre-existing ideas and patterns of behaviour. High profile issues such as the use of the Sewel Convention (Page and Batey 2002; Hassan 2002: Cairney and Keating 2004; Trench et al. 2007) or the dominance of the executive at Holyrood (Arter 2003; Trench et al 2007) demonstrate this. Indeed the Scottish Parliament Procedures Committee (SPPC) reported that 'the obvious tensions between the Westminster model of governance and a more directly participatory model were reflected in much of the evidence which we received. The relationship between the Scottish Executive and the Scottish Parliament will be similar to the relationship between the UK Government and the UK Parliament, reflecting a very traditional view of

democracy, underlined by the former Minister for Parliament's observation that 'the Executive's first and foremost duty is to deliver the programme for government on which it was elected. That has involved and will continue to involve, an ambitious and substantial legislative programme'. These perspectives give credence to the reaction from many external witnesses that, while the Parliament may be implementing the CSG principles, 'the executive does not seem to have changed its culture that much" (cited in House of Commons SN/PC/3000: 7). For consideration of these issues in the light of political traditions see Hall (2009).

2. These reforms include the Scotland Bill 2010, the referendum on extending the powers of the Welsh Assembly in May 2011 and the Con-Dem coalition's commitment to reforms including the power of recall, a referendum on the introduction of the Alternative Vote, and the completion of Lords' reform.

Bibliography

Abercrombie, Nicholas, and Warde, Alan (2001) *The Contemporary British Society Reader,* London: Polity.
Abercrombie, Nicholas et al. (2002) *Contemporary British Society,* London: Polity.
Anderson, B (1983) *Imagined Communities,* London: Random House.
Anderson, Benedict (1991) *Imagined Communities,* London: Verso.
Anderson, P (1987) *The Figures of Descent,* reproduced n Anderson (1992).
Anderson, Perry (1992) *English Questions,* London: Verso.
Anderson, Perry [1964] *Origins of the Present Crisis,* reprinted in Anderson, P. (1992).
Annas, Julia (1981) *An Introduction to Plato's Republic,* Oxford University Press.
Arblaster, Anthony (1994) *Democracy,* Milton Keynes: Open University Press.
Archer, Margaret (1995) *Realist Social Theory: The Morphogenetic Approach,* Cambridge University Press.
Archer, Margaret (2000) *Being Human: The Problem of Agency,* Cambridge University Press.
Arter, D (2004) The Scottish Committees and the goal of a new politics: A verdict on the first four years of the devolved Scottish Parliament, in *Journal of Contemporary European Studies,* 12, 1 (71–91).
Ashcraft, Richard (1986) *Revolutionary Politics and Locke's Two Treatises of Government,* Princeton University Press.
Aughey, Arthur (2001) *Nationalism, Devolution and the challenge to the United Kingdom State,* London: Pluto Press.
Bache, Ian, and Flinders, M. (2004) *Multi-Level Governance,* Oxford University Press.
Bagehot, W. (1867) *The English Constitution,* Oxford: Oxford University Press.
Baker, Philip and, Vernon, Elliot (2011) *Foundations of Freedom,* Basingstoke: Palgrave.
Barker, Chris (2003) *Cultural Studies: Theory and Practice,* London: Sage.
Batters, Elizabeth (2005) *Freedom of Information and the British Political Tradition,* unpublished PhD thesis: University of Birmingham.
Beer, Samuel (1965) *Modern British Politics,* London: Faber and Faber.
Beer, Samuel (1982) *Britain against Itself,* London: Faber and Faber.
Belchem, J (1981) 'Republicanism, constitutionalism and the radical platform in early nineteenth century England', *Social History,* 6, 1.
Bennie, Lynn, Brand, James, and Mitchell, James (1997) *How Scotland Votes,* Manchester University Press.
Bentley, Michael (1999) *Politics without Democracy: England 1815–1918,* London: Blackwell.
Bevir, Mark (1999) *The Logic of the History of Ideas,* Cambridge University Press.
Bevir, Mark (2000) 'On Tradition' Humanitas, xiii, 28–53.
Bevir, Mark and Rhodes, Rod (2002) 'Interpretive Theory' in Marsh and Stoker (eds).
Bevir, Mark and Rhodes, Rod (2003) *Interpreting British Governance,* London: Routledge.

Bevir, Mark and Rhodes, Rod (2004) 'Interpreting British Governance' in BJIPR Vol. 6 No. 2.
Bevir, Mark and Rhodes, Rod (2006a) 'Interpretive Approaches to British Government and Politics' in British Politics Vol. 1 No. 1.
Bevir, Mark and Rhodes, Rod (2006b) *Governance Stories*, London: Routledge.
Bevir, Mark and Rhodes, Rod (2006c)'Disaggregating Structures: An Agenda For Critical Realism' in British Politics Vol 1, No. 3.
Bevir, M. and Rhodes, R. (2008a) 'Politics as Cultural Practice', *Political Studies Review*, Vol 6, Issue 2, pp. 170–177
Bevir, Mark and Rhodes, Rod (2008b) 'The Differentiated Polity as Narrative' in BJPIR, Vol. 10, 729–34.
Birch, Anthony (1964) *Representative and Responsible Government*, London: Allen and Unwin.
Birch, Anthony (2001) *The British System of Government* 10th edn, London: Routledge.
Blaikie, Norman (2007) *Approaches to Social Enquiry*, London: Polity.
Blair (1994) Speech to the Labour Party Conference on 4 October 1994
Blyth, Mark (2002) 'Institutions and Ideas' in Marsh and Stoker (eds).
Blyth, Mark (2003) *Great Transformations: Economic Ideas and Institutional Change in the Twentieth Century*, Cambridge University Press.
Bogdanor, Vernon (1979) *Devolution*, Oxford: Oxford University Press.
Bogdanor, Vernon (1991) The *Blackwell Encyclopaedia of Political Science*, Blackwell: Oxford.
Bogdanor, Vernon (1999) *Devolution in the United Kingdom*, Oxford University Press.
Bogdanor, Vernon (ed.) (2003) *The British Constitution in the Twentieth Century*, Oxford University Press.
Boggs Carl (1976) *Gramsci's Marxism*, London: Pluto Press.
Bond, Matthew (2007) 'Elite Social Relations and Corporate Political Donations in Britain', Political Studies Vol. 55, 59–85.
Bonney, Norman (2003) 'The Scottish Parliament and Participatory Democracy: Vision and Reality', Political Quarterly Vol. 74, No. 4, 459–67.
Bourdieu, Pierre (1980) *The Logic of Practice*, Cambridge University Press.
Bottomore, Tom (ed.) (1983) *A Dictionary of Marxist Thought*, London: Blackwell.
Bottomore, Tom (1987) *Sociology: A Guide to its Problems and Literature*, London: Harper Collins.
Boyce, D George (1996) *Nationalism in Ireland*, London: Routledge.
Bradbury, Jonathan (1997) 'Conservative governments, Scotland and Wales: A Perspective on Territorial Management', in Bradbury and Mawson (eds).
Bradbury, Jonathan and Mawson, John (1997) *British Regionalism and Devolution: The Challenge of State Reform and European Integration*, London: Jessica Kingsley Publishers.
Bradbury, Jonathan, and Mitchell, James (2001)'Devolution: New Politics for Old', Parliamentary Affairs 54, 257–75.
Breuilly, John (1993) *Nationalism and the State*, Manchester University Press.
Brown, Alice, McCrone, David and Paterson, Lindsay (1996) *Politics and Society in Scotland*, Basingstoke: St Martins.
Brown, Alice, McCrone, David, Paterson, Lindsay and Surridge, Paula (1999) *The Scottish Electorate*, London: Macmillan.
Bryson, Valerie (1992) *Feminist Political Theory*, London: Macmillan.

Bullock, Alan and Deakin, Frederick (eds) (1964) *The British Political Tradition:* 8 Volumes, Oxford University Press.
Bullock, A and Trombley, S (1999) *The New Fontana Dictionary of Modern Thought*, London: Harper Collins.
Bulpitt, Jim (1983) *Territory and Power in the United Kingdom: An Interpretation*, Manchester University Press.
Burke, Edmund (1790) *Reflections on the Revolution in France*, Oxford University Press.
Burke, Edmund (1791) *Appeal from the New Whigs to the Old Whigs*, London: Bobs Merill.
Burnham, Peter (2006) 'Marxism, the State and British Politics' in *British Politics* Vol. 1 No.1.
Butterfield, H (1965) *The Whig Interpretation of History*, London: WW Norton & Co.
Butler, D, Adonis, A and Travers, T (1994) *Failure in British Government*, Oxford: Oxford University Press.
Cahoone, Lawrence (1996) *From Modernism to Post-modernism: An Anthology*, London: Blackwell.
Cairney, P and Keating, M (2004) 'Sewel Motions in the Scottish Parliament' in *Scottish Affairs* 47 (Spring).
Callinicos, Alex (2007) *Social Theory: A Historical Introduction* 2nd edn London: Polity.
Cannadine, David (2000) *Class in Britain*, London: Penguin.
Cannon, John (1972) *Parliamentary Reform 1640–1832*, Cambridge University Press.
Caterrall, Peter, Kaiser, Wolfgang and Walton-Jordan, Ulrike (2000) *Reforming the Constitution*, London: Frank Cass.
Catterall, Peter (2000) 'The Politics of Electoral Reform since 1885' in Catterall, P. et al.
Chadwick, A (2000) Studying Political Ideas: a Public Political Discourse Approach Vol 48, Issue 2, pp 283–301.
Chapman, Richard (1997) *The Treasury in Public Policy-making*, London: Routledge.
Coates, David (1975) *The Labour Party and the Struggle for Socialism*, Cambridge University Press.
Coates, David (1984) *The Context of British Politics*, London: Hutchinson.
Cobham, Alfred (1950) *The British Political Tradition Volume II: The Debate on the French Revolution*, Oxford University Press.
Cohen, Robin (1994) *Frontiers of Identity*, London: Longman.
Colley, Linda (2003) *Britons: Forging the Nation 1707–1837*, London: Pimlico.
Colls Robert and Dodd, Philip (1986) *Englishness: Politics and Culture 1880–1920*, London: Routledge.
Conniff, James (1994) *The Useful Cobbler*, New York: State University of New York Press.
Cowling, Maurice (2005) *Disraeli, Gladstone and Revolution*, Cambridge University Press.
Cress, Donald (1987) *Jean Jacques Rousseau: The Basic Political Writings*, Indiana: Hackett.
Crompton, Rosemary (2000) *Class and Stratification: An Introduction to Current Debates*, Polity: London.

Cronin, James (2004) *New Labour's Pasts*, London: Pearson.
Cunningham, Hugh (1986) 'The Conservative Party and Patriotism' in Colls and Dodd (eds).
Curry, O (2003) Get Real: evolution as metaphor and mechanism, *BJPIR* Volume 5, Issue 1 pp 112–117.
Cuthbert, Jim and Cuthbert, Margaret (2009) *'SNP Economic Strategy: Neo-Liberalism with a Heart'* in Hassan (ed.).
Davis, John and Tanner, Duncan (1996)'The Borough Franchise after 1867', Historical Review 69, 306–27.
Dean, Mitchell (1999) *Governmentality: Power and Rule in Modern Society*, London: Sage.
Dearlove, John and Saunders, Peter (2000) *Introduction to British Politics*, London: Polity.
Derry, J (1967) *The Radical Tradition*, London: Macmillan.
Devine, Thomas M, (ed.) (2008) *Scotland and the Union 1707–2007*, Edinburgh University Press.
Dicey, Albert Venn (1885) *An Introduction to the Study of the Law of the Constitution*, London: Macmillan.
Dicey, Albert Venn and Rait, Robert (1920) *Thoughts on the Union between England and Scotland*, London: Macmillan.
Dickinson, Harry T, (1985) *British Radicalism and the French Revolution*, Oxford University Press.
Dickinson, Harry T and Lynch, Michael (2000) *The Challenge to Westminster*, London: Tuckwell Press.
Dorey, Peter (2008) *The Labour Party and Constitutional Reform*, Basingstoke: Palgrave.
Dryzek, John and Dunleavy, Patrick (2009) *Theories of the Democratic State*, Basingstoke: Palgrave.
Dunleavy, Patrick (1999) 'Electoral Representation and Accountability: The Legacy of Empire' in Holliday et al.
Dunleavy, Patrick (2009) 'Assessing how far Charter 88 and the constitutional reform coalition influenced voting system reform in Britain', *Parliamentary Affairs*, Vol. 62, No. 4, 618–44.
Dunleavy, Patrick and O'Leary, Brendan (1987) *Theories of the State*, Basingstoke: Palgrave.
Dunleavy, Patrick et al. (2003) *Developments in British Politics 6*, Basingstoke: Palgrave.
Dunleavy, Patrick et al. (2005) *Developments in British Politics 7*, Basingstoke: Palgrave.
Dunleavy, Patrick et al. (2006) *Developments in British Politics 8*, Basingstoke: Palgrave.
Eastwood, David (1997) *Government and Community in the English provinces 1700–1870*, Basingstoke: Palgrave Macmillan.
Economic and Social Research Council (2005) 'The Labour Party and Devolution' Briefing No. 14.
Edwards, Owen (ed.) (1989) *A Claim of Right For Scotland*, Edinburgh: Polygon.
Elwyn Jones, G (1994) *Modern Wales: A Concise History*, Cambridge: Cambridge University Press.

Erdos, David (2009) 'Charter 88 and the Constitutional Reform Movement: a Retrospective' in Parliamentary Affairs Vol. 62 No. 4, 2009, 537–51.
Erdos, D (2009) Charter 88 and the Constitutional Reform Movement: Twenty Years On (Parliamentary Affairs Special Edition).
Evans, Mark (1995) Charter 88: A Successful challenge to the British Political Tradition, Dartmouth: Dartmouth Publishing Company.
Evans, Mark (2003) Constitution-making and the Labour Party, London: Palgrave.
Fielding, S (2003) The Labour Party: Continuity and Change in the Making of New Labour, Basingstoke: Palgrave.
Fine, Ben (1985) The Peculiarities of the British Economy, London: Lawrence and Wishart.
Finlay, R (2008) 'Thatcherism and the Union' in Devine ed (2008).
Finlay, Richard (2009) 'The Early Years: From the Inter-war Period to the 1960s' in Hassan (ed.).
Finlayson, Alan (2003) Contemporary Political Thought: A Reader and a Guide, Edinburgh University Press.
Flinders, Matthew (2006) 'The Half-hearted Constitutional Revolution' in Dunleavy et al.
Flinders, M. (2009) 'Charter 88, New Labour and Constitutional Anomie', Parliamentary Affairs Vol. 62, No. 4, 645–62.
Forgacs, David (1999) The Antonio Gramsci Reader, London: Lawrence and Wishart.
Forman, Nigel (2002) Constitutional Change in the UK, London: Routledge.
Foster, Robert (ed.) (2001) The Oxford History of Ireland, Oxford University Press.
Foster, R et al. (2001) The Oxford History of Ireland, Oxford: Oxford University Press.
Foxley, Rachael (2004) 'John Lilburne and the Citizenship of 'Free-Born Englishmen', The Historical Journal 47:4, 849–74.
Fulcher, James and Scott, John (2007) Sociology: 3rd edn, Oxford University Press.
Furlong, Paul and Marsh, David (2007) 'On Ontological and Epistemological Gate-keeping: A Response to Bates and Jenkins' Politics Vol. 27 No. 3.
Gallagher, Thomas (1987) Paddy's Lament: Ireland 1846–1847, London: Harcourt Brace.
Gallagher, Thomas (ed.) (1991) Nationalism in the Nineties, London: Polygon.
Gamble, Andrew (1990a) Britain in Decline, London: Macmillan.
Gamble, Andrew (1990b) 'Theories of British Politics' Political Studies, 38.
Gamble, Andrew (1994) The Free Economy and the Strong State 2nd edn, London: Macmillan.
Gamble, Andrew (2000) 'Policy agendas in a multi-level polity', in Dunleavy et al.
Gamble, Andrew, and Wright, Tony (2009) 'The Britishness Question' in Britishness: Perspectives on the British Question, Political Quarterly Special Issues.
Gamble, Andrew, Marsh, David and Tant, Tony (1999) Marxism and Social Science, Basingstoke: Palgrave.
Gardiner, Michael (2004) The Cultural Roots of British Devolution, Edinburgh University Press.

Garner, Robert and Kelly, Richard (1998) *British Political Parties Today*, 2nd edn, Manchester University Press.
Garrard, J. (2002) *Democratisation in Britain: Elites, Civil Society and Reform since 1800*, Basingstoke: Palgrave.
Gash, N (1979) *Aristocracy and People: Britain 1815–1865*, Massachusetts: Harvard.
Giddens, Anthony (1994) *Beyond Left and Right: The Future of Radical Politics*, London: Polity.
Gilmour, I (1978) *Inside Right: A study of Conservatism*, London: Quartet Books.
Gilmour, Ian (1992) *Dancing with dogma: Britain under Thatcherism*, London: Simon and Schuster.
Gramsci, Antonio (1971) *Selections from the Prison Notebooks*, London: Lawrence and Wishart.
Greenleaf, W. H. (1983a) *The British Political Tradition: The Rise of Collectivism Vol I*, London: Meuthen.
Greenleaf, W. H. (1983b) *The British Political Tradition: The Ideological Heritage Vol II*, London: Meuthen.
Greenleaf, W. H. (1987) *The British Political Tradition: A Much Governed Nation Vol III*, London: Meuthen.
Hall, Matthew (2008) 'Interpretation and Explanation: The poverty of the New Interpretivism', unpublished paper: Available from author.
Hall, Matthew (2009) 'Political Traditions and Scottish Devolution', unpublished thesis available online.
Hall, M. (2010) 'Political Traditions and Continuity in UK Politics', unpublished paper: Available from author.
Hall, P (1986) *Governing the Economy*, Oxford: Oxford University Press.
Hall, Stuart and Jacques, Martin (eds) (1983) *The Politics of Thatcherism*, London: Lawrence and Wishart.
Hall, Stuart (1998) 'The Great Moving Nowhere Show' in New Left Review Special Edition.
Hall, Stuart (2003) 'New Labour has picked up where Thatcherism left off', *Guardian*, 6 August 2003.
Halpin, David, Power, Sally and Fitz, John (1997) 'In the Grip of the Past? Tradition, Traditionalism and Contemporary Schooling', *International Studies in Sociology of Education*, 17 (1), 3–20.
Hanham, Harold J. (1969) *The Reformed Electoral System in Great Britain 1832–1914*, London: Historical Association.
Hanson, Albert and Walles, Malcolm (1990) *Governing Britain*, 5th edn, London: Fontana. (1990).
Haralambos, Michael and Holborn, Martin (2004) *Sociology: Themes and Perspectives*, 6th edn, London: Collins.
Hare, Thomas (1861) *A Treatise on the Election of Representatives, Parliamentary and Municipal*, London: Longman, Green and Roberts.
Harris, Ronald W (1963) *Political Ideas 1760–1792*, London: Victor Gollancz.
Harvie, Christopher (1994) *Scotland and Nationalism*, 2nd edn, London: Routledge.
Hassan, Gerry (ed.) (2004) *The Scottish Labour Party*, Edinburgh University Press.
Hassan, Gerry (ed.) (2009) *The Modern SNP: From Protest to Power*, Edinburgh University Press.

Hay, Colin (1995) *Structure and Agency* in Marsh and Stoker (eds), Basingstoke: Palgrave.
Hay, Colin (1996) *Re-stating Social and Political Change*, Milton Keynes: Open University Press.
Hay, Colin (1997) 'Political Time and the Temporality of Crisis', unpublished paper delivered to the PSA Conference.
Hay, Colin (1999a) 'Continuity and Discontinuity in British Political Development', in Marsh et al.
Hay, Colin (1999b) 'Crisis and Political Development in Post-war Britain' in Marsh et al.
Hay, Colin (1999c) 'Marxism and the State' in Gamble et al.
Hay, Colin (2002a) *Political Analysis*, London: Palgrave.
Hay, Colin (ed) (2002b) *British Politics Today*, London: Polity.
Hay, Colin (2004) 'Taking ideas seriously' in BJIPR Vol, 6 No. 2.
Hay, Colin, Lister, Michael, and Marsh, David (2006) *The State: Theories and Issues*, Basingstoke: Palgrave.
Hayes, William (1982) *The Background and Passage of the Third Reform Act*, Garland: London.
Hazell, Robert (ed) (1999) *Constitutional Futures*, Oxford University Press.
Hechter, Michael (1998) *Internal Colonialism*, London: Transaction.
Held, David (1996) *Models of Democracy*, London: Polity.
HM Government (1997) *Scotland's Parliament*, London: HMSO.
HM Government (2001) *Memorandum of Understanding and Concordats/Devolution guidance*, available online.
Heywood, Andrew (2000) *Key Concepts in Politics*, London: Palgrave.
Hill, Brian W (ed.) (1975) *Burke: On Government and Society*, London: Fontana.
Hill, Christopher (1984) *The World Turned Upside Down*, London: Penguin.
Hilton, Rodney (2003) *Bond Men Made Free*, Routledge: London.
Hitchens, Peter (1999) *The Abolition of Britain*, London: Quartet.
Hobbes, Thomas (1651) *Leviathan*, London: Penguin.
Hobsbawm, Eric (1967) *Labouring Men*, London: Weidenfeld and Nicholson.
Hobsbawm, Eric (1983a) 'Introduction' in Hobsbawm and Ranger (eds).
Hobsbawm, Eric (1983b) 'Mass-Producing Traditions: Europe 1870–1914' in Hobsbawm and Ranger (eds), Cambridge: Cambridge University Press.
Hobsbawm, Eric and Ranger, Terence (eds) (1983) *The Invention of Tradition*, Cambridge University Press.
Holliday, Ian et al. (1999) *Fundamentals in British Politics*, London: St Martins Press.
Holliday, Ian (1999) 'Territorial Politics' in Holliday et al.
Holton, Sandra (2002) *Feminism and Democracy*, Cambridge University Press.
Hofstadter, Richard (1948) *The American Political Tradition and the Men Who Made It*, New York: Vintage.
Hoppen, K. Theodore (1998) *Ireland since 1800: Conflict and Conformity*, Longman.
Hoppen, K. Theodore (2000) *The Mid-Victorian Generation*, Oxford University Press.
House of Commons (2004) 'Devolution in Scotland' SN/PC/3000, available online.
House of Commons (2005) 'Social Background of MPs' SN 1528, available online.

Howarth, David (1995) 'Discourse Theory' in Marsh and Stoker (eds).
Ingham, Geoffrey (1984) *Capitalism Divided*, London: Macmillan.
Ingle, Stephen (1999) *The British Party System*, London: Cassell.
Jackson, Alvin (2003) *Home Rule: A History*, London: Weidenfeld and Nicholson.
Jameson, F (1991) *Postmodernism: Or the cultural logic of late capitalism*, London: Verso.
Jennings, Ivor (1936) *Cabinet Government*, Cambridge University Press.
Jennings, I (1941) *The British Constitution*, London: Cambridge University Press.
Jenkins, Brian (2006) *Irish Nationalism and the British State*, Montreal: McGill-Queens University Press.
Jenks, Chris (1993) *Culture*, London: Routledge.
Jessop, Bob (1988) *Thatcherism*, London: Polity.
Jessop, Bob (1990) *State Theory*, London: Polity.
Johnson, Neville (2004) *Reshaping the British Constitution*, Basingstoke: Palgrave.
Jones, B et al (2004) *Politics UK*, 5th ed, London: Longman.
Joseph, Jonathan (2006) *Marxism and Social Theory*, Basingstoke: Palgrave.
Jowell, Jeffrey and Oliver, Dawn (2000) *The Changing Constitution*, Oxford University Press.
Judd, Denis (1977) *Radical Joe*, London: Hamish Hamilton.
Judge, David (1999a) *Representation: Theory and Practice in the UK*, London: Routledge.
Judge, David (1999b) 'Representation in Westminster in the 1990s: The Ghost of Edmund Burke', *The Journal of Legislative Studies*, Vol. 5, 12–34.
Judge, D (2005) *Political Institutions in the United Kingdom*, Oxford University Press.
Judge, David (2006) 'This is What Democracy Looks Like': New Labour's Blind Spot and Peripheral Vision', *British Politics*, Vol 1, No. 3.
Kavanagh, Denis (2003) 'British political science in the inter-war years: the emergence of the founding fathers', *BJPIR*, Vol. 5 No. 4. 594–613.
Kay, Adrian (2003) 'Evaluating Devolution in Wales', *Political Studies*, Vol. 51, 51–66.
Keating, Michael (2005) *The Government of Scotland*, Edinburgh University Press.
Keating, Michael and Loughlin, John (1997) *The Political Economy of Regionalism*, London: Frank Cass.
Kee, R (2000) *The Green Flag*, London: Penguin.
Kellas, James (1973) *The Scottish Political System*, Cambridge University Press.
Kennedy-Pipe, Caroline (1997) *The Origins of the Present Troubles in Northern Ireland*, London: Longman.
Kenny, Michael (1999) 'Ideas, Ideologies and the British Political Tradition' in Holliday et al.
Kennedy, Ellen and Mendus, Susan (1987) *Women in Western Political Philosophy*, London: Harvester and Wheatsheaf.
Kerr, Peter (1999) 'The Post-War Consensus: A Woozle that wasn't' in Marsh et al.
Kerr, Peter (2001) *Post-War British Politics: From Conflict to Consensus*, London: Routledge.
Kerr, Peter (2002) 'Saved from extinction: evolutionary theorising, politics and the state', *BJIPR* Vol. 4, No 2.

Kerr, Peter (2003) 'Keeping it real! Evolution in political science: a reply to Kay and Curry', *BJPIR* Vol. 5, No 1.
Kerr, Peter and Kettell, Steven (2006) 'In Defence of British Politics: The Past, Present and Future of the Discipline', *Journal of British Politics*, Vol. 1 No.1.
Kettell, Steven (2006) *Dirty Politics: New Labour, British Democracy and the Iraq War*, London: Zed Books.
Kinealy, Christine (1994) *This Great Calamity: Irish Famine 1845–1852*, Basingstoke: Gill and Macmillan.
King, Anthony (1985) 'Margaret Thatcher: The style of a PM' in King (ed.).
King, Anthony (ed.) (1985) *The British Prime Minister*, Basingstoke: Macmillan.
Kingdom, J (2003) *Government and Politics in Britain*, 3rd ed, London: Polity.
Kinzer, Bruce (1982) *The Ballot Question in Nineteenth-century English Politics*, London: Garland.
Koch, John T (2006) *Celtic Culture: A Historical Introduction*, California: ABC-CLIO Ltd.
The Labour Party (1997) 'Because Britain Deserves Better'
Laclau, Ernesto and Moffe, Chantal (1985) *Hegemony and Socialist Strategy: Towards a Radical Democratic Politics*, London: Verso.
Laffin, Martin and Shaw, Eric (2007) 'British Devolution and the Labour party', *BJIPR* Vol. 9 No. 1.
Lijphart, Arend (1999) *Patterns of Democracy*, Yale University Press.
Lindsay, Ian (1991) 'The SNP and the lure of Europe' in Gallagher (ed.), London: Polygon.
Lloyd, John (2004) *What are the Media doing to our Politics?*, London: Constable.
Ling, Tom (1998) *The British State since 1945*, London: Polity.
Locke, J (1690) *Two Treatise On Government*, Cambridge: Cambridge University Press.
Lopez, Jose and Scott, John (2000) *Social Structure*, Buckingham: Open University Press.
Loughlin, John and Peters, B. Guy (1997)'State Traditions, Administrative Reform and Regionalization' in Keating and Loughlin (eds).
Ludlam, Steven and Smith, Martin (eds) *New Labour in Government*, Basingstoke: Palgrave.
Ludlam, Steven and Smith, Martin (2004) *Governing as New Labour*, Basingstoke: Palgrave.
Lukes, Steven (2005) *Power: A Radical View*, 2nd edn, Basingstoke: Palgrave.
Lynch, Philip (2002) *SNP: The History of the Scottish National Party*, Cardiff: Welsh Academic Press.
Lynch, Philip (2007) 'Party system change in Britain: Multi-Party Politics in a Multi-Level Polity', *British Politics*, Vol. 2, Issue 3.
MacInnes, A (2008) 'The Treaty of Union: Made in England' in Devine ed (2008).
Macintrye, Alisdair (1984) *After Virtue*, Duckworth: London.
Macintyre, A (1984) *After Virtue*, Notre Dame: University of Notre Dame Press.
McAnulla, Stuart (2002) 'Structure and Agency' in Marsh and Stoker (eds).
McAnulla, Stuart (2006a) *British Politics: A Critical Introduction*, London: Continuum.
McAnulla, Stuart (2006b) 'Challenging the New Interpretivist Approach: Towards a Critical Realist Alternative', *British Politics*, Vol. 1 No. 1.

McAnulla, Stuart (2007) 'Understanding Tradition in British Politics and Beyond' POLIS Working Paper No. 24 (Leeds).
McCormick, John (2003) *Contemporary Britain*, London: Palgrave.
McCrone, David (2001) *Understanding Scotland* 2nd edn, London: Routledge.
McGarvey, Neil and Cairney, Paul (2008) *Scottish Politics: An Introduction*, Basingstoke: Palgrave.
McGee, Owen (2007) *The IRB: The Irish Republican Brotherhood, from the Land League to Sinn Fein*, London: Four Courts Ed.
McGregor, J. F. and Reay, Barry (1984) *Radical Religion in the English Revolution*, Oxford University Press.
McLean, Ian (2004) 'Labour in Scotland since 1945: Myth and Reality' in Hassan (ed). McLellan, David (1977) *Karl Marx: Selected Writings*, Oxford University Press.
Mackintosh, John (1977) *The Politics and Government of Britain*, London: Hutchinson.
Manning, Brian (1991) *English People and the English Revolution* 2nd edn, London: Bookmarks.
Marquand, David (1988) *The Unprincipled Society*, London: Fontana.
Marquand, David (2008) 'The Strange Career of British Democracy': John Milton to Gordon Brown', *The Political Quarterly*, Vol. 79, No. 4, 477–5.
Marsh, David (1999a) 'Introduction: Explaining change in the Post-war period' in Marsh et al.
Marsh, David (1999b) 'Resurrecting Marxism' in Gamble, Marsh and Tant (eds).
Marsh, David (2002a) 'Pluralism and the study of British Politics: It is Always Happy Hour for White Men with Money, Knowledge and Power' in Hay (ed.).
Marsh, David (2002b) 'Marxism' in Marsh and Stoker (eds).
Marsh, David (2003) 'Institutions and ideas: The British Political Tradition and Constitutional Reform under New Labour', unpublished paper, available online.
Marsh, David (2007) 'Stability and Change: Beyond the Last Dualism?', unpublished paper, available online.
Marsh, David (2008a) 'Understanding British Government: Analysing competing models', *BJIPR* Vol. 10 No. 2, 251–68.
Marsh, David (2008b) 'What is at stake? A Response to Bevir and Rhodes', *BJIPR* Vol. 10 735–9.
Marsh, David, and, Furlong, Paul (2002) 'A Skin Not a Sweater: Ontology and Epistemology in Political Science' in Marsh and Stoker (eds).
Marsh, David, and, Hall, Matthew (2006) '*Political Traditions: Beyond Bevir and Rhodes*', unpublished paper, available online.
Marsh, David, and, Hall, Matthew (2007) '*The British Political Tradition: Explaining the fate of New Labour's Constitutional Reform Agenda*', British Politics Vol. 2 No. 2.
Marsh, David, Richards, David, and, Smith, Martin (2001) *Changing Patterns of Governance in the UK*, London: Palgrave.
Marsh, David, and, Stoker, Gerry (1995) *Theory and Methods in Political Science*, London: Macmillan.
Marsh, David and Stoker, Gerry (2002) *Theory and Methods in Political Science* 2nd edn., *Basingstoke*: Palgrave.

Marsh, David and Tant, Tony (1989) 'There is No Alternative: Mrs Thatcher and the British Political Tradition', Essex Paper No. 69.
Marsh, David, et al. (1999) *Post-war British Politics in Perspective*, London: Polity.
Marsh, David, O'Toole, Therese and Jones, Sue (2007) *Young People and Politics in the UK*, London: Palgrave.
Marsh, David, Richards, David and Smith, Martin (2003) 'Unequal Plurality: Towards an Asymmetrical power model', *Government and Opposition* 38.
Marsh, David, Batters, Elizabeth and Savigny, Heather (2004) 'Historical Institutionalism: Beyond Pierson and Skocpol', unpublished paper: available online.
Marx, K (1851) 'The 18th Brumaire of Louis Bonaparte' in McLellan (1977).
May, T. Erskine (1844) *Parliamentary Practice*, London: Butterworth and Co.
May, T Erskine (1862) *Constitutional History*, London: Rothman and Co. (reprint).
McCaulay T.B. (1848) *The History of England*, London: Penguin.
McKibbon, R (1990) *Ideologies of Class*, Oxford: Clarendon Press.
McLellan, D (1977) *Karl Marx: Selected Writings*, Oxford: OUP.
Meiksins Wood, Ellen (1992) 'Locke against democracy: Representation, Consent and Suffrage in the Two Treatises', *History of Political Thought* XIII 4 Winter 1992.
Meiksins Wood, Ellen (1998) *The Retreat From Class*, London: Verso.
Meiksins Wood, Ellen and Wood, Neal (1997) *A Trumpet of Sedition*, London: Pluto Press.
Midwinter, A, Keating, M and Mitchell, J (1991) *Politics and Public Policy in Scotland*, London: Macmillan.
Miliband, R (1962) *Parliamentary Socialism*, London: Allen Unwin.
Miliband, Ralph (1972) *Parliamentary Socialism*, London: Merlin.
Miliband, Ralph (1973) *The State in Capitalist Society*, London: Quarter Books.
Miliband, Ralph (1982) *Capitalist Democracy in Britain*, Oxford University Press.
Miliband, Ralph (1991) *Divided Societies: Class Struggle in Contemporary Capitalism*, Oxford University Press.
Miliband, Ralph (2004) *Marxism and Politics*, London: Merlin.
Mill, John Stuart (1861) *Considerations on Representative Government*, London: Prometheus.
Mill, John Stuart and Taylor, Harriet (1869) 'On the Subjection of Women', available online.
Minkin, L (1980) *The Labour Party Conference*, Manchester: Manchester University Press.
Mitchel, John (1860) *The Last Conquest of Ireland*, available online.
Mitchell, J (1996) *Strategies for self government: The campaigns for a Scottish Parliament*, Edinburgh: Polygon.
Mitchell, James (1998) 'The Evolution of Devolution: Labour's Home Rule Strategy in Opposition', *Government and Opposition*, 479–96.
Mitchell, James (2000) 'New Parliament, New Politics', in *Parliamentary Affairs* Vol. 53 No. 3, 605–21.
Mitchell, James (2002) 'Towards a New Constitutional Settlement' in Hay (ed.).
Mitchell, James (2007) 'The United Kingdom as a State of Unions: Unity of Government, Equality of Political Rights and Diversity of Institutions', in Trench (ed.).

Mitchell, James (2009) 'From Breakthrough to Mainstream: The politics of potential and blackmail' in Hassan (ed.).
Moran, Michael (2006) 'The Unanticipated Consequences of Reigning Ideas: Samuel Beer and the Study of British Politics', *British Politics* Vol. 1, No.1.
Morgan, David (1979) *Suffragists and Liberals*, London: Basil Blackwell.
Morton, Graeme (2000) 'The first Home Rule Movement in Scotland 1886–1918' in Dickinson and Lynch (eds).
Mooers, Colin (1991) *The Making of Bourgeois Europe*, London: Verso.
Murray, Gerard and Tonge, Jonathan (2005) *Sinn Fein and the SDLP: From Alienation to Participation*, London: C Hurst and Co.
Nairn, Tom (1964) 'The British Political Elite', *New Left Review* 23, 19–25
Nairn, Tom (1976) 'The Twilight of the British State', *New Left Review* 101/2, 3–61
Nairn, Tom (1981) *The Break-up of Britain* 2nd edn, London: Verso.
Nairn, Tom (2000) *After Britain*, Granta: 2000.
Nairn, Tom (2000) 'Ukania under Blair', *New Left Review*, Vol. 30 No. 1, 69–103.
Nelson, Cary and Grossberg, Lawrence (1988) *Marxism and the Interpretation of Culture*, Basingstoke: Palgrave.
Nelson, Craig (2007) *Thomas Paine: His Life, His Time and the Birth of Modern Nation*, London: Profile.
Norton, Philip (1984) *The British Polity*, London: Longman.
Norton, Philip (1989) 'The changing constitution Part 2', *Contemporary Record* Vol. 3.2, November.
Norton, Philip (2005) *Parliament in British Politics*, Basingstoke: Palgrave.
Norton, Philip (2007) 'Tony Blair and the Constitution' in *British Politics* Vol. 2 No. 2.
Oakeshott, Michael (1962) *Rationalism in Politics and Other Essays*, Indianapolis: Liberty Fund.
O'Brien, Conor (2002) *Edmund Burke*, London: Vintage.
O'Day, Alan (1998) *Irish Home Rule, 1867–1921*, Manchester University Press.
O'Gorman, Frank (1973) *Edmund Burke: His Political Philosophy*, London: Allen Unwin.
O'Gorman, F (1989) *Voters, Patrons, and Parties: The Unreformed Electorate of Hanoverian England 1734–1832*, Oxford University Press.
O'Neill, Michael (2000) 'From Dicey to Devolution' in *Parliamentary Affairs*, Vol. 53, 1, 69–95.
O'Neill, Michael (2004) *Devolution and British Politics*, London: Longman.
Oliver, Dawn (2003) *Constitutional Reform in the UK*, Oxford University Press.
Page, A and Batey, A (2002) 'Scotland's Other Parliament; Westminster Legislation about Devolved Matters since Devolution', *Public Law*, Autumn, pp. 501–23.
Paine, T (1776) *Common Sense*, London: Penguin.
Paine, Thomas (1791) *The Rights Of Man*, London: Penguin.
Paine, T (1792) *The Rights of Man Part II*, London: Penguin.
Paine, T (2008) *The American Crisis*, Forgotten Books.
Paluski, Jan and Waters, Malcolm (1996) *The Death of Class*, London: Sage.
Paterson, L (2000) 'Scottish Democracy and Scottish Utopias', *Scottish Affairs* No 33, Autumn 2000.
Pattie Charles, Seyd, Patrick and Whiteley, Paul (2004) *Citizenship, Democracy and Participation in Contemporary Britain*, Cambridge University Press.
Payne, Geoff (ed.) (2006) *Social Divisions*, London: Palgrave.

Pearce, Malcolm and Stewart, Geoffrey (2002) *British Political History 1867–2001: Democracy and Decline* 3rd edn, London: Routledge.
Pelling, Henry (1996) *A Short of History of the Labour Party*, London: Macmillan.
Philips, Anne (1999) *Which Equalities Matter?*, London: Polity.
Pierre, Jon (ed.) (2000) *Debating Governance*, Oxford University Press.
Pierre, Jon and Stoker, Gerry (2000) 'Towards Multi-Level Governance' in Dunleavy et al.
Pilkington, Colin (1997) *Representative Democracy in Britain Today*, Manchester University Press.
Pitkin, Hanna (1967) *The Concept of Representation*, Berkeley: University of California Press.
Popper, Karl (1989) *Conjectures and Refutations*, London: Routledge.
Poulantzas, Nicos (1978) *State, Power, Socialism*, London: Verso.
Preston, P (1997) *Political/Cultural Identity*, London: Sage.
Preston, Peter (2004) *Relocating England*, Manchester University Press.
Punnett, R (1987) *British Government and Politics*, Dartmouth: Dartmouth Publishing.
Radice Lisanne, Vallance, Elizabeth and Willis, Virginia (1987) *Member of Parliament*, London: Macmillan.
Ramsden, John (ed.) (2002) *The Oxford Companion to Twentieth Century British Politics*, Oxford University Press.
Rhodes, Rod (1996) 'The New Governance: Governing without Government', *Political Studies* 44, 652–67.
Rhodes, Rod (1997) *Understanding Governance*, Milton Keynes: Open University Press.
Rhodes, Rod (2000) 'Governance and Public Administration' in Pierre (ed.).
Rhodes, Rod, Wanna, John and Weller, Patrick (2009) *Comparing Westminster*, Oxford University Press.
Richards, David and Smith, Martin (2001) 'New Labour, the Constitution and the Reforming State' in Ludlam and Smith (eds).
Richards, David and Smith, Martin (2002) *Governance and Public Policy in the UK*, Oxford University Press.
Richards, David, and, Smith, Martin (2004) 'The Hybrid state: Labour's Response to the Challenge of Governance' in Ludlam and Smith (eds).
Rhodes-James, Robert (1978) *The British Revolution*, London: Methuen.
Roberts, Ken (2001) *Class in Modern Britain*, Basingstoke: Palgrave.
Rogers, Robert and Walters, Rhodri, (2004) *How Parliament Works* 5th edn, London: Pearson.
Rokkan, Stein and Urwin, Derek (1982) *The Politics of Territorial Identity: Studies in European Regionalism*, London: Sage.
Rousseau, Jean Jacques (1762) *The Social Contract*, Oxford University Press.
Royle, Edward (1996) *Chartism*, London: Longman.
Royle, Edward (2000) *Revolutionary Britannia: Reflections on the Threat of Revolution in Britain, 1789–1848*, Manchester University Press.
Royle, Edward and Walvin, James (1982) *English Reformers and Radicals 1760–1848*, London: Harvester.
Rustin, Michael (2009) 'Revisiting Charter 88' in *Parliamentary Affairs* Vol. 62, No. 4, 568–79.

Schimdt, Vivian (2006) 'Institutionalism' in Hay, Lister and Marsh (eds).
Scott, John (1991) *Who Rules Britain?*, London: Polity.
Scott, John (1992) *The Upper Classes: Property and Privilege in Britain*, London: Macmillan.
Scott, John (1997) *Corporate Business and Capitalist Classes*, Oxford University Press.
Scott, John (2001) *Power*, London: Polity.
The Scottish Office (1998) 'Shaping Scotland's Parliament' Report of the Consultative Steering Group on the Scottish Parliament 1998, London: The Scottish Office.
Shils, Edward (1981) *Tradition*, London: Faber and Faber.
Simon, Roger (1991) *Gramsci's Political Thought: An Introduction*, London: Lawrence and Wishart.
Smiles, S (1859) *Self Help*, London: W Clowes & Sons.
Smith, Martin (1999) *The Core Executive in Britain*, Basingstoke: Palgrave.
Smith, Martin (1999) 'The Institutions of Central Government' in Holliday (ed.).
Smith, Martin (2008) 'Re-centring British Government: Beliefs, Traditions and Dilemmas in Political Science', *Political Studies Review* Vol. 6, Issue 2, 143–54.
Smith, Paul (1996) *Disraeli*, Cambridge University Press.
Stanworth, Philip (2006) 'Elites' in Payne (ed.).
Stedman-Jones, Gareth (2003) *Languages of Class*, Cambridge University Press.
The Sutton Trust (2005a) 'State Admissions to Our Leading Universities: An update to the missing 3000', available online.
The Sutton Trust (2005b) 'The Educational Backgrounds of The UK's Top Solicitors, Barristers and Judges', available online.
The Sutton Trust (2005c) 'The Educational Backgrounds of Members of the House of Commons and House of Lords', available online.
The Sutton Trust (2006) 'The Educational Background of Leading Journalists', available online.
Swartz, David (1997) *Culture and Power: The Sociology of Pierre Bourdieu*, University of Chicago Press.
Sztompka, Piotr (1993) *The Sociology of Social Change*, Cambridge: Blackwell.
Tant, Anthony (1993) *British Government: The Triumph of Elitism*, Dartmouth: Dartmouth Publishing Company.
Taylor, Miles (1995) *The Decline of British Radicalism 1847–1860*, Oxford: Clarendon Press.
Thain, Colin (2004) 'Treasury Rules OK? The Further Evolution of a British Institution', *BJPIR* Vol. 6, 121–8.
Thain, Colin and Wright, Maurice (1995) *The Treasury and Whitehall*, Oxford: Clarendon Press.
Thatcher, M (1993) *The Downing Street Years*, London: Harper Collins.
The Power Inquiry (2006) *Power to the people*, York: York Publishing.
Thompson, Dorothy (1984) *The Chartists*, London: Pantheon.
Thompson, Edward P (1980) *The Making of the English Working Class*, London: Penguin.
Thorpe, Andrew (2001) *A History of the British Labour Party*, London: Palgrave.
Tilly, C (1990) *Coercion, capital and European states*, London: Blackwell.
Tivey, Leonard (1988) *Interpretations of British Politics*, London: Harvester Wheatsheaf.

Townsend, Charles (2006) *Easter 1916: The Irish Rebellion*, London: Penguin.
Trench, Alan (ed.) (2007a) *Devolution and Power within the United Kingdom*, Manchester University Press.
Trench, Alan (2007b) 'The Framework of Devolution. The Structure of Devolved Power' in Trench (ed.).
Trench, A (2007c) 'The Politics of Devolution Finance and the Power of the Treasury' in Trench (ed.).
Trench, A (2007d) 'Washing Dirty Linen in Private: The Processes of Intergovernmental Relations and the Resolution of Disputes' in Trench (ed.).
Trevelyan, George M, (1922) *History of England*, London: Longman.
Vallance, E (2009) *A Radical History of Britain*, London: Little Brown.
Verney, Douglas (1991) 'Westminster Model' in Bogdanor (ed.),
Vernon, James (1993) *Politics and the People: A Study in English Political Culture, 1815–1867*, Cambridge University Press.
Ward, John (1973) *Chartism*, London: Batsford.
Ward, Paul (2004) *Britishness since 1870*, London: Routledge.
Webb, Darren (2004) 'The Bitter Product of Defeat? Reflections on Winstanley's Law of Freedom', *Political Studies*, Vol. 52, 199–213.
Weber, Max (1958) 'The Three Types of Legitimate Rule', *Berkeley Publications in Society and Institutions*, 4 (1): 1–11.
Westergaard, J (1995) *Who gets what?: The hardening of class inequality in the late twentieth century*, Basingstoke: Macmillan.
Westergaard, John (2001) 'The Persistence of Class Inequalities' in Abercrombie and Warde (eds).
Whateley, Christopher (2008) 'The Making of the Union of 1707' in Devine (ed.).
Wickham, Chris (ed) (2007) *Marxist History Writing*, Oxford University Press/British Academy.
Williams, R (1965) *The Long Revolution*, London: Penguin.
Williams, Raymond (1977) *Marxism and Literature*, Oxford University Press.
Williams, Raymond (1983a) *Keywords*, London: Fontana.
Williams, Raymond (1983b) *Culture and Society*, Columbia University Press.
Wollstonecraft, Mary (1795) *A Vindication of the Rights of Woman*, London: Penguin.
Wood, Neal (1984) *John Locke and Agrarian Capitalism*, Los Angeles: University of California Press.
Worden, B (2001) *Roundhead Reputations*, London: Allen Lane.
Wright, David G (1988) *Popular Radicalism*, London: Longman.
Wright, Tony (1996) *Socialisms*, London: Routledge.
Wright, Tony (2000) *The British Political Process: An Introduction*, London: Routledge.
Young, Michael (1988) *The Metronomic Society: Natural Rhythms and Human Timetables* (London: Thomas and Hudson).

Index

Accountability, 12, 13, 21, 28, 74, 128–129, 136, 138, 141, 143, 144, 151, 175, 176, 222, 229, 231, 255
Act of Union (1707), 17
Act of Union (1800), 146, 194, 198
Active Citizens Transform, 190
Agency, 5, 25, 28, 33–36, 38–40, 44, 96, 108, 111, 112–113, 115, 122, 162, 225, 234, 252, 257, 260
Bevir and Rhodes approach 52, 55–56, 58, 62, 64–68, 70, 72–73, 77, 83–86, 90
Alternative Vote (AV), 1, 157, 190, 251
Anglo Irish Treaty, 201
Anti-Poll Tax Federation, 207
Archer, Margaret, 44, 46, 53, 54, 65, 68, 96, 98, 112, 113
Asymmetrical Power Model (APM), 2, 57, 63, 221, 222, 224, 234, 261
Asymmetrical resonance, 4, 75, 85, 88, 90, 105, 106, 118, 174, 213, 219, 235
Athenian Democracy, 175, 179, 229
Attlee, Clement 150, 247, 259

Bagehot, Walter, 3, 8, 16, 78, 134, 136–138, 140, 147, 228, 230, 232, 252
Ballot Act 1872, 183, 184, 197, 201, 230
Barnett, Anthony, 189
Beer, Samuel, 4, 18, 22–24, 28, 41, 42, 43, 44, 45, 46, 47, 49, 56, 109, 117, 124, 141, 144, 159, 228, 252, 262
Bevir, Mark, 99
Bevir and Rhodes, 26, 38–29, 40, 42, 45, 51–52, 55–76, 83–86
Agency, 55–57, 62–68
Continuity and Change, 76, 83–86
Dilemma, 59–60, 73–76
Ontology and epistemology, 55, 61–62
Tradition, 57–59, 68–73

Birch, Anthony, 4, 18, 19–22, 23, 24, 25, 27, 28, 39, 40, 41, 42, 43, 44, 45, 47, 56, 117, 123, 136, 141, 151, 222, 228, 253
Blair, Anthony, 1, 12, 240, 253
The Blue Books, 209, 210, 249
Bourdieu, Pierre, 46, 65, 96, 97, 124, 155
British Political Tradition (BPT), 122–152
Classical approaches, 18–28
Critical approaches, 28–35
Criticisms, 35–49
Impact on political life in the UK, 153–172
Socio-Economic elites and, 162–165
Structured Inequality and, 165–171
British Civil Wars, 175
British exceptionalism, 2, 10, 19, 47, 48, 111, 125, 146, 147, 148, 218
Britishness, 16, 48, 49, 109, 121, 146–148, 151, 154, 160, 195–197, 198, 201, 203, 209, 210, 211, 213, 219, 232, 242, 243, 246, 248
Burke, Edmund, 18, 20, 23, 87, 88, 89, 99, 125, 126–129, 130–132, 125, 136, 137, 138, 140, 141, 147, 176, 179, 180, 229, 230
Burkeian, 20, 28, 88, 133, 137, 179, 230
Butt, Issac, 201

The Calman Commission, 215, 245, 250
Cameron, David, 235
Campaign for Freedom of Information (CFOI), 31, 32, 40, 120, 187, 188, 219, 229
Can't Pay, Won't Pay Campaign, 207
Cecil, Robert Gascoyne-, 89, 184, 201
Chamberlain, Joseph, 184, 201, 240

268 *Index*

Change and Continuity, 2, 3, 9, 39–41, 73, 76–78, 123, 125, 165, 186, 216, 217, 229, 236
  Bevir and Rhodes approach, 83–86
  In British politics, 78–81
  Tradition and, 111–116
Chartism, 135, 161, 174, 181, 182, 183, 192, 228, 236, 239
Chartists, 135, 170, 182, 239, 242
Charter 88, 28, 33, 115, 120, 174, 182, 187, 188–192, 219, 236, 241, 248
Choosing Scotland's future: The National Conversation, 208
Civic Republicanism, 175, 236
Class, 53, 144, 161, 163, 165, 168, 182, 228, 234, 238, 245
  Capitalist, 162, 163, 164, 169, 234
  Commercial, 164
  Decline of, 3, 162, 165
  Dominant, 148
  Landed 107, 131, 137, 147, 230, 238
  Lower, 132, 160
  Middle, 135, 164, 166, 177, 192, 230, 239, 249
  Upper, 148, 166
  Working, 135, 137, 139, 141, 144, 147, 149, 160, 161, 177, 189, 192, 229, 234
Class Struggle, 160, 236
Cole, G D H, 87
Coleridge, Samuel, 177
Collectivism, 24, 25, 26, 37, 41, 47, 48
Conservative, 17, 18, 20, 31, 36, 69, 72, 74, 77, 86, 98, 102, 104, 107, 110, 114, 116, 117, 144, 145, 206, 227, 240, 241
Conservatives, 48, 94, 99, 110, 139, 141, 142, 144, 149, 156, 166, 191, 205, 212, 222, 240, 248, 249, 250
The Conservative party, 20, 150, 191, 213, 215, 240, 241
Conservative–Liberal Democrat coalition, 1, 156, 184, 193, 220
Constitutional Reform, 33, 34, 35, 72, 74, 84, 85, 89, 115, 125, 150, 177, 189, 190, 191, 206, 218, 219, 222, 224, 232, 236, 240, 242
Constitutionalization, 150, 227

Consultative Steering Group, 190, 241
Cook, Robin, 189
Corrupt and Illegal Practices Act 1883, 230
Critical realism, 63, 67, 78, 83, 122
Cromwell, Oliver, 176, 245

Darling, Alistair, 189
Davitt's Land League, 201
Democracy, 3, 44, 47, 104, 109, 124, 126, 129, 130, 134, 135, 140, 143, 146, 157, 166, 201, 222, 225, 227, 235,
  Athenian, 175, 229
  Deliberative, 236
  Elite, 4, 28–29, 30, 32, 33, 34, 35, 144, 149, 150, 151, 155, 217, 219, 231, 241
  Participatory, 31, 33, 40, 41, 135, 142, 149, 151, 174–193, 219, 239, 235
  Radical, 236
  Representative, 235
Democratic Collectivist Tradition, 87, 89
Democratic deficit, 72, 84, 197, 198, 206, 212
Democratic Republican Tradition, 87, 88, 90, 117
Devolution, 1, 12, 17, 72, 89, 187, 189, 196, 197, 206, 207, 208, 212, 213, 214, 215, 243, 244, 245, 247, 248, 249, 250
  Scottish, 1, 72, 125, 190, 208, 233, 246, 247, 250
  Welsh, 213, 245, 250
Dialectical, 24, 26, 39, 43, 45, 66, 67, 79, 80, 83, 112, 122
Dicey, A.V., 8, 14, 15, 16, 24, 33, 34, 78, 143, 144, 221, 231, 232
The Differentiated Polity Model (DPM), 2, 12, 52, 57, 158, 224, 233
Discourse concerning change, 132, 133–134, 142, 187, 195, 196, 217
Discourse concerning national distinctiveness, 146–149, 153, 160, 195, 196, 218, 242
Discourse concerning representation, 125–138, 139, 140, 145, 184, 226

Discourse concerning responsibility, 143–146, 156
The Diggers, 176, 192, 237
Disraeli, Benjamin, 136, 231
Dual Polity, 15, 16, 154

Easter Rising 1916, 200
Electoral Reform, 1, 156, 157, 184, 190, 222, 233, 240
Electoral Reform Society, 184, 229
Elitism, 2, 28, 30, 31, 33, 37, 45, 48, 50, 126, 132, 134, 138, 139, 140, 142, 145, 148, 150, 155, 157, 158, 165, 169, 171, 179, 180, 181, 183, 185, 186, 191, 192, 197, 232
Ellis, T.E., 210
Epistemology, 53–55, 224
  Bevir and Rhodes, 61–62
Evans, Gwynfor, 212
Evans, Mark, 33–35, 36, 41, 42, 43, 44, 45, 48, 71, 117
Evolutionary approaches, 81, 83, 112
Evolutionary change, 81, 87
Ewing, Winnie, 205

Fabian, 68, 87, 149
Fawcett, Henry, 237
Fawcett, Millicent, 185
Fenian Rising, 200
Francophobia, 147
Free Wales Army, 212, 249
'Freeborn Englishmen', 176, 199
Freedom of Information Act (2000), 1, 40, 188

Gaelic Tradition, 199
Giddens, Anthony, 94, 227
Gladstone, William, 136, 184, 201, 230
General Election 2010, 167
The Glorious Revolution (1688), 9, 133, 176, 178, 240
Government of Wales Bill (1922), 211
Governmentalities, 65
Governance, 11–13, 56–57, 66, 104, 158, 221
Gramsci, Antonio, 41, 79, 96, 100, 108, 164
Grattan, Henry, 198
The Great Famine 1845–52, 197–199

Greenleaf, W H, 24–28, 37, 39, 41, 42, 43, 45, 47, 48, 116, 117
Grey, Earl, 133
Glyndwr, Owain, 209

Habitus, 97
Hardy, Thomas, 177
Hay, Colin, 28, 37, 45, 51, 53, 54, 76, 81–82, 85, 112, 223
Historical Institutionalism, 38, 228
Hobbes, Thomas, 125, 129, 144
Hobsbawm, Eric, 36, 93, 101, 106, 107, 110, 192, 226, 227
Holyrood, 167, 207, 208, 215, 244, 249, 250
Home Government Association, 201
Home Rule, 200, 201–202, 204, 210, 213, 244, 245, 247
Home Rule Bill (1886), 201
House of Commons, 127, 129, 131, 143, 145, 156, 167, 190, 204, 231, 251
House of Lords, 1, 11, 104, 126, 127, 131, 143, 179, 231
Human Rights Act (1998), 1, 190

Institute for Public Policy Research (IPPR), 189
Institutionalism, 38
Intentionalism, 56, 67, 78, 225
Internal colonialism, 196
Interpretivism, 4
  Bevir and Rhodes, 52, 55, 68, 86, 223
  Definition, 53–54
  'new', 4, 61, 217
Ireton, Henry, 176
Irish National Liberation Army (INLA), 200, 242
Irish Nationalism, 195, 197, 199, 202, 245
Irish Parliamentary Party (IPP), 201
Irish Republican Brotherhood (IRB), 200
Irish War of Independence, 201
Irishness, 196

Jack Cade's Rebellion (1450), 175
Jennings, Ivor, 16, 78, 134, 140, 141
Jessop, Bob, 65, 79, 112
John, E.T., 210

Kensington Society, 183, 239
Kerr, Peter, 41, 45, 81–83, 85, 112, 113
Kett's rebellion (1549), 175
Keynesianism, 41, 82
Kilbrandon Report, 212

Lab-Lib coalition, 156
Labour party, 31, 34, 72, 105, 141, 142, 149–150, 182, 186, 189, 191, 192, 206, 207, 213, 227, 246, 247, 248
Laws of Wales Act, 208
Levellers, 176, 192, 237
Lewis, Saunders, 211
Liberal, 72, 117, 138, 140, 143, 144, 153, 188, 191, 22, 235, 250
Liberals, 19, 31, 136, 139, 142, 144, 149, 150, 210
The Liberal party, 160, 191, 239, 240
Liberalism, 116
Libertarianism, 24, 25, 26, 37, 41, 117
Lilburne, John, 176, 237
Lijphart, Arend, 9, 221, 236, 237
Limited liberal discourse on representation, 130, 138–143, 144, 145
Lloyd George, David, 210
The Llyn Incident, 211

McAnulla, Stuart, 12, 36, 44, 46, 48, 50, 52, 55, 61, 62, 63, 93, 112, 223, 227, 232
MacCormick, John, 205, 246, 247
Magna Carta (1215), 188
Major, John, 156
Make Votes Count, 190
Marquand, David, 4, 52, 86–90, 91, 117, 217, 232, 242
Marsh, David and Tant, Tony, 28–29, 38, 44, 228
Marsh, David, 39, 52, 223
Marsh, David and Hall, Matthew, 39, 46, 50, 52, 61, 62, 68, 71, 75, 143, 166, 222, 224, 228, 242
Marsh, David, Richards, David and Smith, Martin, 2, 8, 10, 16, 105, 113, 165
Marxism, 79, 100, 101, 103, 225
Material-Ideational, 45, 46, 67, 68, 77, 94, 119, 225

May, Erskine, 134
Miliband, David, 235
Miliband, Ralph, 78, 101, 102, 107, 139, 141, 148
Miliband-Poulantzas debate, 162–163
Mill, John Stuart, 137, 183, 184, 196, 239
Mill, John Stuart and Taylor, Harriet (1869), 185, 239
Miners Strike 1984, 197, 212, 249
Ministerial Responsibility, 9, 10, 12, 99, 143, 144, 213, 231
  Collective, 21
  Individual, 21
Multi-level governance (MLG), 13–14, 215

National Association for the Vindication of Scottish Rights (1853), 203
National Party for Scotland, 196, 204
Nationalism
  British, 48, 49, 232, 243
  Cultural, 210
  Ireland, 198, 199, 200, 243
  Political, 200, 212, 213, 242
  see also Irish nationalism, Scottish Nationalism, Wels Nationalism
New Labour, 69, 85, 125, 196, 222, 236, 242
New Politics Network, 190
Non-conservative persuasion, 100, 105
North Sea Oil, 197, 205, 244
Northern Ireland Assembly, 214, 233
Norton, Philip, 19, 47, 78, 102, 114, 134

Oakeshott, Michael, 18–19, 27, 36, 47, 49, 94, 99, 114
Ontology, 53–54, 224
  Bevir and Rhodes, 61–62
Oxbridge, 166, 167, 168

Paine, Thomas, 177, 178–179, 180, 181, 183, 187, 191, 199, 238, 239, 245, 249
Pankhurst, Sylvia, 185
Parliament for Wales Campaign, 211

Parliamentary Labour party (PLP), 150
Parliamentary reform, 132, 135, 137, 177, 178, 181, 182, 183, 184, 238, 239
Parliamentary sovereignty, 8, 10, 12, 14, 15, 16, 34, 43, 85, 124, 125, 143, 145, 153, 154, 155, 195, 217, 218
Parnell, Charles, 201, 245
Participatory Democracy, see democracy
Participatory Tradition, 35, 48, 120, 150, 173, 193–197, 198, 241, 248
Path dependency, 38, 44, 66, 71, 75, 80, 82, 83, 84, 85, 86, 113, 142, 214, 220, 227
Peasants Revolt 1381, 175
The People's Charter (1838), 181, 188, 239
'The Peers vs. People' campaign, 184
Peterloo Massacre 1819, 133, 181
Plaid Cymru, 196, 197, 211–213
Pluralism, 2, 9, 234, 236
Political Traditions, 116–121
  Competing, 109, 120, 142, 173
  Definitions, 116–118
  Predominant, 116–119, 123–151, 152–172, 173, 190, 203, 217–219, 244
Poll Tax, 197, 206, 207, 232, 247
The Ponting Case (1985), 188
The Poor Law Amendment Act (1834), 182
Popper, Karl, 94
Poulantzas, Nicos, 79, 234
Power blocs, 161, 162, 163, 164, 172, 219, 234
Power 2010, 175, 190, 229, 236, 241
Preston, Peter, 46, 49, 97, 103, 106, 107, 109, 121, 147, 148, 155
Proportional Representation Society, 184
Protestantism, 147, 245
Provisional IRA, 200
Putney Debates, 176

Radical Democracy, 175, 236
Rainsborough, Thomas, 176, 237
Realists, 54

Reform Act (1832), 133, 134, 181, 152
Reform Bill (1867), 183
Reform League, 135, 182, 239
Reform Union, 135, 182, 239
Representation, 123–126, 135–137, 138–143, 151, 176–177, 179, 217, 228
  Actual, 128, 138
  Beer, 22–24
  Birch, 19–20
  Burke's view, 127–130
  Marsh and Tant, 28
  Territorial, 194
  Virtual, 126, 128, 138, 176
Responsibility, 123–124, 143–146, 151, 156, 222, 228
  Beer, 22–24
  Birch, 21–22
  Marsh and Tant, 28
Rhodes, Rod, 12, 17, 135
The Royal Commission on the Constitution (1968), 205, 212
The Rule of Law, 8, 18, 25, 235, 241

Salisbury Lord, see Gascoyne–Cecil, Robert
Salmond, Alex, 208, 248
The Scotland Act (1998), 125, 207, 248, 250
The Scotland Bill (2010), 215, 245, 250, 251
Scottish Constitutional Convention (SCC), 189, 207, 244, 248
Scottish Home Rule Association (SHRA), 204
Scottish National Convention, 124
The Scottish National Party (SNP), 196, 204, 208, 211–212, 242
The Scottish Office, 203, 243, 244, 246
Scottish Nationalism, 204
Scottishness, 109, 196, 203, 242, 246
Shils, Edward, 77, 97, 99, 100, 103, 227
Simple Plurality System (SPS), 156
Single Transferable Vote, 184, 233
Sinn Fein, 196, 200, 201, 211, 241, 242
Smiles, Samuel, 136
Smith, John, 189, 207

Social and Democratic Labour party (SDLP), 202
Socialist, 57, 69, 71, 72, 74, 86, 104, 117, 118, 149, 191, 201, 204
Society of United Irishmen, 198, 245
Socio-economic elites, 3, 130, 145, 151, 152, 161–165, 166, 168, 169, 170, 233
Strategic Selectivity, 73, 75, 79, 82, 82, 84, 108
Structuralism, 67, 78, 79, 225, 234
Structure-Agency, 44, 66, 68, 77, 112
Structured Inequality, 3, 4, 65, 75, 101, 104, 105, 129, 130, 131, 157, 161, 165–169
Suffragettes, 187, 237
Suffragists, 185, 262
Welsh Sunday Closing Act (1881), 210
Sunningdale Agreement (1974), 202
The Supreme Court (2005), 1
The Sutton Trust, 167, 168, 235
Sztompka, Piotr, 80, 95, 110, 111, 115

Tant, Tony, 30–33, 36, 38, 44, 45, 48, 72, 99, 105, 149, 150
Tawney, R H, 87
Thatcher, Margaret, 12, 82, 184, 206, 212, 240, 241, 244
Thatcher government, 40, 48, 188, 243
Thatcherism, 57, 187, 197, 213, 244
Thatcherite, 212
Thomas, D.A., 210
The Tisdall Case (1983), 188
Tories, 19, 125, 126, 130, 131, 133, 142, 175, 191
Tory democracy, 144, 231
Tory Nationalist Tradition, 87, 89
Tradition, 92–121
Treasury view, 164, 170
Trusteeship, 127, 128, 129, 179, 229
The Tryweryn Affair (1965), 21, 249

Unlock Democracy, 120, 175, 190, 219, 229, 236
Union of the Crowns (1603), 146, 194
The Union State, 146, 194
The Unitary State, 12, 14–15, 17, 34, 43, 120, 124, 146, 153, 154, 158, 195, 196, 217, 222

Virtual Representation, 126, 128, 138, 176

The Wales Act (2006), 244, 245
Wars of the Three Kingdoms (1639–1651), 198
Webb, Sidney, 89
Weir, Stuart, 189
Welsh Devolution Referendum (2011), 250
Welsh Language Society, 197, 211, 213
Welsh Nationalism, 197, 210–213
Welshness, 109, 196, 209–210, 212–213
'Westminster and Whitehall knows best', 129, 141, 143, 151, 155, 157, 159, 169, 179, 195, 201, 217, 230, 232, 241
The Westminster Model (WM), 2, 7–10, 13, 18, 33, 42, 52, 63, 64, 66, 92, 144, 153, 154, 155, 158, 195, 221, 236, 250
Westminster Parliament, 8, 14, 103, 126, 167
Whig discourse, 126, 130, 132, 133, 135, 138, 140, 180, 228
Whig Imperialist Tradition, 86–89, 119
Whig Interpretation of history, 2, 3, 78, 133, 149, 180, 187, 225
Whiggish Developmentalism, 2, 47, 49, 78, 86
Whigs, 19, 125, 126, 131, 133, 142, 175, 176, 191, 229
Wilkes, John, 177
Williamite War (1689–1691), 198, 245
Williams, Raymond, 93, 95, 100, 101
Wilson, Harold, 150, 205, 212, 249
Winstanley, Gerrard, 176, 237, 238
Wollstonecraft, Mary, 177, 178, 180, 185, 186, 191, 238
Women's Suffrage Movement, 184, 185, 192, 242

Young Irelanders, 198
Young Wales Movement, 210
Your Right To Know White Paper (1997), 188